To Peter +

Fair winds

From Jenny Coghlan

Winter in Fireland

NICHOLAS COGHLAN

Winter in Fireland

A PATAGONIAN SAILING ADVENTURE

THE UNIVERSITY OF ALBERTA PRESS

Published by

The University of Alberta Press

Ring House 2

Edmonton, Alberta, Canada T6G 2E1

LIBRARY AND ARCHIVES CANADA CATALOGUING
IN PUBLICATION

Coghlan, Nicholas, 1954-

    Winter in Fireland : a Patagonian sailing
adventure / Nicholas Coghlan.

(Wayfarer series)
Includes bibliographical references and index.
ISBN 978-0-88864-547-0

    1. Coghlan, Nicholas, 1954- —Travel—Tierra
del Fuego (Argentina and Chile). 2. Tierra del Fuego
(Argentina and Chile)—Description and travel. 3.
Coghlan, Nicholas, 1954- —Travel—Patagonia
(Argentina and Chile). 4. Patagonia (Argentina and
Chile)—Description and travel. I. Title. II. Series:
Wayfarer series (Edmonton, Alta.)

F2986.C64 2011   918.2'76047   C2011–900763–0

The University of Alberta Press is committed to
protecting our natural environment. As part of
our efforts, this book is printed on Enviro Paper: it
contains 100% post-consumer recycled fibres and is
acid- and chlorine-free.

The University of Alberta Press gratefully
acknowledges the support received for its
publishing program from The Canada Council
for the Arts. The University of Alberta Press also
gratefully acknowledges the financial support of the
Government of Canada through the Book Publishing
Industry Development Program (BPIDP) and from
the Alberta Foundation for the Arts for its publishing
activities.

Canadä   Canada Council   Conseil des Arts
for the Arts   du Canada

Alberta Foundation for the Arts

For Debra: Bosun Bird*'s mission control.*

Contents

Prologue   IX

— 1   Far Away and Long Ago   I

— 2   Fitting Out   47

— 3   Rolling Down to Rio   79

— 4   Three Fronts, a Pampero, and a Zonda   113

— 5   Bright and Fierce and Fickle is the South   153

— 6   Winter in Fireland   185

— 7   More Anxieties and Hardships   217

— 8   In the Wake of the Dresden   245

— 9   To the Gulf of Sorrows   279

— 10   Wizards, Witches, and Ghost Ships   307

— 11   Under the Wide and Starry Sky   335

Epilogue   353
Select Bibliography   357
Index   363

LIST OF MAPS

Bosun Bird's *track: Cape Town to Puerto Montt.* XII–XIII
Tierra del Fuego and adjacent waters. 230
The Chilean channels: Strait of Magellan to Puerto Edén. 280
The Chilean channels: Puerto Edén to Puerto Montt. 305

FRIDAY, FEBRUARY 25, 2006; latitude 54.08 south, longitude 65.26 west. It's a cold and drizzly late afternoon, and *Bosun Bird* is under a full press of sail off the eastern coast of Tierra del Fuego. Forty miles ahead lies the Strait of Le Maire, the narrow passage between the main island of Tierra del Fuego and Staten Island that will allow us to turn west and into the more protected waters of the Beagle Channel. Le Maire has a fearsome reputation, with its twice-daily reversing currents of up to eight knots, which, when opposed to the southwesterly gales that are all too frequent hereabouts, can create ten-metre-high standing waves. It has probably sent more ships and men to the bottom than Cape Stiff—the Horn itself, only a hundred miles farther on.

For two years now, Le Maire has haunted us: while our voyage to the southern tip of the world will no doubt provide many other adventures and difficulties, it is here that things have the greatest potential to go wrong.

Now the wind is favourable: a cold northerly coming in on our port quarter. If we are to have a smooth passage we will need to hold that wind and start passing through the strait exactly an hour after high water, which occurs twice a day: wind and current in the same direction. For the twentieth time in an hour Jenny, who is down below over the dimly lit chart table, checks the GPS to see if we are holding our speed. I take yet another look at the Argentine tide tables to be sure we have calculated slack—03:39—correctly.

And, not for the first time on this voyage, I wonder if we have taken on more than we can handle.

Bosun Bird's *track: Cape Town to Puerto Montt.*

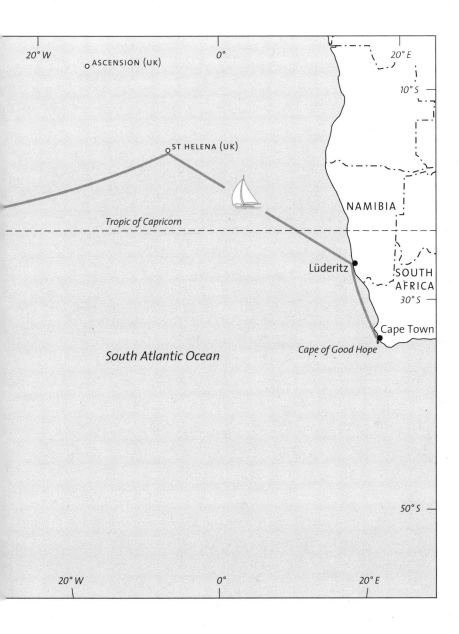

20° W

ASCENSION (UK)

0°

20° E

10° S

ST HELENA (UK)

Tropic of Capricorn

NAMIBIA

Lüderitz

SOUTH AFRICA

30° S

Cape Town

Cape of Good Hope

South Atlantic Ocean

50° S

20° W

0°

20° E

—1

Far Away and *Long Ago*

MARCH 1978. I was twenty-three, living with my girlfriend, Jenny, in a damp and chilly pair of basement rooms in a Victorian house on Arthur Street, Nottingham. We shared a bare-concrete floored kitchen with four students and tried to pay no attention to the fresh mouse droppings we found on every surface in the mornings. Our bedroom, where we slept on a mattress on the floor, was painted deep purple. In the bathroom a huge red and yellow poster featuring *The Band* hung limply on a peeling wall. Despite the decoration, it wasn't tempting to linger in the bath, with each inch of tepid water in the four-legged bathtub costing us five pence in the meter. On the top floor was a communal TV room where, at 7:30 every Thursday, as I had for years, I'd try to catch *Top of the Pops*; Blondie was at Number One that week with "Denis."

The rent was five pounds a week. It wasn't unreasonable, even for those days, but, as students will, we still made every effort to be out when we thought Mrs. Kalirai, our formidable Indian land-lady—bulky, glowering, with a red dot on her forehead—was due to be collecting. When she unilaterally upped our payment to seven pounds fifty we appealed to the rent tribunal.

Nine months earlier I'd graduated from Oxford University with a degree in French and Spanish and now I was training to be a teacher in Nottingham, where Jenny—two years older, with her own degree in bio-statistics—was working for Boots the Chemist. We'd met a few years earlier when I was secretary of the Oxford University Cave Club and she was president. Once a week the club officials took turns in serving pies and baked beans to the members as we jointly planned the next weekend's "trip" to Yorkshire or South Wales. Most of the girls who went caving were either very robust and large or reluctant participants in their boyfriends' obsession. Jenny, who already had one degree from Cambridge, was not over-sized and she liked caving because it was physically challenging and had an edge of danger: she would become angry whenever anyone—imagining she was not quite up to it—would try to pull her up the longer ladder pitches or push her through especially tight squeezes. After a flirtation among the limestone grykes and clints of County Clare, Ireland, our romance was consummated one night in a small canvas tent on a roundabout in northern France, on the university's Spring Expedition to the Jura Mountains.

I spent the first term at "Nottie" mainly in the lecture theatre, with a couple of mornings a week helping out at a local primary school. Although I wouldn't be going on to teach kids of this age group, it was hard not to be affected by the enthusiasm, energy, and innocence of these seven- and eight-year-olds. But in the second term we were all brought down to earth. I was assigned to a sprawling 2,000-pupil comprehensive school near Sheffield, sufficiently large for each faculty to have its own separate staffroom. I recall being shown around.

"This is the French staffroom," said my tired mentor as he shuffled ahead of me into a large rectangular room with a table overflowing with test papers and piles of textbooks.

There was a smell of coffee that had been brewing too long, stale pipe tobacco, and damp sweaty football jerseys; the windows could not have been opened in years. A portly bearded man was slumped into an armchair; he wore a tweed jacket with leather patches on the elbows and a knitted tie. He opened one eye, grunted "Hmmph," shifted, and went back to dozing. From behind the pile of papers, a mousy-looking and bespectacled blonde no older than myself looked up briefly, smiled nervously, and went back to her marking.

"And this is my future," I thought.

Most of the teachers hated their jobs, and the tough fifteen-year-olds from this working-class area sensed it, reacting with truculence and outright hostility. Trainee teachers like me were baited with particular relish: as yet we had little idea of how to react to tried tricks such as co-ordinated coughing fits, the hiding of chalk and blackboard erasers, and blatant copying in tests. As I made my way back home every rainy and dark evening, swaying on the top deck of the green and white double-decker bus, the prospect of enduring this for the rest of my life was not enticing.

One day between classes I picked up a copy of *The Times Educational Supplement*, known in the business as the TES, which includes advertisements for teachers needed at private schools (confusingly known as public schools in Britain). Reasoning that classes were likely to be smaller, students more motivated, and discipline better at such schools, I found myself idly scanning for posts in modern languages. One ad in particular caught my attention.

Three months later, I drove down to suburban Cambridge in Jenny's Mini for an interview in the front room of a mock-Tudor semi-detached.

"Hello there, I'm Roger," said my gruff and red-faced host as he plied me with a gin and tonic (at ten o'clock in the morning) and gestured to me to me sit down.

Roger wore a crested college tie: one of those signals that a middle-class education in England trains you to look for. Although I heard rustling from the direction of the kitchen, there was no sign of his wife. After clearing his throat very loudly, Roger came straight to the point.

"You went to Ampleforth? Good rugby school, if I recall. Chum of mine at Caius was there; seems to have survived the bloody monks without too many scars. But what about cricket? D'you think you'll be able to handle the junior team?"

There was no discussion of my qualifications or what I might be teaching; Roger spent most of the time rambling on amiably about Oxford and Cambridge's sports rivalry, with occasional unrelated tirades against Britain's labour unions.

A week or two later, a telegram dropped through the door at Arthur Street, just as I was on the way out of the door to catch the bus to the university campus. It was a job offer.

"So what are you going to do?" asked Jenny, unseen and sounding casual, from the bedroom.

"Well I don't know really...I went for the interview, so I suppose I'd better take it."

Silence.

"Err...I didn't actually tell Roger about you."

More silence.

"I think we'll have to get married if you want to come along."

May and June were frenetic. I don't recall proposing or Jenny accepting, but we did go out to the local Indian restaurant the day the telegram arrived, and we got married one warm English Spring day in Berkshire. Our wedding presents included a climbing rope and a commemorative set of colour slides from the leader of the last big caving expedition I'd been on, to the world's third deepest pothole. We crammed as much as we could (including a dozen deflated rugby balls and some cricket balls, a last-minute request by the headmaster) into two tin trunks that we despatched to Harwich for onward shipment and said our goodbyes.

We boarded a British Caledonian DC-10 at Gatwick Airport. Barely had we taken our seats on the aircraft when, to my embarrassment, Jenny showed her mettle by loudly insisting that the man behind us desist from smoking; she won the applause of half the passengers. We then spend twenty minutes shedding several of the four or five layers of clothes that we had not been able to fit into our suitcases, and stowing the rope under the seat in front.

Off we set, via a short honeymoon in Rio de Janeiro, to Buenos Aires and St. George's College (established 1898).

⌁ I didn't know too much about Argentina, Jenny even less. Unlike most of our caving friends, I at least knew that Buenos Aires, not Rio, was the capital city. At Oxford I'd studied the intriguing short stories of Jorge Luis Borges and a minor classic of gaucho literature, *Don Segundo Sombra*. I also had the twin album of Andrew Lloyd Webber and Tim Rice's *Evita*, featuring Julie Covington singing "Don't Cry for Me Argentina," which Jenny and I had listened to during illicit overnight stays at her college in North Oxford. I was vaguely aware that the album was banned in Argentina, but I wasn't quite sure why. Although *Evita* was not flattering to Juan Perón and his glamorous first lady, weren't the generals now in power of the same inclination? I knew Argentines were pretty good at football, too: my farewell visit to my brother and sister-in-law at their suburban Birmingham home had coincided with the

5

Argentina–Holland World Cup final, won by the host country amid scenes of very un-English jubilation. Occasionally the cameras would home in on the presidential box. A thin-faced man with a Hitler moustache and a long camel-hair overcoat looked on impassively for most of the game; this, the commentators noted, was General Jorge Videla; evasively and uninformatively, they said, "He is not universally appreciated."

I was politically unaware. I was too young to have been a student activist in the late sixties. The only issue that ever exercised my fellow students at Oxford was when several colleges threatened to raise the rent for college rooms. Egged on by the then-president of the National Union of Students, one Jack Straw (yes, that one), we held a brief sit-in, but most of us knew that our middle-class parents would stump up the modest increase if our efforts should fail. If pressed, I would have said that I didn't think military governments were a good thing, but a cursory check of the vicinity now reminded me that the governments of Brazil, Uruguay, Chile, Bolivia, and Paraguay—Argentina's neighbours—were all military, as well, apparently with the complaisance of Western governments.

At the last minute before we set out for Buenos Aires, browsing through a bookshop, I bought Bruce Chatwin's *In Patagonia*; I hadn't heard of it, but I liked the cover—the pale-blue vertical wall of a glacier—and the stark simplicity of the title.

~ We were met at Ezeiza airport by the headmaster and his wife: Harry and Margaret. Harry was tall, wore thick glasses, and was more serious and academic than Roger; Margaret—toothy, a little gushy—had probably been captain of the girls' hockey team.

After we had climbed into the back of Harry's rust-red Ford Falcon and exchanged a few pleasantries, what seemed to me to be an uneasy silence descended. I was right. Fifteen minutes out, Harry half-turned over his shoulder to say abruptly:

"You didn't tell us there were going to be two of you."

Margaret and Jenny looked stolidly ahead as I mumbled something incoherent.

"You'll find the flat very small for two."

The rest of fifty-minute ride through the suburbs of Buenos Aires to Quilmes, twenty kilometres southeast of the city centre, passed without a word except for Harry's explanation that Roger was Harry's best friend from university days. I sensed I had let everyone down.

The flat consisted of two tiny rooms on the top floor of a large, rectangular, brick-built block known as School House. In the much larger ground-floor apartment lived the housemaster, Jimmy and his wife, Jolie, and immediately below us were Alan and Barbara, from the USA. Jimmy, Alan, and I would be jointly responsible for the day-to-day supervision of the sixty or so thirteen- to eighteen-year-old boys whose four spartan dormitories occupied the rest of the building. Just across from School House was the other boys' residence, shared by Cutts and Lockwood Houses. It was a ten-minute walk across the rugby fields to the main school complex, where forty girls were also housed.

St. George's, founded by Canon Stevenson, was not the only school in Buenos Aires dedicated to catering jointly to the city's large Anglo-Argentine community and to well-off Argentines who wanted a British-style education for their offspring. But it was the oldest, the most traditional, and the only one to take mainly boarders. This was largely of necessity: over the course of the twentieth century, Quilmes had become an unfashionable suburb, and most of the school's likely clients now lived in plush areas like Olivos, at the other extreme of the city and nearly two hours away.

The pupils all wore uniforms: grey trousers, blue cord jackets, and house ties for the boys; blouses and red tartan kilts for the girls. I was only five or so years older than some of the girls, and they seemed a lot more spectacular than the dumpy and slouching sixth-formers it had been my misfortune to teach at Sheffield.

School House at St. George's College, Buenos Aires, 1980. The author is front row, sixth from the left.

About two thirds of students, known for administrative convenience as the National College (NC), took the Argentine national curriculum in the mornings, taught in Spanish by Argentine staff. The remainder, who included most of the children of expatriates or diplomats for whom Argentina was not their permanent home, and who were known as the English Side, were taught in English for British exams ("O" and "A" levels) by expatriate British staff like me. In the afternoons and on Saturday mornings both "sides" studied together in English for a more limited range of British exams.

In order to encourage fluency in English among NC students, it was forbidden to speak anything other than English on campus after lunch and on the weekends. A bizarre by-product of this forced bilingual environment was a Spanglish developed by Argentine-born students not fluent in English. One day early on I

overheard a colleague reprimanding two boys on the lawn outside
our apartment:

> "Pérez, Godward, what are you two boys doing here when you
> should be doing your prep?"
>
> "Desolated, sir," replied one of them. "What happens is that the
> watch of Pérez lost itself and now we are retarded."

Argentine colloquialisms, such as *nada que ver* ("nothing like,"
or "nothing to do with it") would be translated literally and be
expressed as "nothing to see." If an Argentine-born student needed
to translate a verb into English but couldn't quite find the term,
he or she might just add "-ate" to the Spanish term; thus *despegar*
("to take off," as an airplane does) would become in English
"despegate." So infectious were these habits that many of the staff,
expatriate and Argentine alike, picked them up; the city's English-
language paper, the *Buenos Aires Herald*, ran a weekly spoof column
written entirely in Spanglish.

The staff was under standing orders not only to enforce the
language regulations but also to prevent proximity between boys
and girls and award black marks accordingly. Bewildered novice
teachers were advised to consider "no physical contact" as the
operative rule. I recall the second or third staff meeting I attended,
in the dark-panelled, book-lined staffroom next to the school
theatre. After a little brisk paper rustling and clearing of throat,
Harry looked over his heavy black-framed glasses to announce:
"Item Number One today: hand-holding."

For twenty minutes or more we held an earnest discussion
over whether this constituted an acceptable exception to the "no
contact" rule.

When I would recount these debates to Jenny, she acted initially
with incredulity and hilarity, but, with admirable adaptability,

A Sunday asado *(barbecue), St. George's: Jenny with some of the English-Side students.*

soon learned to play the part that was expected of a master's wife: alternately stern and mothering to the younger boys, and a source of unlimited fresh cookies, cakes, and aspirin for all. Of course, I didn't always tell her how uncomfortable I was in reprimanding dusky and knowing-looking pampas heiresses who were standing an inch or two too close to their boyfriends; but she surely guessed.

While the fifteen- to eighteen-year-old boys of St. George's were as interested in the opposite sex (or more so) as boys of this age anywhere are, I learned that the risk of things going "too far" was not that high. Upper-middle- and upper-class girls of the kind who attended St. George's had it impressed upon them firmly at home that they would never find a young man prepared to marry them unless they kept their virginity until their wedding night. Meanwhile the boys were actively encouraged by their fathers to relieve their frustrations with their domestic staff at home, or with prostitutes for whom Daddy might even pay. When several members of the Under-16 (under sixteen!) rugby team on tour to Chile had to be rescued from a Santiago brothel by the team coach (insufficient funds), the news was greeted with equanimity by parents and staff alike. The only consequence of the affair was that the school nurse checked the entire team for sexually transmitted diseases on their return to Argentina.

Years after my stint at St. George's I watched the movie *Miss Mary*, starring Julie Christie. This story of an English governess on an isolated estancia in the pampas in the 1920s was a glimpse of the world from which many of our boys and girls came, but which was fast disappearing by the late 1970s.

My teaching load in the mornings, when we expats taught only the English Side, was not demanding. For French A level, I had only two students, while for O level there were six or seven. The fact that the school fees were over 15,000 USD per annum didn't guarantee that the students were especially bright or well-schooled. Many had already attended five or six different schools as their peripatetic parents travelled the world, and they had picked up what seemed to be only random elements of learning. Fourteen-year-old Gina Robertson, pale-faced, with long black hair and an invariable twinkle in her eye that had you thinking she was about to tell you a joke, had been taught—until she came to St. George's—first in a one-room school at the tiny community of Fox Bay West in the Falklands, where her father was the farm manager, and subsequently by radio. It was going to be a struggle to get her through French.

In the afternoons, when the NC students joined in, classes were a lot larger and more challenging. As a result of a ploy by the second master, who should have known better, I was assigned remedial English with the school leavers. With my class invariably occurring as the last class of the day, and in a makeshift location—the chemistry lab—where the only seats were stools and there were many interesting distractions on the lab benches (such as gas outlets) for my charges to fiddle with idly, this was an ordeal. After a few weeks I would find myself starting to feel physically queasy when Friday's last period—NC5A: Extra English—approached.

The day began with the duty master (or mistress) ringing the wake-up bell, ensuring that everyone took showers and, summoned respectfully by each duty prefect in turn, inspecting the thirty-bed dorms for well-made beds, combed hair, shining shoes, and properly tied ties. He would then supervise all 150 or so students over breakfast; the staff not on duty ate in an adjoining staff dining room, served by white-jacketed waiters. Most mornings there would then be a short ecumenical chapel service in the college's beautiful brick-built chapel. This, complete with its brasses and embroidered kneelers, could have come from a small English village (the bricks, it was said, had in fact come over in an English ship as ballast.) We sang English hymns; staff departing for the UK at the end of their postings were traditionally sent off with a mournful rendition of "For Those in Peril On The Sea."

The English Side student body was located in cubbyholes all around the campus. I often gave my classes in the wooden, prefab geography room, which had been donated to the college by Ernest Shackleton as surplus to requirements on one of his expeditions to Antarctica. At lunch, which usually consisted of prime Argentine steak, the duty master would sit in splendour with the headmaster and head boy at the high table, while the rest of the staff headed tables according to the houses to which they were assigned. English speaking was enforced over lunch, which meant that the less articulate students competed to be at the end of the table farthest from the staff.

In the afternoons it was all hands on deck, with the relatively small number of expat staff now having to deal with the entire student body: almost everyone was pressed into teaching English at some level or another, as well as their specialties. Following this, there was compulsory sport, depending on the season: rugby, field hockey (for the girls), soccer, swimming, cricket, and so on. As at the most traditional British schools, inter-house matches were a highlight of the year, and the entire school was expected to turn out for the year's big rugby matches against our traditional rivals; here, at least, it was permitted to express enthusiasm in Spanish.

Many memories of my time at the college are of afternoons on the sports fields. They were enclosed by mature eucalyptus trees, and in summer they were mown once a week: now, whenever I smell either freshly mown grass or eucalyptus, I'm taken back to long afternoons in the sun, with the sound of cricket balls striking willow and the excited cries in mangled Spanglish: "*Corra, Murphy! Necesitamos sólo tres runs para ganar este innings!*"

Some weekend evenings, depending on the Buenos Aires "season," we would take a group of students to a concert in the city, taking the cheaper seats on the seventh level (the *paraíso*, or "Gods") of the Scala-like Colón opera house, where traditional claques would still gather to bravo or boo their favoured or hated performers. More adventurously, we received reluctant permission to take some of the older boys and girls to Earth, Wind and Fire at Luna Park, the more modern events-hall where Juan Perón famously first met Evita at a benefit concert. We'd usually go for a pizza afterward at Los Inmortales, the 1930s-era restaurant around the corner from the Colón, or wait until we got back to the Pizzería Udine, near Quilmes station, where you could choose from sixty-five toppings. Either way we would rarely be back at the college before 1:30 A.M.

A couple of times a term, discos would be organized in the small wooden assembly hall. To try to even up the sex ratio, girls from Northlands school, on the other side of the city, would be bussed in for these events. Unlike at British or North American schools—where the boys would all have stood at one end of the gym for ninety minutes, only plucking up courage to approach the opposing team in the last few minutes—the boys were not shy and would be in passionate clinches soon after the discos began. *Saturday Night Fever* and the Village People were in vogue but, as in North America, "Stairway to Heaven" was often the favoured finale. And at the end of every school year there was the graduation dance, held in the dining hall. This was a sight to behold: the boys in elegant but traditional dinner jackets (none of the frilly or coloured shirts favoured in North America), the girls in full-length silk gowns that a few had specially ordered from Paris. Alcohol was served, of course, but I do not recall a single instance of drunkenness. In Argentina you were expected by fifteen or sixteen to be able to handle drink sensibly, and peer pressure was such that getting visibly drunk would have been a major source of embarrassment.

I was also responsible for the outdoors club. This required imagination in the two hours allotted to me on a weekday afternoon, four hundred kilometres from the nearest hill. We rappelled off the water tower, pretended the large plane trees that dotted the campus were rock faces and climbed them with pegs and ropes, practised Eskimo rolls in the swimming pool, and orienteered our way around the campus. But most long weekends we would try to get away. Five or six of the boarders who lived too far from Buenos Aires to travel home formed a core group of adventurers, and I remember them all to this day.

Paula Ferrante, a big girl with a long blonde mane, invariably cheerful but a little clumsy—we had to keep her away from the water tower; Paula's tomboy sister, Gabi, whose main ambition was to outdo whatever the boys did (their parents owned a plastics company and they kept us supplied with free plastic plates and mugs); petite but tough Shirley Bárcena Rudd, one of the school's exclusive Patagonian clan, from distant Río Gallegos; twins Jean and George Godward from Saõ Paolo, so far away that Jenny and I were asked to take them along on every outing rather than have them languish alone at the school over long weekends and half-term breaks.

With our backpacks and armed with a supply of pre-cooked milanesas (breaded beef) and boiled eggs supplied by Jorge, the school chef, we would on a Thursday afternoon take the pale-blue Number 580 bus that passed the school gates to our closest suburban train station: Quilmes. From here it was a thirty-minute ride into the main terminal at Plaza Constitución, where we could catch a long-distance overnight train deep into the province of Buenos Aires. Or we would cross the city by Subte (subway) to Retiro terminal to take another overnighter to Córdoba and its nearby mountain ranges.

We had no maps. Mostly we went to places because they sounded interesting and we'd heard second- or third-hand that there was some nice walking. Frequently we would get lost. On our first trip, to a jagged massif known as Los Gigantes, about one hundred kilometres outside Córdoba, darkness caught us in a set of ravines far from where we had pitched our camp, and we spent a night in sub-zero temperatures huddled together under a rock overhang. Another time, with six kayaks on a makeshift trailer in tow, we headed south from Quilmes across the pampas until we crossed a likely looking stream, and put the boats in. For two days we paddled gently downstream though the old haunts of the Anglo-Argentine writer W.H. Hudson, spotting herds of rheas under an enormous sky and eventually emerging into the Atlantic at Samborrombón Bay.

A favourite spot became the isolated mountain range of Sierra de la Ventana, which rises abruptly from the otherwise flat pampas four hundred kilometres south of the capital. We would get off at dawn at the tiny train station of the same name, cross the tracks, and head straight for the hills. On sun-filled days trekking through the yellowish tussock grass, we would first hear then see—far on the horizon—herds of shy guanaco. On one trip a local farm dog attached itself to us and embarrassingly kept digging up terrified armadillos from their holes and presenting them to us as offerings.

We would always finish our trek at the same lone restaurant on Sierra de la Ventana's main drag; here they served rough red wine from brown porcelain penguins.

My final distraction was, for two years and after our neighbour Alan left, directing the school plays. I had no experience whatsoever but, as Harry sternly put it, "someone has to do it." For my first major production we put on the old chestnut *Doctor in the House*, the following year the much more ambitious *Enter a Free Man*, by Tom Stoppard. The pool of talent available was limited: I was forced to cast a tiny and very innocent little blonde girl called Molly as a prostitute, kitted out in a mini-skirt and silver lamé stockings. But acting appealed to the naturally extrovert Argentine children, and, moreover, the increasing pressure of rehearsals as performance time grew near gave them an excuse to get out of evening prep. The facilities were minimal. There was a stage in the assembly hall, but for each production we had to rig up makeshift footlights with a row of masked light-bulbs; the two available floodlights had to be manoeuvred as required by a small boy perched high in the rafters, which could only be reached by ladder. The set was built and painted by our eighty-year-old woodwork teacher, Mr. Gwozdz; bald, with false teeth, he had come to Argentina from his native Poland in 1945 and spoke negligible Spanish and even less English. Objectively speaking it is doubtful whether the enormous investment we all made in these productions was worth it: the eventual audience consisted only of the remaining students and the doting parents of cast members (if they lived within reach of the campus).

I loved nearly all of it: the sheer exoticism of Argentina, the consciousness of living a unique, slightly bizarre way of life that could scarcely have been further removed from that dreary Sheffield staffroom. What I did not always like was the teaching itself. I know now that I was far too eager to please and to be popular with the students. Boys and girls of that age ruthlessly sense any such vulnerability and home in on it.

Jenny took things much more stolidly, in her stride. With only a modicum of schoolgirl Spanish, she found a job with a systems analysis outfit in downtown BA, riding the bus or train an hour each way every day. The hazards for women travelling on public transport were *piropos*, just-audible ribaldries uttered by men with the dual purpose of amusing other men and eliciting a reaction—any reaction—from their target. As Jenny was blonde and moderately well-endowed she elicited her fair share of these; but she soon learned to feign the necessary utter indifference.

Coming to Argentina wasn't her idea, of course, and by doing so she gave up hope of a steady career in the UK. This would turn out to be the pattern of our later life. For me the grass was always greener somewhere else; there were always different places to go and new things to see. Jenny often wouldn't comment at all when I came up with some new plan, but she invariably came along, found her own groove, and—just when I was ready to move on again—would discover she had become deeply attached to the place. She also took care of all those mundane things like money, health, and remembering relatives' birthdays.

I don't know where my wanderlust comes from, but it could have something to do with having been sent away to boarding school at the early age of seven and never having much of a sense of home. One of my recurrent dreams has me in a hotel wandering the corridors and taking one elevator after another, unable to remember which is my room; in another version I'm back at boarding school and I can't remember which dorm I've been assigned to. Jenny says she doesn't dream at all.

$\backsim$ Argentina—the outside world—meanwhile suffered under perhaps the most repulsive regime experienced by any country in Latin America in the twentieth century.

The country, despite the clearly fascist inclinations of its leaders during the Second World War, had remained nominally neutral during almost all of the conflict and was, when former General Juan Domingo Perón won the presidency in 1946, one of the most prosperous in the world. Greatly assisted by his charismatic and glamorous wife, Evita, a former actress, Perón was for some time able to keep both the powerful military and the labour unions on his side and deliver a program that gave women the vote, put in place a wide and ambitious range of workers' rights and benefits, and nationalized many lucrative foreign-owned companies. But by the mid-fifties, Argentina, which did not have the oil resources that would later allow Venezuela's Hugo Chávez to implement similarly populist policies, was ceasing to be competitive, the military and the much-abused private sector restive. The talismanic and popular Evita already having died of cancer, Perón was deposed in a coup in 1955.

Over the next eighteen years there were three military and two civilian governments; left-wing subversion began to gain a toehold. Perón made a spectacular return from exile to reclaim the presidency in October 1973 only to die nine months later. Left in charge was his widow and the nation's vice-president, María Estela Martínez de Perón, known as Isabelita. Incompetent and reputedly in the thrall of a sinister, Rasputin-like minister who practised necromancy, Isabelita could only preside over the country's further decline into economic and political chaos, with the extreme left now beginning to resort to bombings and kidnappings. When a military junta, led by General Jorge Rafael Videla, deposed her in March 1976, it was given a cautious welcome by many.

Videla and his cohorts failed to capitalize on this faint goodwill. Instead they launched a savage repressive campaign against the incipient guerrilla. They botched the economy, too. Hyperinflation took hold. Simple transactions, such as buying a ticket on the bus, involved so many zeroes that people adopted names for the higher denomination notes: ten thousand pesos, a red and black note, became *un palo*, a stick. Second-hand car dealers ceased posting their prices on the car windshields because they would rise several times a day. The college staff had standing permission to go to the bank the moment they knew their salaries had been deposited—even in the middle of a class—because a delay of a few hours in withdrawing the cash (and converting or investing it) could cost them several per cent of its value.

The routine was always the same. Referring to the school bursar by name, some first-year boy with poor English would knock timidly on the classroom door and, when summoned, announce timidly, "Seer, Mister Nield say is bank time."

Many of us chose to play the currency market: you could buy bonds that the government would buy back at three or four times their face value within a month (but would inflation be 300 per cent or 500?). On behalf of the boys, we would routinely invest their meager pocket money allowance and, when withdrawal time came near, the daily talk in the school corridors was all about inflation rates.

It's a cliché, and I am uneasily aware that many Germans who lived under Hitler said more or less the same, but most Argentines and expatriates living in Argentina at the time were not aware of the gross human rights abuses that were taking place. Others, I suspect, had an inkling but remembered the chaos under Isabelita. The common refrain at dinner parties in Olivos and the other posh suburbs, where we would meet parents or other teachers over gin and tonics, was: "Well, you know, you have to remember what it was like before. It's possible that some excesses have been committed. I don't think so myself; that's just left-wing propaganda. But so what if they have? Have you any idea of what those subversives used to do? Kidnappings, bombings...you couldn't go out."

For the friends and relatives of the at least 30,000 civilians who were illegally "disappeared" (Argentina gave this new transitive verb to the Spanish language), the horrors were immediate and real, but even they did not understand, at the time, the extent of the nightmare. Media censorship was rigorous, and it was only in the dying months of the regime that many realized the trauma they had gone through was not something private and exceptional.

Occasionally, at night or early in the morning we would lie in bed in our tiny apartment and hear helicopters flying overhead.

"What's that noise?" Jenny might say groggily.

"Must be doing traffic reports for the radio," I'd mumble.

Eventually I enquired whether BA radio stations actually did this. The answer was no. Incuriously, I stopped thinking about it. Much later we learned that they were probably dumping bodies of torture victims into the nearby River Plate. It was said that sometimes the passengers were embarked alive; the first would be pushed out from 2000 metres without a word being spoken; the second would be briefly interrogated and again pushed out if he or she was not immediately co-operative; the third usually talked.

Jenny, with her job downtown, got to know the city much better than I did. For nearly thee years her daily bus route took her past the doors of Naval Mechanics School. Usually there were a couple of smartly uniformed cadets on duty, and she might see an officer stepping in with a briefcase. Afterward, we read that this was the principal detention and torture centre of the regime; now it is a macabre national monument.

Once in a while her train to town would be delayed and the rumour would go around that some guerrilla group had placed a bomb on the line. And very occasionally an entire block would be sealed off by the army and the papers of every individual in the street examined. Coming as we did from a country where no one has papers we thought this an imposition, but to remember to carry our little red residents' carnets was not onerous. If driving at night, you were supposed to leave your interior lights on, so that the police and military could inspect you as you passed by; but as we had no car this did not concern us either. As was proudly pointed out to us by many Argentine friends, an upside of this heavy military presence was that it was entirely safe to travel on public transport, anywhere in the city at any time. We often came back from a late movie or concert in downtown BA on the 1:30 A.M. train and thought nothing of it.

Only a couple of times did the dark undercurrents of violence and repression wash briefly up against our little island of tranquility. The young, bearded, and fierce-looking school chaplain, Paul Battersby—known to the rest of the expat staff as The Bish or The Vicar—was an unlikely incumbent in this bastion of high-church conservatism. He and his wife, Sheila, were from the North of England; they both spoke with strong Lancashire accents and took a very down-to-earth, pragmatic, and often humorous approach to caring for the spiritual welfare of their upper-class charges. Now I realize that they were much more aware of what was going on outside the college gates than any of the rest of us were, but they were careful not to be too outspoken. Until one day Paul made a reference in class to Amnesty International, at that time a banned organization in Argentina. A few days later a fire was set outside the door of his home. Rumours began to circulate and reached the attention of the college's board of governors. In response to their formal enquiry, Paul freely avowed that he was a member of Amnesty. His contract was terminated.

There remains with me, too, a conversation I once had with one of my star Spanish A-level pupils. Every school day, at both the college and its junior school, things began with the raising of the blue and white Argentine flag, with all of the pupils lined up by class by the tuck shop. The flag was also taken down ceremonially at dusk, albeit without a full school assembly. Only honour students were accorded the privilege of slowly raising or lowering the flag, and it was a proud day for this little girl when, at age twelve or thirteen, she was allowed to lower it.

"I was as happy as can be," she recalled when I asked her about it two or three years later. "All my classmates were envious: no one could remember when anyone so young had been given this privilege. I remember it was a windy evening. I was a bit nervous but the flag came down properly, nothing snagged. But it was a big flag, you see. Everyone was watching. I couldn't fold it up—it kept blowing around. I thought it would be best to lay it out on the lawn and fold it properly..."

There was a shocked silence. The girl was bundled away and the next day summoned to account before the headmaster and a senior uniformed government official; in tears, she was severely reprimanded and informed that to put the national flag in contact with the ground was a grave offence; the *agravio* ("insult to the nation") would not be forgotten.

In a similar but more amusing incident a year or two before my time, a young teacher at the prep school had early one Saturday morning staggered back to his room in the school buildings in an advanced state of inebriation. Mistaking the severe bust of General Belgrano that stands before the main door for an old friend, he had embraced the general, dislodged him from his pedestal and caused him to fracture into several pieces. In a panic, he gathered up the pieces and hid them under his bed. There was a furor, and it was only a matter of hours before he was undone: a cleaning lady found the fragments. Again, there was much official talk about *agravios*, and grovelling apologies had to be made by all concerned (including an arcane ceremony of *desagravio*). The teacher was also shipped home, and, just in case anyone had not received the message, an armoured car was parked outside the college gates for several weeks.

The death knell for the generals came when, as a distraction from their own incompetence and in a desperate bid to unite the nation behind the one issue on which all Argentines agree (even today), they launched an ill-advised military occupation of the Falkland Islands, known in Spanish as the Islas Malvinas.

New staff tended to treat the oft-repeated vows of the nation's leaders to "recover" the islands from Britain as a joke. We soon learned, though. At the staff's favourite watering hole in Quilmes, the Casa Vieja, other patrons had three St. George's staff ejected for discussing the question among themselves in a frivolous manner. Once a year, like every other school in Argentina, we had to observe Malvinas Day, which meant teaching the students the ins and outs of Argentina's territorial claim and the manifest weakness of Britain's, which was based mainly on Spain's failure to exercise its claim and Britain's de facto occupation since 1832. The bookshelves of the geography department were periodically inspected by eagle-eyed government officials, and woe betide the geography teacher if an atlas was found that said anything other than "*Islas Malvinas (Arg.)*." The two or three pupils from the Falklands that the student body usually included were quietly excused from Malvinas Day.

Official stridency on the Falklands was just one manifestation of an extreme nationalism that the government deliberately fostered in the hope of obscuring or excusing its excesses in other areas. But observers of the national scene (especially those in the British Embassy who were paid to watch and analyze such things) should have foreseen that the more dire things became domestically, the more likely the generals were to talk up the Falklands issue, and that they could even be foolish enough to do something about it.

In late 1978, a few months after our arrival, there was a direct warning, a dress rehearsal.

Over the course of the mid-nineteenth century, Chile had been the winner in a long-running dispute over who should control the shores of the Strait of Magellan, which, in the days before the Panama Canal opened, was strategically and commercially much more significant than it is today. You would logically have expected Argentina to be awarded control of the eastern entrance from the Atlantic, Chile the western exit to the Pacific. But over the long period during which no one had really bothered about who owned what in the extreme South, Chile had established a presence well to the east of Cabo Froward, which is the southernmost tip of the

mainland: first at Fuerte Bulnes and then at the penal colony of
Punta Arenas. Moreover, Chile argued, unless it were awarded both
shores, and all the way along the strait, it would be denied guaranteed access to Europe. Chile won out; an international arbitration
gave her what she wanted, plus the western half of Tierra del Fuego
and "all land south of the Beagle Channel," which separates Tierra
del Fuego from the islands of the Cape Horn group.

The agreement left one matter vague: the precise limits of the
Beagle Channel. Chile claimed that a southbound ship would
enter the Beagle as soon as it rounded the eastern tip of Tierra del
Fuego—Cabo San Diego—and turned west. With the big island
of Tierra del Fuego to starboard, it would first pass Lennox and
Nueva islands to port, then Picton and the much bigger Navarino.
Argentina claimed the channel dipped south between Picton and
Navarino, and that the three smaller islands were therefore theirs.

For many years this difference of opinion didn't matter too
much to anyone. First gold miners, then sheep farmers, and finally
fishermen made temporary homes on Picton, Nueva, and Lennox.
But Argentina asked the International Court of Justice to look at the
issue. In 1977, to the surprise only of the leadership in Buenos Aires,
it ruled in Chile's favour.

The generals decided to make an issue of it and said they rejected
the court's decision. This looked like a surefire cause insofar as the
public was concerned, a flag to rally round. "Victors of the Beagle"
would look great on their epitaphs. Chile, it was thought, would
roll over and let Argentina have its way. In the unlikely event of it
coming to a fight, it was true that the rival air force was half-decent.
Mythology had it—incorrectly—that President Salvador Allende
had been shot dead at his desk in the national palace in Santiago
in 1973 by a strafing fighter pilot. But Chile's nearest roadhead and
port to the disputed islands (Punta Arenas) was two hundred kilometres distant, via a maze of tortuous channels, while the large
Argentine port of Ushuaia, with a good airstrip, was almost in sight

of Picton. And Argentine troops could theoretically reach, overland and through Argentine territory, a point only two miles across the Beagle Channel from Chile's only presence in the entire region: the tiny naval outpost of Puerto Williams.

In 1978 righteous demands were made by Buenos Aires of Santiago. Newspaper headlines blared: "*Son nuestras!*" (They're ours!)

The junta prepared for their photo ops: it was noted gleefully in the Argentine papers that there would be one island for each of the commanders in the triumvirate. But, lest the Argentine public take all this for granted and possibly not appreciate the magnitude of their leaders' achievement, we were warned that Chilean mountain troops were massing just across the Andes, and instructions were given to hold air raid practices in Buenos Aires.

Chile's General Pinochet was far wilier and—at this time—much more secure in his job than his trans-Andean counterparts. Recognizing he would likely lose the first round of any military encounter, he promptly appealed for further arbitration to the one referee whom he knew the Argentine generals, as good Catholics, would not dare impugn, and who was likely to take his time: the Pope. The matter would not be definitively resolved (in Chile's favour) until 1985, by which time Buenos Aires had lost all interest in it.

Nationalism was fostered in more innocuous ways as well. The euphoria of Argentina's 1978 World Cup victory over Holland was given full rein, and for months there were celebratory street parties on which the usually dour soldiers on every corner looked smilingly. You might be out walking when someone suddenly shouted: "*El que no salta es un holandés!*" (If you don't jump, you're a Dutchman!) There would be a minute or two of spontaneous euphoria as everyone jumped on the spot.

Social historians later argued that the feel-good factor the football victory engendered bought the junta at least another year's free ride. At the movies, sonorous propaganda newsreels ran, claiming that while Argentina had missed its chances before, *"Ahora podemos ocupar nuestro lugar en el primer mundo!"* (Now we can take up our place in the First World!).

Many seemed to believe it. For Porteños—the inhabitants of Buenos Aires—this was the greatest and most sophisticated city in Latin America. Not that the competition (Rio? Mexico City?) was too much to write home about, they would hasten to add; it would be more apt to describe BA in terms of Paris or Rome. The generals were more than happy to play along, even if they looked uneasy and out of place, in their medal-bedecked uniforms, at the Colón Opera House or indulging their new-found passion for football.

You could tell a lot about how the better-off Argentines saw themselves in those years by the jokes that their bemused and humbler fellow Latin Americans told about them: "Why does an Argentine rush out of the room and into the garden when there's thunder and lightning? Because he thinks God has come to take a flash photo of him."

≈ Over prep, I had been reading Chatwin's *In Patagonia*. His comparison of Buenos Aires to Russia didn't seem too apposite to me. (Did he mean Cold War Moscow? Tsarist St. Petersburg? It was a stretch either way.) And when I tried a random scan of the BA telephone directory, as he did, it turned up not Radziwills and Romanows ("exiles," as Chatwin put it) but mainly Italian and Spanish names.

But the book was a great read, and Jenny and I were inspired. This was before the days that the clothing company of the same name had become common currency. The very word Patagonia conjured up for me the sound of wind howling over lonely and little-known empty places and was resonant with romance and adventure. Argentine writers and poets had always been drawn to the South: for many years the country's leading literary review was called *Sur*. Just as the soul of Canada is felt to reside in its far frozen North, Russia's in the empty expanses of eastern Siberia, so it seemed that if you were going to live in and know Argentina, you must head south.

Most of our Argentine friends were dismissive: "Why would you want to go down there? It's full of drunken Scotsmen and Welsh, and a lot of sheep. No real Argentine would ever want to live in Patagonia..."

The thirty-six-hour train ride south and west, in early December as the three-month summer holidays began, became an annual ritual for us. This was the General Roca line, named after the soldier who had in the nineteenth century led what is known in national mythology as the Conquest of the Desert; actually it was the extermination of Argentina's Aboriginal inhabitants. Three or four trains a week left from the huge echoing terminal at Plaza Constitución, which must have been modelled on the great Paris or London stations, and they were dead on time. They had brown-painted carriages, drawn by red and yellow diesel electrics, with shiny faux-leather seats on which you could stretch out to sleep at night. As we rode along we'd jam open the windows so that the clackety-clack made it difficult to talk; over the smell of diesel smoke, and once we had escaped the pungent slums of Buenos Aires, that wonderful smell of eucalyptus would waft in again.

Our first year we were accompanied by Brian Hoskins, a fellow teacher at St. George's, born in Argentina but about to move to Britain ("home" as he wryly put it). Brian, short, wiry, and prematurely balding, spoke a clipped and efficient-sounding Spanglish as a matter of course and was often unable to distinguish between English and Spanish words. He had held the "outdoors" mantle at the college for years and was anxious to show us something of the Andes before he left.

Brian taught us many things: the surprisingly long life of pre-cooked cold milanesas, if properly wrapped; how to make a tuna-based spaghetti tuco; where to buy heavy longlife German bread in Quilmes; how to hitchhike (not the traditional thumb in the air; instead, the would-be freeloader holds out an arm and index finger and points downwards, as if toward a pothole in the middle of the road). But, above all, he had a disarmingly simple approach to problems like our collective lack of knowledge about any of the places we were going, not to speak of our lack of maps and adequate equipment for the conditions. "*Ché, boludo,* why don't we just go and see." This was long before *Lonely Planet* and other guides to trekking in South America existed.

Our principal objective in December 1978 was the ascent of Lanín Volcano, in the Andes. Brian had once seen a postcard of it and assured us it was very beautiful and didn't look too steep; he had since lost the postcard, but we found a school atlas that showed it to be 3800 metres high.

The train first cuts south, across the pampas. Except for Sierra de la Ventana, the landscape is green and pancake-flat. Gauchos do not roam anymore here, for the largest estancias have been broken up. Fences, narrow dirt tracks, and strangely cut-off rows of tall poplars indicate where one property begins and another ends. Oven-birds make their distinctive spherical baked-earth nests on the fence and telegraph posts that click past rhythmically. The small towns are confusingly similar: fifteen or twenty blocks of single-storey buildings laid out on a grid pattern, a plaza with a bust of San Martín or Belgrano, and a grand railway station with the name of the town in raised white letters on large black boards. In the signal hut the brass levers and dials gleam as if the British engineers who laid out this network had never left. The businesses are of the kind you would find on the prairies: hardware stores, a gas station, three or four bars, an agricultural equipment dealership. From the train you glimpse in the streets models of cars that everywhere else have been obsolete for thirty years or more.

After Bahía Blanca the tracks turn west; the towns become fewer, farther in between, and poorer; the landscape more scrubby, arid but just as flat. There is an occasional oasis of green, such as at Neuquén where fruit is grown, but mostly you see a few cattle, some sheep—and almost no one. Then suddenly, as the train briefly curves one way or the other, you realize there is a great, grey-blue wall, topped with white, rising up ahead: *la cordillera*, as everyone calls it (not *los Andes*).

It seemed logical that we should approach our target through the picturesque San Martín de los Andes and Lanín National Park. We were lucky enough to be able to hitch a ride into the park with a National Parks vehicle—there didn't seem to be too much other traffic—and as we bumped along a dirt track approaching the mountains, we could see that Brian had indeed chosen a spectacular peak. "There it is! *Hijo de puta,* it's not bad…"

Lanín, a recently extinct volcano, is perfectly conical and towers a good thousand metres above the neighbouring mountains, with its uppermost eight hundred metres snow-covered. With a base camp on Lago Lácar, we bushwhacked up to the snowline in one very long day without too many problems, smoothed out a flattish area on the glacier for our two-person canvas tent (it was cozy with three), and witnessed a spectacular sunset over Chile and the Pacific. Next day we were up before dawn. We had had the foresight to bring our wedding rope, and we had two sets of crampons and two ice axes between the three of us. Brian gallantly insisted on using his hickory walking stick and hobnailed leather boots on the rock-hard, 45-degree slopes.

We headed straight for the top but were thwarted by vertical ice-cliffs with no way around them. Brian spent much of the time stoically sliding downhill, until the sun started to warm the snow, at which point we began to sink in to our thighs. I had neglected to bring sunglasses, and by noon I was effectively blind and had to be led by the other two. It was time to head down.

After some rest and recovery at the lakeside, we moved to a pleasant grass verge on the edge of the dirt road and, taking turns to stand up and be alert for vehicles, waited for a ride out. Three days later, my sight having been restored, I had finished my Dostoyevsky Penguin Classic, Jenny was well on her way through it, and Brian was reading the labels on the tuna tins. Not a single vehicle had passed. Reluctantly—food was running out—we walked the sixty kilometres out.

At the exit to the park, where there was a small National Parks booth, there was a commotion. Half a dozen uniformed personnel rushed out in evident panic.

"Who are you? Where have you been?" a young captain shouted repeatedly. "Are you Chilean? You must be spies..."

One actually brought out a pistol, although it didn't look as though he knew how to use it.

We explained. There was a long silence and everyone looked at each other. Someone went to make a phone call as the silence lengthened.

"*Okey. Está bien*," was the final, deflated response. "Why don't you have some maté with us..."

Over maté everything became clear. In the course of the week or so we had been in the park, political tensions with Chile over the islands in the Beagle had reached new heights, the park had been closed, and a Chilean invasion was expected any time. Our friends were reassured when we said that we had seen no signs of armoured divisions massing on the slopes of Lanín, but the captain warned us: "You never know. Be sure to take precautions. The enemy never sleeps..."

By next season, Brian had left: gone "home" to teach chemistry at Denstone College in the English Midlands. Jenny and I were keen to return and try for the summit again. This time, I had the foresight to buy a map. This was not as helpful as Jenny and I had hoped. It showed about one third of the cone of Lanín; the

In the loft at Tromen Pass, below Lanín Volcano, Argentina.

remaining two thirds falling in Chile were left blank. But it indicated we would have been better off attempting the volcano from
the Tromen Pass on the northern side, that is to say outside Lanín
National Park. Now we mounted a larger expedition, including
several of the older students from St. George's. Their names were
more like what Chatwin found in the phone directory: Bobby
Olsonosky, Gonzalo Blanc-Sánchez, Juan Taylor, Andrew Westcott.
We made an altogether more professional attempt; there were to be
no more walking sticks.

The first several days were spent living in the loft of the Argentine
customs post on the border at Tromen, waiting for a break in the
weather. We were allowed to do this only on the condition that we ·
remain silent and hidden when the officers had to process any
vehicles crossing the border. All went well until on the third day
the daily passenger bus came through. We had just made lunch.

Anxious lest the soup go cold, Jenny quietly reached for her mug, stretched for it—and knocked it over. Hot tomato soup dripped down like blood through a wide crack in the floor and to our horror (we watched this through another crack) splashed onto the logbook in which our friend the chief of customs was laboriously recording the names and passport numbers of every passenger. To his credit, he did not even look up.

When the lenticular clouds indicating high winds on the summit cleared, we made a successful three-day ascent, accompanied by a friendly white dog whose claws were effective on hard snow but whom we felt guilty about not feeding. A cane marked the highest point. When we dug beneath it, we found that the last successful expedition had been from the Argentine military and they had left, wrapped up in plastic, a board-mounted colour photograph of a field gun with an elegant brass plaque affixed to it; as is traditional (or so we thought) we took the plaque and left our own memento, a small St. George's flag. On the way down, we had to spend several more days in a tiny and freezing metal emergency shelter on the edge of an ice-cliff, waiting for a blizzard to abate; you had to lash yourself to the door-post if you wanted to go out and pee.

⌇ After our first attempt on Lanín in 1978, we had made our way farther south, overland, hugging the eastern edge of the cordillera. With those Chileans still reported to be poised for invasion, just out of sight behind the skyline on our right, there was almost no vehicle traffic for the first couple of weeks. We had to walk most of the hundred kilometres or so of the famous Seven Lakes route south to the largest town in the area, Bariloche. Our already depleted food supplies soon gave out, and we trudged for the last couple of days buoyed up only by the fact we had a standing invitation to join Paul and Sheila Battersby for a traditional Christmas lunch at the villa they had rented in Bariloche. We arrived late, of course, exhausted and footsore at 3:00 P.M. on Christmas afternoon. Paul, florid and

boisterous, ushered us in enthusiastically. Sheila came out from
the kitchen, eyed us with her hands on her hips, and said to her
husband in her blunt northern accent, "Tell 'em, Paul. They're too
late. We've eaten the bloody lot."

Bariloche was a tourist trap: faux Swiss-German gabled houses,
nativity scenes made out of chocolate in the windows of the expensive cafés and chocolate shops, *Tannenbaum* and *Stillenacht* echoing
tinnily though loudspeakers in the streets at night. Still, it was sufficiently authentic to attract many German and Austrian retirees,
some of whom, it was widely known, were ex-Nazis. But the tacki-
ness of the town could not detract from the sublime, luminous
beauty of its surroundings: the deep blue, mountain-fringed Lake
Nahuel Huapí, the jagged spires of Cerro Catedral, and the softer
outline of Tronador.

There were tourists, of course: a few very wealthy Europeans
or Americans staying at the luxurious Llao-Llao Hotel, and upper-
class Argentines who would rent a place here for a month or two
to escape the heat of Buenos Aires in summer. But Argentina and
Chile were too expensive for the backpackers. The gringo trail
ended in Bolivia and Peru, and once you got away from the two or
three set circuits offered by the local tourist agencies, you could
have this wilderness quite to yourself. One day we splashed out
and bought tickets on an ancient but elegant white steamer, the
Modesta Victoria, to visit some islands in the lake; one of them, our
guide told us earnestly, was the inspiration for Walt Disney's *Bambi*.

We rode the red and white Don Otto bus onward and when
the road ran out we boarded a prop plane of Argentina's military
airline, LADE, to the small plains outpost of El Calafate and hitched
and walked to the Fitzroy massif.

As a boy unhappily at a monastic school in rainy and claustrophobic England, I was entranced alternately with sailing and
mountaineering adventure books. As well as Chichester's adventure around the Horn, I'd read all the accounts of the early attempts

on Fitzroy and the neighbouring, spike-like Cerro Torre. This had been the setting of the biggest scandal in mountaineering history. Italian climber Cesare Maestri claimed to have reached the summit of then-unclimbed Cerro Torre in 1959. Although his companion, Toni Egger, died in an avalanche, Maestri's feat was hailed by some as the greatest climb ever. But then doubts began to creep in. There were discrepancies in Maestri's various versions of the ascent; he had lost his camera; and there was no living witness to the climb. To spite his critics, Maestri then bludgeoned his way to the top by using a steam hammer to place bolts every couple of metres all the way up Torre's near-vertical face. He made it, but the climbing community never forgave him for what was seen as a horrific breach of mountaineering etiquette, compounding further his perceived lies about the earlier climb.

We chose a smaller neighbouring peak for our own more modest adventure. At its summit we were rewarded with a unique view of Torre, Fitzroy, and the glacier between them, with a pair of condors circling below us. The sense of excitement made me almost breathless: here we were, at the end of the world, where climbing history was made and where nobody we knew had ever been. With perverse pleasure, I remembered those cold rainy nights, riding the bus in Nottingham under the orange street lights. Jenny was more stoic; I think she had learned by then that we would be forever moving on to somewhere more distant, more exotic, and she would always be accordingly parsimonious in her enthusiasm.

The farthest south we went was Ushuaia (Oosh-WHY-er), which, with its back to a spectacular mountain range, sits on the north shore of the blue-grey Beagle Channel, looking across at Chile's equally rugged Hoste Island, only a couple of miles away. Sixty miles farther south is Cape Horn. Ushuaia was a quiet place of one-storey buildings, many clad in brightly painted tin, in the Patagonian style, and dirt roads. We camped on a piece of waste ground at the end of one, three or four blocks up from the harbour, and spent most of our days walking in the mountains behind. We trekked along the rocky shore of the channel itself, and one hot afternoon even went swimming, although the sea was frigid. At Lapataia, we gathered mussels for dinner and camped by a sign that informed us we were at the end of Ruta Tres, 3000 kilometres from Buenos Aires. At night the Southern Cross was high in the clear sky. Every afternoon a westerly wind piped up hard in the Beagle Channel; it was like Scotland, but bigger and emptier.

I had a cheap camera that Jenny had got for us at a discount from Boots. I photographed everything in sight. In hindsight, this was the beginning of an unhealthy obsession with recording all the new and exciting things I see, not so much to show the pictures off later to friends and relatives, but somehow to capture what I anxiously know to be fleeting, transitory. Jenny has no such obsession and long ago gave up her own photographic career; as a result I suspect, she now recalls truly memorable places and happenings in a better way than I do.

We worked our way back up the flat, windswept, eastern side of Tierra del Fuego, crossing back into Chile to catch the converted pale-blue landing craft that served as a ferry from Porvenir across the Strait of Magellan to the large Chilean city of Punta Arenas. We hitchhiked two hundred kilometres north on a dirt road to the much smaller town of Puerto Natales. A fat man in a blue flatbed truck, unshaven and reeking of cheap alcohol, gave us a ride, but we almost immediately had to help him when we careered off the road with a puncture. I noticed he had a handgun tucked under his belt. When we got back in, he saw I was eyeing the gun nervously. "*Qué?*" he asked aggressively. "Have you never seen a gun before?"

I didn't confess that, coming from safe, gun-free England, I had never examined one closely.

"Take it," he said as we bumped along the road, prising the weapon out from below his paunch. He belched loudly.

"If you see something, you can fire it. Just don't shoot any shepherds!" and he laughed loudly at his own joke.

Next stop was Paine (pronounced "piney") National Park. A ranger told us it was possible to walk all the way around the remarkably shaped and coloured "horns" of the Paine massif. For eight days we followed his verbal instructions, sleeping several nights in abandoned shepherds' huts, others in our canvas tent high on mountain passes as blizzards raged outside. We got lost repeatedly and saw no one.

Back in Punta Arenas, we were adopted by a young evangelical priest and a family from his congregation. "You are most welcome in this humble home of God," said our host in rather ornate Spanish at the door of his single-storey, three-room home. "This house is yours. We are deeply honoured by your visit." They taught us the ABCs of life under Chile's Pinochet.

"He says he is a Man of God," said Padre Armando ruminatively. "But he is not. He is an evil man. Do you understand? Yes, very evil. I think he may be like Hitler. Do you know who Hitler was? But we must all pray for him."

The city had a uniquely mixed population, he explained: third- and fourth-generation Croats, who had originally come to mine gold; tough, hard-drinking, king crab–fishermen, proud to work the roughest and coldest waters in the world; transient sheep-farm labourers between contracts; retired merchant marine captains; a handful of died-in-the-wool Anglos who had forgotten to go home; small but dynamic and business-minded Indian and Arab communities. Their common denominator was their independent-mindedness, cussedness even. As on the Argentine side of the border, there was in this remote region of Chile a tradition of strong and bloody-minded unions and little sympathy for central government. So, more than most cities of its size elsewhere in Chile, Punta Arenas had over the first five years of the Pinochet government seen harsh repression of dissent, and there had been many "disappearances."

Armando summoned me over to the window one overcast afternoon. At the bottom of a steep dirt road lined with tin shacks you could see the open grey waters of the Strait of Magellan and, on its far side, a smudge of low land. "That's Dawson Island. Maybe you have heard of it."

On Dawson, he explained, the military managed a combined torture and concentration camp. It was, Armando added, built on the ruins of the last Salesian mission to Tierra del Fuego, where well-meaning but misguided Italian priests had presided over the extinction of the island's Selknam people.

"*Muy triste. Muy triste.* What has become of my country?"

By this time it was February. School would be back in a few weeks. From the wharf at Punta Arenas we took the *Río Baker* up the Chilean coast to Puerto Montt. The *Baker* was an old rust bucket with a permanent list to starboard. On the bridge there was a framed paper certificate stating that she had been built at Le Havre in 1943; the last inspection of her fire and safety systems had been in 1965. Most of the forty or so passengers were housed in a green-painted, square room with no portholes, far below deck: it was unventilated, insufferably hot, and an hour or two after departure already smelled ripely of vomit. We had a tiny, two-bunk cabin that you had to enter sideways and where we surreptitiously cooked porridge on our camping stove in the mornings. Meals were served in rotation at a single, eight-seater table in a corridor, but they were always the same: seaweed soup.

We spent as much time as we could on deck as we headed first south—around Cape Froward, the southernmost tip of the mainland—then northwest up the Strait of Magellan, and finally north and into the maze of narrow natural waterways known as the Chilean channels. The cloud was low, the waters steely grey, the mountainsides (rarely more than a mile away on either side) lush and steep as they disappeared upward into the mist. We made only one stop: two days out, at dawn, at the only human settlement in seven hundred miles of intricate navigation, tiny Puerto Edén. The cloud was at first so low that, when we anchored, we could not see the shore.

Five or six crudely constructed rowing boats came out and banged up against our steel sides: dark-faced Indians, the very last of the Alacaluf people, peddled mussels, limpets, and strange-looking, square cakes of dried kelp. In one of the boats, three or four empty oil barrels were tightly wedged: a hose was run down from the large white tank on our deck and five hundred litres of San Pedro red wine were decanted. The captain came and stood by us at the rail: "*Esos pobres indios*," those poor Indians, he said lugubriously.

By eight in the morning we were off again, and Puerto Edén was left to its own devices for another six weeks or so.

At the southern end of the open-water Golfo de Penas (Gulf of Sorrows), we hove to for half a day while rain and gale-force winds lashed the bridge and we rose and fell in deep long swells that reached from the ocean into our narrow channel. Our ever-pensive and philosophical captain sighed and shrugged melodramatically: "The sea does not forgive. It is better to wait..."

But by next morning sky and sea were utterly blue: seagulls turned and dived in our wake. Far away, ahead and to starboard, we could see the familiar volcanoes of the central Andes.

≈ The volatility of the peso/dollar exchange rate was in this period extreme. Some months, in dollar terms, my salary was derisory; but sometimes we got lucky and my monthly deposit would amount to several thousand dollars. After a bonanza in late 1979 we decided to splash out and take a cruise to Antarctica.

The Río Baker *crossing the Golfo de Penas.*

At this time there was only one commercial company—Lindblad—offering cruises to the Antarctic peninsula. But the *Lindblad Explorer* was small, booked up years ahead, and out of even our price bracket. This was discouraging. After weeks of enquiries we got wind of a possible alternative: every year the Argentine navy sent a supply ship down to its bases in the region and it normally accepted a small number of passengers. We signed up.

You had to pay in cash, dollars only and in advance. Counting on Argentine thieves' propriety, Jenny put 5,000 USD into her bra and we rode the train and subway one morning to the naval offices at Dársena Norte, in BA's vast and crumbling docks, to pay up.

It was an area with which we were already familiar. Once a year David Nield, St. George's Anglo-Argentine bursar, would summon us to his office, give us a bottle of Johnnie Walker Red Label at the college's expense, and despatch us to the immigration offices at Dársena Norte to renew our residence permits. I never quite got over the feeling of guilt, but the mere sight of the bottle ensured we were ushered to the very head of what was usually a queue of several hundred dispirited persons and thus saved the school several days of our time. You never had to say anything; you just put the bottle on the table without making any eye contact and left it there when the transaction was finished.

Our vessel for the Antarctic trip was the 5000-tonne *Bahía Buen Suceso*, named—like her sister-ship the *Bahía Aguirre*—after a bay in Argentine Tierra del Fuego. Although painted in military grey and black and manned by navy personnel, she was an all-purpose supply ship, built in Halifax and surplus to the Canadian Navy at the end of the Second World War, and was not armed.

For this trip she carried fifty civilians, whose average age I calculated to be about seventy. We were accommodated in cramped, four-bunk cabins, most of which were below the waterline, segregated by sex. On-board entertainment was mostly of the do-it-yourself variety, notably round-the-clock card games, but three or four times the purser cleared the main saloon for tango dancing sessions; the chef permitted visits to his galley at all hours, and the captain operated an open bridge. One evening an 8mm film on the wildlife of Antarctica was projected onto a bedsheet in the saloon; it was well-photographed but spoiled by a saccharine commentary with the refrain, as different species were covered: "*Ciao, pinguinitos!*"

Winding our way out from Buenos Aires through dredged channels in the brown and shallow River Plate, we were in a few hours in the open ocean, heading first south then west. First stop was the naval base at Bahía Blanca: nothing to see on shore, and we weren't allowed to take any pictures anyway. Next was Puerto Madryn, founded by Welsh colonist Parry Madryn when he landed here with 150 other immigrants in 1865. The place seemed bleak, dusty, and windswept. Our hosts were unknowledgeable about the Welsh—"*Son galeses. No son muy interesantes.*"—but told us that Gaimán, smaller, farther south, and a little inland, still organized an annual Eisteddfod and had a couple of pseudo-Welsh tearooms. I remembered that one of the secretaries at St. George's came from hereabouts; her name was Monica Williams and she spoke better Welsh than English.

We were given packed lunches and—while the *Buen Suceso* took on cargo at the town wharf—sent off to see the wildlife on nearby Valdés Peninsula. At this time the local authorities were just beginning to catch on to the idea that in the huge sea lion and elephant seal colonies of the peninsula, and in the large seasonal populations of killer and humpback whales, they had something that people might want to come a long way to see. Unfortunately, in what was to become a pattern, our guides could tell us little beyond the obvious: "Those are sea lions."

Our fellow voyagers, after brief exclamations of "*Qué lindo!*" were anxious to get back and make up at the dinner table for what they considered to be paltry lunches.

We ploughed on south, past the entrance to the Strait of Magellan, through the Strait of Le Maire and into the Beagle Channel. Our next and final stop in South America was Ushuaia, which we had visited overland the year before.

Two of my pupils at St. George's were Anne and Abby Goodall (it did not escape the attention of their friends that Anne and Abby were also the first names of the two most widely syndicated agony

41

columnists in the USA). Their home was Estancia Harberton, near Ushuaia. This was the first European settlement in this the remotest part of Patagonia and the setting for one of the most remarkable books about pioneering in any part of the world: Lucas Bridges's *Uttermost Part of the Earth*.

Bridges's father, Thomas, had come out from Britain, via the Falkland Islands, as an Anglican missionary in 1871. Earlier attempts to bring Christianity to the wild and primitive Yahgan and Selknam people of this wet, cold, and windswept place had met with unmitigated disaster. But Thomas and his young bride, Mary, from the Devon village of Harberton, faced the challenge with quiet stoicism and pragmatism. Drawing on his father's journal, Lucas reconstructs the scene that first met his mother:

> This Ushuaia, of which she had heard so much, was new, strange and rather frightening. Behind the shingle beach the grassland stretched away to meet a sudden step less than a quarter of a mile from the shore. Between shore and hill were scattered wigwams, half-buried hovels made of branches roofed with turf and grass, smelling strongly, as she was to find later, of smoke and decomposed whale-blubber or refuse flung close outside. Round the wigwams dark figures, some partially draped in otter skins, others almost naked, stood or squatted, gazing curiously at the little boat as it approached the beach...

It is difficult to overstate how remote this part of the world was at that time. There was no communication with the nearest Chilean town, Punta Arenas, for there was no known overland route over the high wall of mountains bordering the north shore of the Beagle Channel. The sea route involved either an impracticable beat to windward through three hundred miles of narrow and hardly charted channels to the west and north, or a risky sail up the

exposed eastern coast of Tierra del Fuego and through the double
narrows of the Strait of Magellan. Such outside communication, as
it existed, was with the Falklands.

Mary Bridges's voyage from the mission base at Keppel Island
(itself days away from the "capital," tiny Port Stanley) in the eighty-
tonne *Allen Gardiner* took forty-one days. They battled huge seas
and were twice driven back by the violent currents of the Strait
of Le Maire before turning tail and attempting to reach the Beagle
Channel by passing south of Staten Island.

Until 1884 neither Chile nor Argentina appeared to show any
interest in this territory they theoretically shared: indeed it fell
to Thomas Bridges first to hoist the Argentine flag when a motley,
four-vessel flotilla sent from Buenos Aires unexpectedly showed up
here in that year.

The book is both a wonderful Tom Sawyer–like adventure
story of a young white boy growing up among indigenous people
who were barely emerging from the Stone Age and a sad treasure
for anthropologists. Thomas Bridges and his children witnessed,
within their lifetimes, the extinction of not one but two Aboriginal
cultures. Thomas was no fanatical evangelical. Reading between
the lines of *Uttermost Part of the Earth*, we sense that at some unde-
fined point he realized the futility of thrusting the Christian Bible
down the throats of these hardy but warlike and uncomprehending
people. He decided instead to offer to those who wished it a refuge
from the encroachments of "civilization," which they surely could
not long resist. And so he created an estancia at Harberton, where
they could simply come and work and receive medical attention, as
they wished. Instead of spending his time preaching, he set himself
to documenting in written form the Yamaná (or Yahgan) language.
His 32,000-word *Yamaná-English Dictionary*, initially stolen by a
colourful passing fraudster called Frederick Cook who passed it off
as his own, then lost during the two World Wars in Europe, is—like

Tommy Goodall moving sheep, Estancia Harberton, Argentina.

his son Lucas's saga—a masterpiece of its genre. (Cook, for his part, went on to even greater deceptions and was briefly hailed as the first man to reach the North Pole before being exposed.)

Anne and Abby's father was Tommy Goodall, their grandmother Clara Mary Bridges, known in the family as Clarita. Born in 1902 she in turn was a granddaughter of Thomas and Mary Bridges, thus a niece of Lucas. The girls' mother, Natalie Prosser, was an American who had first come here on an assignment for *National Geographic* and never left. She was a naturalist and photographer, horsey, a little brash. We'd met her once or twice at St. George's and, although she was obviously tired of talking about the rich history into which she had married, she had not actively discouraged us from our earlier proposal that we pay a short visit to Harberton.

We hitchhiked the eighty-kilometre dirt road from Ushuaia to Harberton, while the *Buen Suceso* unloaded and loaded yet again.

The farm, whose principal building was brought from England in pieces in 1886, looked just as it did in the sepia photographs of my 1948 edition of *Uttermost Part of the Earth*. It was much more like a station in the Falklands than in Devon: slightly ramshackle but brightly painted tin-clad farm buildings set among sheep-cropped grass, with bundles of fence posts and barbed wire lying around, musty fleeces piled up in a shearing shed. Natalie wasn't here nor were the girls. After we had shaken hands with the grey-haired and apparently mute Auntie Clarita, bushy-bearded Tommy—who was a lot shier and quieter than his wife—didn't seem to quite know what to do with us. It was clear that we should have checked in advance.

With Tommy's permission, we camped for a couple of days over-looking the quiet backwater that separates Gable Island from the big island of Tierra del Fuego. Tommy was busy bringing sheep over from Gable, using an old barge lashed to the side of an even older-looking rusty steel sailboat. One of his black and white sheepdogs followed us wherever we went.

Later I learned that Bruce Chatwin was not fondly remembered at Harberton because he had sent an abrupt telegram warning of his arrival. Then, according to Anne and Abby's mother, he had: "...expected to be treated as a celebrity. He was really very rude."

I hoped that Tommy hadn't thought I was another Chatwin.

We sailed onward from Ushuaia late one afternoon. But the days are long in January and it was still light when we sailed past the disputed Picton, Nueva, and Lennox islands before turning south toward the Antarctic peninsula. The captain pointed out the three islands and there was some resigned and unconvincing patriotic grumbling from the few passengers who ventured on deck. The Drake Passage was disappointingly windless, but a huge swell from the west kept us rolling heavily: there is nothing, at this latitude, to break those seas as they process endlessly around the globe.

Alone on the top deck we followed with binoculars Wandering Albatrosses as they swooped and soared over the wavetops.

"They say albatrosses are the souls of drowned sailors," I said to Jenny.

She was unimpressed. "Yes. Just be thankful you're not seasick."

≈ The Antarctic was predictably spectacular. So, in quite a different way—with their abundant wildlife and enormous spaces of untouched moorland—were the Falklands, which we visited two summers running. But it was Patagonia, that vast and underpopulated tract of land south of 40 degrees, uneasily shared by Chile and Argentina, that always drew us back.

You could spend decades exploring here; we decided we'd like to come back one day.

Fitting Out

FAST-FORWARD NEARLY TWENTY-FIVE YEARS. I was standing by our picture window, looking out at the ocean.

"Somehow I get the feeling you're bored again," Jenny finally said.

The motto of St. George's had been *Vestigia Nulla Retrorsum,* which can be translated approximately as "There's no Going Back." It's not a bad principle, I suppose, but how many of us can, as late middle age creeps up on us, resist the temptation to revisit places where we were once happy, even though we know we'll probably be disappointed?

In the years after we left Argentina in 1981, we had lived and travelled all over the world. We immigrated to British Columbia, on the West Coast of Canada, but in 1985 were off again, this time for a four-year circumnavigation of the world in our small, twenty-seven-foot fibreglass sloop, *Tarka the Otter*.

Cruising in a small sailboat, we found, was the ultimate means of travel: it was cheap (especially in the tropics, where clothing on long passages was optional) and it took you to interesting places still unreachable by 747. The jargon of sailing could be intimidating, but it was almost impossible to capsize a properly designed boat with a permanent keel and over twenty-five feet in length. Cruising was 99 per cent common sense, we realized, only 1 per cent specialist knowledge. I recall that we were off Mexico and nine months into our circumnavigation before Jenny figured out why "gybeing" (making a significant course change with the wind from dead astern, bringing the boom crashing over from one side to the other) was necessarily more violent and potentially damaging than making a similar change with the wind coming from ahead ("going about").

The only problem with cruising was that it didn't pay. So shortly after our return to Canada from our sailing trip I joined the Canadian Foreign Service, which, with intermittent spells in freezing Ottawa over fourteen years, allowed me to keep sating my restlessness by sending me successively to Mexico, Colombia, Sudan, and South Africa—all with remuneration. Jenny came along on these ventures as patiently and uncomplainingly as ever, although with every move her career prospects faded a little more.

Once in a while on our peregrinations, we would open up the old school trunk that contained our ever-growing collection of colour slides, and spend an evening projecting them onto the wall. As we watched we would grow nostalgic, above all, for those times in the luminous South. Perhaps it was less to do with the landscape itself than the fact that we had been young and happy there. Whatever the reason, over a period of years, a vague plan began to form. One day we'd buy another sailboat and explore Patagonia once again, this time as it was originally discovered—by sea—and with the narratives of some of those explorers in hand.

After Sudan, I'd been rewarded with the grand title of Consul General and what seemed to everyone else to be a plum posting: Cape Town. But for a political officer the time to have been in South Africa was a decade before, when apartheid was coming down. Now it was quiet, and only a few months into a four-year posting I was indeed bored.

"You know what?" I finally said, looking out beyond Robben Island. "Patagonia's just an ocean-crossing away. We could buy a boat here and sail over."

〜 My duties as Consul General, the "good and trusty friend" of the Governor General of Canada as my parchment charter indicated, were not onerous. Most afternoons I would walk ten minutes or so to the beautiful Parliament buildings where I attended debates and committee meetings of significance. I reported in as interesting and colourful manner as I could to my masters in Ottawa on legislation that might be underway; since the end of apartheid South Africa has been writing new and often innovative laws at a fantastic rate. I assessed the regional investment climate, attended elegant National Day receptions at an average of once a week, and catered assiduously to my boss, the Canadian High Commissioner, whenever she came visiting from Pretoria, which is where much of the dirtier work of government and the harder work of diplomacy went on. Periodically, I would also attend to dead or robbed Canadian tourists and—especially in the summer, which coincided with the depths of Ottawa's notorious winter—arrange light programs for visiting dignitaries from the Canadian capital.

There was plenty of time to look for a boat.

Jenny also had an excess of time. Although in modern South Africa she gained extra points by being a member of one minority—

the female gender—she lost many more on the job trail by being white. We found nothing to complain about in that. One of the most striking moments of our circumnavigation of the world in South Africa's Bad Old Days had been when we walked along the Durban waterfront after a tough sail in from the island of La Réunion. On the beach was a sign in English and Afrikaans, beginning "This beach is reserved for members of the white race..."

We both agreed corrective measures were now in order.

South Africans are keen and very accomplished sailors: they have to be good just to survive this coast. On account of this interest in sailing and of the country's strategic location on the most straightforward round-the-world route (the Red Sea having in recent years become inhospitable) there is a small but well-reputed local boat-building industry and a good market for cruising boats.

We spent several weekends poking around mildewy and little-used boats in various marinas in the Western Cape before we spotted, in the classifieds of the country's main sailing magazine, a boat of a class familiar to us from our last time out, in the eighties.

⌇ It's been said that buying a boat is a bit like buying a car or a house is for most people. But it's more like choosing a wife.

Like it or not, looks are important. Over the years I've inspected dozens of damp, cold-feeling yachts for sale. They all have an unmistakable musty atmosphere that comes from having had the hatches and the curtains closed for too long. But in most cases, by the time I have clambered down the companionway to have a poke around, I've already made my mind up.

With the spec sheet in hand, Jenny might say: "There's a long list of extra goodies the owner will throw in free...*Cruising World* gives these boats an excellent review...She's just had a new engine installed."

But if I didn't like the boat from thirty metres away, when we were still coming along the marina walkway, then I knew I'd never like her.

I tried to flatter Jenny by saying it was the same when I first saw her. She could have been brilliant as Einstein or as funny as Jo Brand, but if I hadn't been attracted by her looks, it would all have been wasted on me. She was not very impressed by this line of argument, even less so when I digressed on what I was looking for in a boat: traditional lines, solidity, and the ability to withstand heavy punishment.

Conversely, when I find a boat I like the look of, its obvious vices will rarely dissuade me. When we test-sailed *Tarka the Otter* off Victoria, we could have died of chlorine gas poisoning when seawater entering the boat through a leaky stern gland filled up the bilge, covered the batteries, and generated clouds of toxic blue smoke. Then when we returned to the marina and I casually tugged the light flag halyard that ran from the port spreader (one of the horizontal arms, halfway up the mast), the spreader fell off. To cap it all, the boat was demeaningly then named *Squeek*. We bought her regardless.

Pipe Dream, as she was named in 2003, was a Canadian design known as a Vancouver 27. It was, like *Squeek,* love at first sight.

Where boats are concerned, the number usually denotes a vessel's overall length, in feet. The name itself is (like a car brand: a Corolla, a Jaguar, a Mini) chosen by the designer or manufacturer. In this case, in the 1970s, British Columbia–based yachting draughtsman Robert Harris had received a commission from a young Canadian couple to design for them a vessel that would take them from the West Coast to New Zealand. Safety, solidity, and ease of handling were to be emphasized over speed, they instructed him, and no pretence was to be made at accommodation for any more than two people.

Exactly the same length as our earlier boat, which was of a very popular class called a Vega 27, the Vancouver—as Harris named his eventual design—weighed twice as much. She had a keel that ran most of the length of the boat, and she was cutter-rigged, that is to

51

say she had one mast, a mainsail, and stays (wire ropes) allowing two sails to be flown forward of the mast, one in front of the other. The design was a successful one, and several hundred were built, about half in Canada and half in the UK; many have now circumnavigated. An indicator of the regard in which the boat is held was that by 2003, which is when we entered the market, twenty- to twenty-five-year-old Vancouvers were still commanding between 50,000 and 90,000 USD, which is a lot of money for a used boat at the small end of the cruising range.

Pipe Dream, bright blue with a white coach roof and deck, lay at Richards Bay, a coal-lading port on the northeastern coast of South Africa, close by the Mozambique border. We met her owners for a nervous drink at the marina restaurant. Richard, tall and thin, bearded and very English-sounding, was a naval architect, his girlfriend, Karin, a small, slight, and lively young nurse. In the sixties or seventies she'd have been a hippie, but I don't think Richard would have ever tried dope. They'd sailed *Pipe Dream* here from Hong Kong, where Richard worked sporadically, with many detours to the Philippines, Malaysia, and Thailand.

As we talked I could tell they had become deeply attached to their boat. I was sympathetic. Selling *Tarka the Otter* had been one of the hardest decisions of our lives ("Harder than dumping me would be?" Jenny once asked quizzically; I didn't answer). I was literally choked up when I signed the bill of sale. She had looked after us faithfully for years; she was now a little tired and battered; it felt like a terrible betrayal to pass her on to someone we didn't know. Richard now talked wistfully and proudly of his and Karin's adventures on *Pipe Dream*. So much so, in fact, that we wondered if he was starting to get cold feet.

Then Richard got up to buy us another round of drinks. Karin leaned in conspiratorially: "He's too embarrassed to tell you the real reason we want to sell. We want a double bed..."

Most versions of the Vancouver indeed had just two separate bunks in the main cabin and a functional, well-designed storage area for sails and other equipment in the bows, an area where boats of this size would conventionally have a double bed known as a Vee-berth. Now Vee-berths were not actually very practical to sleep in at sea: the motion in the bows was violent, and in the case of most designs the area would quickly become very damp as the forward hatch was opened and closed, occasionally letting in waves. But Vee-berths had their uses in port, when the captain and crew were usually in a more relaxed mode and not liable to be interrupted by calls to go on watch or to avoid suddenly observed, oncoming shipping.

This was undeniably a disadvantage, albeit one we knew of in advance and to which we were resigned. The inconvenience of single narrow beds was not, after all insuperable, as we had discovered at college and on French roundabouts.

We had a good rummage around below decks, while Richard and Karin tactfully stayed in the restaurant. Apart from the absence of the Vee-berth, the layout below was traditional: a small galley on the port side, consisting of a sink and propane gas stove (which we soon decided would have to go, in favour of the safer kerosene); a 20hp diesel engine under the cockpit floor, accessed by lifting out the companionway steps; a sturdy folding table between those two bunks; an uncompromising-looking porcelain "head" (toilet bowl) amidships in the forward third of the boat, snugly surrounded by deep sail lockers. Contemplating the head and recalling past mishaps, Jenny said thoughtfully, "The good thing is that if it was rough and you fell off, you'd be alright: you're hemmed in tightly…"

Because this was Richard and Karin's home, it didn't have that mustiness. It was cozy, lived in, and—with its soft kerosene lantern and wood panelling—I sensed the cabin would be a comforting haven on windy and cold nights in the far South.

Back on deck the cockpit was small, which is just what we were looking for: there was less space to fill up should we be boarded by large waves in the Southern Ocean. A sturdy canvas-and-stainless-steel dodger protected the helmsman from oncoming seas; unlike on *Tarka the Otter*, it was solid enough to grab hold of when moving forward and in case of unexpected lurches. Hanging off the stern, outboard of the rudder, was a complicated apparatus whose purpose I understood immediately—a self-steering wind vane—but whose peculiarities would nevertheless take me a long time to master.

Most important, we loved *Pipe Dream*'s lines: a very slight tumble-home the length of the hull; an aggressive, not effeminate bow; a sharply cut-off stern, on which there hung a solid-looking rudder. The downside of an external rudder was that it was vulnerable to impact, but there was a huge plus as well: if anything went wrong it would be immediately visible, and it would be easy to work on (or even replace) the rudder without having to dive. There was a solid, low doghouse in two levels.

Below water level, the heavy keel ran nearly two-thirds the length of the boat; this was unfashionable in modern boats, because it made a boat slow to turn, but I knew it would also mean she would track steadily in heavy seas; and she'd be able to take a moderate grounding without damage to the hull.

When I absently tapped the hull, Richard rummaged around and produced what looked like an enormous set of beads: a dozen or so disks of varying thickness threaded onto a string. The thickest was a good two centimetres. "I like to think of it as my worry beads, especially when things are getting rough," he said, fingering the disk that he had cut from the hull years earlier so as to insert a new fitting. "That's the below-water thickness of the hull." It was four times thicker than any fibreglass used in *Tarka*'s construction.

Next day we went for a test sail in the narrow confines of the port. By that time I had long since been sold. Jenny could tell, but she still insisted for form's sake on rationalizing aloud the boat's virtues.

Richard and Karin weren't prepared to negotiate on the price at all. So enamoured was I by now that I didn't demur in the least. I could understand them: haggling must have seemed demeaning to the boat, cheapening.

Later, we'd stay in regular touch with them. Their pretext was that they wanted to help us out with any features of the boat or engine that might not lend themselves to immediate mastery. And we very much appreciated this. But we knew what had really been going on: they'd been checking us out to see if we'd love *Pipe Dream* as much as they had.

⏤ Years earlier, in December 1987, we had sailed the route from Richards Bay around to Cape Town in *Tarka the Otter*. This coast has a very bad reputation, not just on account of the scarcity of good havens along the 850 miles that separate the two ports, and the infamous twin capes of Agulhas and Good Hope.

The main problem is the Agulhas current, a fast-flowing river-in-the-sea that flows parallel to the coast, southwest-bound, at a speed of two to six knots. As long as you have the wind behind you when westbound to Cape Town, then this current is of enormous assistance and can almost double the usual speed of a twenty-seven-footer. But should the wind switch and start blowing out of the southwest, as it does when major fronts come through, then a classic wind-against-current scenario arises, capable —if the wind is strong enough and it blows long enough—of creating massive ship-destroying seas up to twenty metres high. There is a long list of vessels that have simply disappeared here, including the Australian passenger ship *Waratah* in 1909.

In the build-up to Christmas 1987, we had waited weeks in Durban for ideal conditions to form then had made a hasty dash out of the harbour and a 280-mile run to the next shelter: East London. We made it just in time. Over Christmas Day, it blew at seventy knots from that wrong direction, collapsing the large customs shed on the wharf where we were tied up and creating major difficulties for tankers out in the shipping lanes.

Now, notwithstanding the leisurely pace of things at the office and our slightly uncomfortable awareness that in a year or so we'd be taking our new boat into waters even more difficult than these, we had no desire to again spend weeks sailing this stretch of coastline in a boat with which we were not familiar. The solution was quite simple. We recruited Richard, Karin, and half a dozen others, including Nick and Jan on the Australian-registered *Yawarra*, and, in an atmosphere of bonhomie and co-operation that reminded us of our cruising years in the eighties, took *Pipe Dream*'s mast down, lashed it on deck, and hoisted her by crane onto the back of a flatbed. She did most of the thirty-hour journey to Cape Town at eighty kilometres per hour. Jenny slept on board as the boat roared to windward, emerging only to share a hamburger with her *rooinek* (redneck) Afrikaner driver at the occasional bleak truck stop in the Karoo desert. I flew back in comfort, alleging a need to get back to the office. The only wear and tear on the boat was a large number of flattened mosquitoes on the bow section.

⟿ Naming a boat is a delicate business. Unlike choosing a name for a child or a cat, you cannot (if you wish to cruise internationally) take a name that is already in use, in other words one that exists on your country's national register. This reduces the options drastically.

Powerboat owners favour tacky puns (*Fourplay, Wet Dream*) and incorrect Spanish (*No problemo*). But there was no lack of unfortunate sailboat names out there as well: *Passing Wind* or (this on a French boat we later met in Chile), *Ch't'imagine*, invariably rendered by English-speakers as *Shitty Machine*. We didn't dislike the name *Pipe Dream,* but it didn't seem appropriate as neither of us smoked, and, more to the point, a pipe dream is a dream that is never accomplished. Jenny, for once the romantic, said: "Why don't we try wildlife again?"

Loading Pipe Dream *(later* Bosun Bird) *at Richards Bay, South Africa.*

Storm Petrel, *Shearwater*, and *Kittiwake* were all gone. I liked *Cape Otter*, a gesture to our previous boat and to the local variety of otter, but the crew said, very practically, that we weren't actually from South Africa, so that wasn't appropriate. Jenny also shot down reprises of historic ships, such as *Golden Hinde*, as too pretentious.

Little by little we homed in on *Bosun Bird*. As well as being (we thought) pleasantly alliterative, this is the common name that is given to a beautiful white seabird with distinctively long tail feathers that is known more correctly as a tropicbird. They range far out to sea in the tropical zones of all the world's oceans, and on our previous voyage we had seen them nesting in places as diverse as Tobago, the Galápagos, Cocos Island, and St. Helena. The tropicbird's call is a high-pitched whistle that, to the crews of the sailing ships of old, resembled the whistle with which a bosun welcomed senior officers aboard: hence Bosun Bird.

This critical task accomplished, we spent the next eighteen months preparing our new boat for her cruise.

We unloaded and moored the boat at a quiet marina called Port Owen, which adjoins the twin fishing ports of Laaiplek and Velddrif, on the Berg River and about one hundred miles north of Cape Town. At the prestigious and historic Royal Cape Yacht Club in the city it was forbidden to sleep on boats, and noisy and/or dirty boat-work was frowned upon. More to the point, South African sailing regulations were so strictly enforced that it would be impossible for us, lacking local competency certification, to take the boat out for sea trials. The Royal Cape was also located in an industrial part of town where muggings were common, and it was so large that theft by other boat owners had become a problem.

At Port Owen, by contrast, there were no harbour officials to ask us where we might be going as we motored out of the river mouth on a Saturday morning, the buzz of electric drills was positively welcome and, although the marina was wide open to anyone who might stroll by, there was no security problem at all. There was a tiny yacht club with a bar that opened on Friday evenings, and whose five or six sailboat owners sometimes raced on St. Helena Bay on a weekend. But it was far less pretentious and grand than the Royal Cape.

~ Sailing to and then exploring Patagonia would involve first of all crossing the South Atlantic. Then we would dip south, parallel with the coast of Argentina, and work west into the Pacific by one of three adjacent routes: the Strait of Magellan, the Beagle Channel, or the Drake Passage (south of Cape Horn). Finally we would wind north up the Chilean coast through that intricate maze of natural waterways that we had traversed in the *Río Baker*. We thought long and hard about revisiting the Falklands, under sail; the diversion would only be a minor one. But after much study we concluded the place was simply too windy, even by Patagonian standards, and that we would spend so much time worrying about the safety of the boat that we would not be able to enjoy the wildlife.

Crossing an ocean sounds simple enough. But we would not be able to go in a straight line across the South Atlantic.

Sailing 101 begins by teaching that even the most efficient sailing vessel cannot sail directly into the wind. At best it can usually manage a course 40 degrees to either side of the direction from which the wind is coming. So, if the desired destination is directly to windward, it must patiently zigzag (or tack) its way forward. This is slow, and it is also uncomfortable in that the vessel must pound into oncoming waves. It is much more pleasant and may be quicker in the long run to choose a route where the wind is likely to come from the vessel's side or from astern, even if that route may be much longer in miles. This means that the key to passage-planning is understanding the typical weather on the stretch of ocean to be crossed, for the season in question.

Thus to Meteorology 101. At the risk of oversimplification, it is the never-ending strengthening and weakening of high and low atmospheric pressure areas, and their interaction—the movement of air between them like water flowing from one jug to another— that causes wind. The South Atlantic's weather, like that of the other major oceans, is determined principally by the strength and the oscillating north–south movement of a single, enormous area of high pressure, known in this case as the South Atlantic High, and its interaction with adjacent and passing low-pressure areas.

On a weather map (or "surface analysis") you can see such high- and low-pressure areas represented as if they were mountains or hollows on land, i.e., by very roughly circular contours. Pressure is measured in millibars, with sea-level pressure very rarely straying out of the range 950 to 1050. Each contour shown on the map represents a line of constant pressure; contours are usually spaced every four millibars and are known as isobars. The centre of each high (the summit) or low (the valley bottom) is usually depicted with a bold H or L (A or B in Spanish), along with the figure of the exact estimated pressure at that location.

In the southern hemisphere the winds blow anticlockwise around high-pressure areas but at a slightly oblique angle, pointing outward (or downhill) 10 to 20 degrees from the isobars. They blow clockwise around lows, pointing slightly inward (also downhill) into the centre of the depression. In the northern hemisphere the directions are reversed.

But the surface analysis does not just indicate wind direction: it also is a guide to wind strength. The closer the isobars are to each other, that is to say the steeper the slope to the top of the hill or the bottom of the valley, then the stronger the wind will be. Where the isobars are very widely spaced or where there are none—for example at the very centre of highs or lows—there will be little or no wind.

A typical weather map for the South Atlantic will show the South Atlantic High in mid-ocean, its centre a few hundred miles south or southwest of the island of St. Helena. Its eastern and western perimeters will be bunched up against the two continents, over which lows are predominant. In the north, the contours space out into the nothingness of the doldrums (or, as they are more properly known, the Intertropical Convergence Zone), while in the south they are squeezed upward a little by a procession of lows cartwheeling across from west to east. In summer, as the sun moves south, so does the high; in winter both move north.

All this to say that to sail from—for example—Cape Town to Buenos Aires, which are ports at approximately the same latitude, you must sail first north up the eastern margin of the South Atlantic High, west across the top (following the anticlockwise trend of the wind), then south along its western edge. If you try to go direct from east to west you would, depending on the seasonal shifts of the high, either run into huge areas of calm in the centre of the high or face the strong westerly headwinds that blow along the southern edge of the high. Sailing back from South America is much easier and can be done more directly: you usually only need to dip a little south from Buenos Aires to find yourself running anticlockwise along the bottom of the high to Cape Town, with the wind behind you.

In reality, things are never quite as stable as these scenarios imply, and the typical status quo is affected by a number of factors in addition to the north–south movement of the high with the seasons. Notably, in the southern hemisphere, those cartwheeling low-pressure systems that process around the world from west to east, with "rooster tail" fronts that run to the northwest from their centres and that reach far up into the oceanic highs, can create trouble. As they brush through the lower half of the highs, the fronts bring rain, an intensification of wind strength, and a shift in the wind's direction of 90 to 180 degrees.

And just as important as the position of the high and of fronts in influencing the wind's direction and strength at any given time and in a given place is—in the case of both southern Africa and southern South America—what is going on over the continents. Normally, a low-pressure area sits over both landmasses. As it deepens, so the gradient from the centre of the low to the centre of the high increases; the trend accelerates as and when the high simultaneously builds. It is this gradient that determines the strength of the wind. A deep low adjoining a powerful high will mean very strong winds where the two areas squeeze together; conversely a moderate high adjoining a moderate low will mean that not very much is happening.

The good news about the South Atlantic is that the water temperature is too cold for cyclones, as any revolving storm with wind speeds over sixty-four knots is known. And, unless you seek it out, there is very little in the way of physical obstruction between South Africa and South America. It is solid objects like land or other ships that account for more sailing and shipping disasters than the weather.

So much for our ocean crossing. But what happens to the south of the areas of influence of the various oceanic highs, that is to say in Patagonian waters?

This was the area that troubled me most. At night in our apartment at Sea Point on the Cape Town waterfront, with the loom of the lighthouse at Green Point flashing across the walls of the bedroom every few seconds, I would fret about the Southern Ocean. Sometimes I felt as queasy as when I was teaching those eighteen-year-olds on a Friday afternoon in Argentina. Superstitiously I would touch the headboard of the bed. Common wisdom has it that "touching wood" is a tradition harking back to the wood of the true cross. But after many scared nights at sea, I think that more probably the idea has its origin in what sailors have always done when they are afraid. Wood floats. If you are drowning it will save you.

I never told Jenny about this. On nights when it was blowing especially hard and the rain that lashed our eighth-floor windows was full of salt spray, I didn't sleep at all. I imagined that if she knew I was afraid, she might lose heart, too.

A quick glance at a world map will show that south of about 40 degrees, there really isn't much land. There is just the far southern cone of South America and the Antarctic continent, with a wide ribbon of ocean (the Southern Ocean) running unimpeded all the way around the world, narrowing only where Cape Horn and the Antarctic peninsula face off against each other (the Drake Passage). Very deep lows, typically centred between 55 and 65 degrees south, circle the globe in the Southern Ocean, setting up a band of westerly winds to their north. The lows bring an intensification of wind speed as they approach and a slight fading as they recede, along with directional shifts toward the north and the south respectively. The westerlies very rarely die away completely or lose their predominant westerly component. The top portion of this band, between latitudes 40 and 50, is known as the Roaring Forties, the part closer to the usual centre of the lows as the Furious Fifties.

The Andes temporarily stop the enormous seas generated by
the Roaring Forties but do little to break the incessant wind. In
fact, refreshed by heavy cold air flowing down from the continental ice cap, the Forties are as hard over Argentina's east coast as
they are over Chile's western shores. And to add to the mayhem,
the narrowing of the Southern Ocean south of Cape Horn squeezes
the isobars tighter than anywhere else, the result being that winds
off the southwestern shores of Tierra del Fuego are the strongest
consistently recorded anywhere.

To explore Patagonia, we would have to sail through the Forties
as far as 55 degrees south (the latitude of the Beagle Channel) then
up again.

As I pored over the charts, I wondered if we would make it. Over
the past five hundred years, hundreds of vessels have been lost
here, overpowered by the incessantly hostile winds and unimaginable seas. Gold Rush skippers en route from Europe or New York
to San Francisco knew this route as the Dead Men's Road, and Cape
Horn earned its grim sobriquet: Cape Stiff. More recently, French
sailing guru Bernard Moitessier, the epitome of coolness under
pressure and the inspiration of many of the world's top ocean
racers, wrote that anyone who takes his sailing vessel below 40
degrees cannot guarantee that he will not founder.

More and more sailboats are these days venturing down south,
equipped with increasingly accurate weather forecasting, navigational tools of an accuracy Cook could never have imagined,
and in ever-better designed vessels that can go to windward like a
square-rigger never could. But make no mistake, says the common
wisdom, this remains the Everest of sailing. And if something major
goes wrong, the chances of a successful rescue are about the same
as those of a rescue off the slopes of Everest above 8000 metres.

Sobering stuff. But it did mean that our Decision Number One
was easy: we must negotiate the Forties and Fifties in summer, not

winter. This led straight to Decision Number Two: in order to reach the far south in the southern summer we would have to leave Cape Town in the early spring at the latest—say, August or September. We set our target date for August 2005, and I handed in my resignation; we'd be leaving Cape Town only two years into my assigned four years.

〜 The weather and navigational tests we were sure to encounter not only kept me awake at night, touching the bedstead, but governed many of our purchases and determined most of the upgrades we now made to *Bosun Bird*.

Fortunately for the sake of today's sailors, the behaviour of the world's pressure has over the years been tracked and mapped on sets of Pilot Charts. There exists one twelve-chart set of these for each of the world's oceans, and we still had our sets from the eighties. Each chart shows what natural conditions can typically be expected for each month in the ocean in question: the average position of the highs and lows and their average strength; average wind directions and strengths for each 5-degree square of ocean; percentages of gales and calms for each square; the likely extent of drift ice; average cyclone tracks and so on.

But the Pilot Charts only tell you what you can expect over a given month, and they represent only averages. Immediately prior to a vessel's departure, and also underway, having the latest surface analysis available is of great use, too. Modern technology is such that even small vessels can now receive this information by hooking up a laptop to a high frequency radio set at times made public by most countries' meteorological services. The only snags are that the so-called "weather fax" may take half an hour to come in, may often be blurry in quality, and its reception uses up valuable battery power.

A more efficient variation on the weather fax is to download, either by radio or by satellite phone, any of a number of sophisticated weather models based on information developed and made freely available by the National Oceanic and Atmospheric Administration (NOAA) of the USA. You can also do this on the Internet, but the means do not yet exist to make Internet browsing easy and cheap from a sailing vessel in a remote location. These models use computer technology to meld the latest available weather information with "past performance" information and accordingly predict in graphic form what is going to happen in the selected area for up to seven days ahead. The file packages in which predictions are transmitted to users are known as gribs, and it is now as common to hear sailors discussing "what the gribs show" as "what the weather fax shows."

We figured that given where we were going we could never have too much weather information. We invested in a laptop to hook up to our ancient ICOM 9000 HF radio, practised downloading and reading weather faxes (surface analyses), and later purchased an Iridium satellite phone that gave us access to gribs.

We'd need lots of charts, too. Nowadays, there exist electronic charts for the world's more travelled waters. You can call all up the required area on a laptop and connect it to your Global Positioning System (GPS) in such a way that your boat will appear, in real time, as an icon on the electronic chart. But the process of accurately converting paper charts to electronic ones is a complicated one that involves much more than scanning the old paper versions; it has not yet been done in the case of less-travelled regions, such as southwestern Chile. This meant that we would need to obtain two hundred to three hundred paper charts. New, these can cost between 20 and 30 USD apiece. Happily, over a period of eighteen months we were able to borrow and photocopy a large range of charts from cruising boats that had headed to Cape Town from Chile. We also found a treasure trove of once-used charts for the channels in Cape Town's self-styled "Yacht Grot," a dusty, two-storey warehouse crammed with used sailing junk.

As the foghorn at Green Point moaned eerily, I spent long winter evenings assembling these charts of British, American, Chilean, and Argentine origin, many of which were covered with pencilled annotations from their previous owners or stamped "*Anulado*" (out of date), into a vast mosaic on the dining room table. My aim was to check that we had coverage of some sort for every single mile we would cover and to catalogue them so that we could with confidence pull out the right chart at the right time. Many were works of art, especially the older British Admiralty charts, whose margins were often filled with carefully shaded sketches of sections of coastline as seen from seaward. The original versions of these charts were often developed by HMS *Beagle* and her fellow ships, and for scale they would show a tiny square-rigger at anchor. I realized we were not only sailing into adventure but into history, and sometimes I'd spend hours running my finger along the intricate waterways and calling out to Jenny some of the more intriguing island names.

"Why is this strait called Collingwood?" I'd wonder aloud.

"I wonder where we can get rechargeable AA batteries?" Jenny would counter from her office, where she was compiling endless lists of boat tasks to be accomplished.

The lack of electronic charts for Chile also meant that our GPS would be of very limited use once in these waters. To clarify, it is not that the relevant paper charts are bad; indeed they depict shorelines, reefs, channels, and the relative positions of distinctive features with amazing accuracy, as we were to discover. But, developed as these charts invariably were in the pre-satellite era, cartographers were never able to fix latitude and longitude (especially the latter) as accurately as they can today. In practical terms, this means that if you are sailing down the middle of a three-mile-wide channel and decide to transfer the latitude/longitude reading on your GPS screen to an old paper chart, you may find that it shows you to be on top of the adjacent mountain.

Although few sailboats yet visit Patagonia compared to the world's other (warmer) cruising grounds, some of those that have ventured here over the years have been prolific in documenting their experiences. Apart from Darwin's *Voyage of the Beagle*, we tracked down more modern accounts, and when I was not assembling charts I spent many hours frightening myself with some of these.

They included *Mischief in Patagonia*, a classic and very funny account of H.W. (Bill) Tilman's climbing and sailing expedition to the continental ice cap and the Amalia Glacier (deep in the channels) aboard his Bristol Pilot Cutter *Mischief*, in 1955–56; *Second Chance*, which recounts a 1975 cruise by Maurice and Maralyn Bailey, who had earlier become world famous for surviving 117 days in a rubber dinghy and life raft following the ramming and sinking of their first boat, *Auralyn*, by a sperm whale; *Sailing Alone Around the World*, Joshua Slocum's account of the first singlehanded circumnavigation of the world (via the Strait of Magellan) in 1898; and Gerry Clark's *The Totorore Voyage*, a masterfully understated but gruesome account of a crisis-filled amateur ornithological expedition to Patagonia, the Falklands, South Georgia, and Antarctica between 1983 and 1986.

More practical if less literary were the brand-new *Patagonia and Tierra del Fuego Nautical Guide* by Mariolina Rolfo and Giorgio Ardrizzi, with detailed descriptions, GPS locations derived from personal experience (i.e., reliable), and chartlets for more than four hundred anchorages; and a shorter and older soft-cover guide for the Chilean coast produced by Britain's Royal Cruising Club. Later our copies of these last two books would be very heavily thumbed, exposed to wind, rain, sleet, and snow; almost every sailing boat in the South Atlantic, we were to discover, carried one or both of them, describing them in shorthand as "the Italians" and "the RCC."

As a direct accompaniment for our charts we carried the appropriate blue-cloth covered and gilt-lettered volumes of the British

Admiralty Pilot. These are guide books for commercial vessels, developed over a period of two hundred years, but they contain a wealth of information on natural phenomena and anchorages that is of use to sailing vessels. We would probably be the only boat in the South Atlantic to carry sight reduction tables—dense volumes of figures that allow the navigator to shortcut much of the trigonometry otherwise involved in traditional celestial navigation—but we were determined to not be entirely seduced by push-button navigation of the kind that a GPS permits, and to keep our hand (or eye) in with the sextant.

Other reference books we jammed into our reduced bookshelf space included the usual engine manuals; a tome on meteorology; the very conservative, rather dated, but still sound *Voyaging Under Sail* by Britain's sober and down-to-earth answer to the elegiac Moitessier, Eric Hiscock; and Adlard Coles's scary but useful *Heavy Weather Sailing*. This last, by dispassionately recounting a series of sailing disasters or near-disasters, imparts much practical advice on what to do when the going gets rough. Its photographs of heavy seas in the Southern Ocean should be skipped as quickly as possible by anyone of a nervous disposition. We also had a book called *First Aid Afloat*, which comprised a number of real-life scenarios and featured an image of a hairy, fat, male torso with felt-tip-pen markings showing where to cut; one scenario involved improvising a catheter from an engine fuel line.

As a diversion we bought a couple of dozen paperbacks from the weekend market at the Green Point football stadium, just behind where we lived. At almost every port of call we were able to trade what we had read on the previous passage for more light material, even though the quality dropped with each trade, from Penguin Classics to Judith Krantz and Sidney Sheldon. With weight and space considerations looming larger with every weekend visit we made to *Bosun Bird*, we limited ourselves to twenty of our favourite CDs and a dozen or so tapes. At the last minute—accurately foreseeing that the weather would often keep us inactive on board—we stuffed in a word board game, Scrabble.

Our reading and our preparation became progressively more frenetic as departure time loomed.

I never articulated it to Jenny, but my constant fear was that—as captain—I was just not up to it, and that I was risking both our lives on this venture. I searched ever more desperately for accounts that suggested it could all turn out to be plain sailing, but found myself lingering anxiously on stories of great storms and near disasters: what if there was some tip buried deep in one of these accounts that could save us one day? Neither of us ever talked openly about what I suspect we both felt. Perhaps it was just as well. Otherwise we would never have gone.

～ Our principal exterior job on *Bosun Bird* was dealing with about one square metre of mushy deck just forward of the mast: a phenomenon caused by water seeping, over the years, through improperly sealed screw and bolt holes in the fibreglass shell, and into its three-centimetre-thick, balsa-wood core. The only effective way to treat this was drastic: excising and stripping off the outer fibreglass skin with a circular saw, scraping out all the wet balsa, replacing it with new dry wood, sealing everything up with epoxy, and sticking the outer skin back on. Neither of us are very practical, but it is best, on a boat, not to put maintenance jobs off, hoping that everything will hold together. When survival conditions are developing, the last thing you want is to be regretting not having done a job like this when you were safe and dry on land.

Jenny watched me switch the circular saw on and recoil, with a morbid fascination. "Are you sure you know what you are doing?" she asked unhelpfully.

Inside the boat, the most time-consuming and messy job was installing closed-cell foam insulation wherever we could access the

bare fibreglass hull: this would be critical in making the boat livable over a southern winter and would, we hoped, help reduce condensation and mildew. We also put in a Canadian-built kerosene Force 10 cabin heater, connecting it to the same tank that supplied our two-burner kerosene stove and oven. We tore out the existing propane stove and associated tank: kerosene is more difficult to light but much safer on a small boat than gas.

Another area for preventive maintenance was the engine. Richard and Karin had experienced a serious problem with the 20 hp Bukh diesel engine in that the small, externally mounted water pump that pushes seawater around the jacket of the engine to cool it, periodically allowed seawater to creep past its seals and into the engine, where it contaminated the lubricating oil. This was a problem with which I was depressingly familiar from our previous boat.

Their solution was to detach the pump from the body of the engine, seal up the link to the camshaft—which drove the pump— and rig the pump so as to be powered by the same V-belt that also runs from the flywheel to the alternator (thus recharging the batteries). This was a logical enough step to take but, of course, if it was that brilliant an idea the designers of the engine would have thought of it in the first place. The problem lay in aligning the water pump with both the alternator and the flywheel. If it was at all out of true then on the one hand it would wear the rubber belt, sending fine black dust into the air, heating the belt and causing the alternator to overheat and shut down. And on the other it tended—almost imperceptibly—to pull the water pump's stainless steel drive shaft out of its rubber impeller, thus causing the pumping function to cease.

It took months of unaccountable pump and alternator stoppages for us to work all of this out. The stoppages would usually occur at

< *Excavating rotten balsa wood from the roof of* Bosun Bird.

stressful moments, such as when we were returning to our marina slip under power and against the wind, with dusk coming on. We did not achieve a definitive solution while still in South African waters, but at least we reached a definitive diagnosis, and that is often half the battle.

⌁ In order to test the efficacy of our various maintenance projects and so as not to forget how to sail, many weekends we went out cruising in the protected waters of St. Helena Bay, into which the Berg River empties. The sea here is cold—at certain times of year we would see penguins—but the beaches are pristine white, the rocky coves deserted. Not once in two years did we share an anchorage with another sailboat. A favourite location was Slipper Bay, a small indentation in the extreme southwestern corner of the larger bay; there was a pilchard-packing plant on shore and a wind-blown and forlorn township behind the beach. Usually we saw nobody, but one day a shivering young Coloured boy paddled out on a surfboard.

"I'm with the Slipper Bay Baywatch," he said tentatively, bobbing against the hull.

We must have both looked puzzled.

"You know, mon...Pammie Anderson and all that. We save lives. Gimme 50 Rand."

At Britannia Bay, farther to the west and facing the open South Atlantic, there were luxury faux-fishermen's cottages, quaintly thatched, whitewashed, and owned by wealthy families from Joburg, but again there was almost never anyone in sight.

Sailing nearly thirty miles to the southwest to rugged Cape Columbine and the isolated village of Paternoster exposed us to five-metre ocean swells and tested our navigation skills keenly, while a night at anchor at Stompneus Bay, when it blew forty knots and our bows were dipping into the oncoming waves, increasing our confidence in our anchoring technique and gear. Now instead of the bedstead, I found myself touching *Bosun Bird*'s wooden bulkhead every few minutes.

Most days—usually in the afternoons—it blew very hard, in summer almost always from the southeast. Some days the wind would rise from mirror calm to thirty-five knots in a matter of ten minutes. This meant we were able to try using our roller-furling genoa, and we also practised putting in up to four reefs in the mainsail, i.e., reducing its size progressively so as to offer less area to the wind.

Most textbooks say that if the wind is still too strong to continue and after all combinations of reduced sail have been exhausted, then the remedy is to heave to. This means arranging the vessel's sails and tiller in such a way that she comes to an effective stop, pointing at maybe 60 degrees from the wind and rising and falling with the oncoming waves: the objective is to present the vessel's strongest profile, the bows, to the wind. Experimenting in the bay, we found that *Bosun Bird*, aided by her long keel, hove to very well, with her stay-sail backed (i.e., hauled across to the "wrong" side, with its clew to windward), her mainsail sheeted in hard, flat and with three or four reefs, and the tiller tied to leeward. When the wind was still stronger she would also remain nicely hove-to with just the mainsail up. In these conditions the boat does drift to leeward (downwind), so you do need plenty of room, but the smooth slick she thus leaves serves as protection against boarding waves.

According to the frighteningly cool Adlard Coles and others, there remain two further strategies as and when the wind is too high to fly any sail at all: lying ahull and running before the wind.

Lying ahull is what it sounds like: just taking everything down and sitting there. The problem with this is that you end up broadside on to the waves and vulnerable to being rolled completely, possibly losing your mast in the process, and quite probably dying.

The final strategy, if you have room, is to turn and run downwind, either with no sails at all or towing lines and other material ("warps") behind you to slow yourself down. This latter variation is fraught with controversy: some believe that towing warps only serves to make the boat slow to respond to the tiller, and if the following seas are big enough they will just wash all that rope and chain over you again. But if you run without warps the boat can attain such speeds that there is a real risk of pitchpoling: somersaulting into the back of the wave in front. This is usually disastrous to the rig, more so than a conventional sideways capsize.

We duly tried towing an expensively acquired drogue (a kind of canvas windsock designed to sink below water level and create drag) behind us, in lieu of warps. It snagged the bottom and ripped to tatters. Enough was enough. We consoled ourselves with the wry note by Adlard Coles that occurs toward the end of his book:

> Whatever decision you make, if you get into trouble you may be sure that someone who was not there will come up with something you should have done.

~ On July 1, 2005, I quit work—thus missing the National Day diplomatic cocktails not only in honour of Canada but also of the USA and France.

It was midwinter in Cape Town and northwesterly storms were bashing the Cape Peninsula once or twice a week, with the Cape Point lighthouse often reporting fifty knots or higher. Watching the big ships straining at anchor in Table Bay did nothing for our confidence. My every dream was now of high waves and of the boat falling to pieces. Jenny gently snored on.

Once our books, ornaments, and all my suits and ties were packed away and shipped back to Canada, we decamped to the boat. By now we were out "on the hard" (i.e., sitting on dry land) at the tiny boatyard adjoining the Port Owen marina, preparing to paint the boat's bottom with red anti-fouling paint. This meant climbing a rickety ladder into the cockpit, having to use land toilet facilities, and remembering not to drain cooking pots down our sink. There was also the usual dust and grit of the boatyard to deal with, and a herd of eight or ten stray cats to be dodged when negotiating the clutter in the dark. One of them, named Mascara by Colin, who ran the boatyard, learned to climb our ladder and was a frequent visitor to the cabin on colder nights.

Once we'd stripped the old paint off the bottom, a new but not completely unexpected problem presented itself: fibreglass osmosis. This is a phenomenon from which many fibreglass boats sooner or later suffer, especially those that have been kept in warm waters for a long period, as ours had. The chief symptom is a rash of blisters that can range between one-cent- and saucer-size and which, when pierced with the tip of a screwdriver emit an acrid, vinegary liquid. There is no easy remedy, but the usual one consists of gouging out the rotten material from each hole, thoroughly drying the vicinity with acetone and moderate heat, refilling with some kind of epoxy filler, coating the whole bottom again with epoxy paint, and then adding the anti-fouling. It's a very messy job. For the first and only time we had a few unkind words for Richard and Karin: hadn't they seen this problem coming?

Nearly all our blisters were tiny, but we had several hundred on each side, so that by the time I had finished drilling out each with a blunt, rounded drill piece, poor *Bosun Bird* looked as though she had a severe case of acne. The refilling was tedious. With many of the hundreds of the tiny craters facing downward, we needed a mix of epoxy that would adhere upside down but that allowed a reasonable working life. When we came to repaint the surface with liquid epoxy, the challenge was a related one: to achieve a mix that was thin enough to paint on smoothly and that would set overnight, neither too quickly nor too slowly, in the cool climate at this time. We got all but one batch right. Of this batch Jenny kept saying, as she tested it hopefully with her finger on the side of the boat: "The epoxy's drying."

Painting Bosun Bird's *bottom.*

After four days it manifestly was NOT. The only remedy was
to paint a second layer over the top and hope that the new layer
would react with the old and harden it all the same. Later we came
to use the phrase "the epoxy's drying" in stressful situations, when
hoping for the best but tending to believe in the worst.

As we worked on the boat, passers by—often with children in
hand—would come and watch, usually engaging Jenny and me in
conversation just at some critical moment and/or when we were
having a disagreement over what do next with regard to the osmosis. Comments ranged from the gormless "Why has your boat got
so many holes in it"—to the depressing—"We had some friends
who did what you're doing; a year later it had all gone bad and they
abandoned the boat..."

More positively, we were able to start connecting with the infor-mal worldwide support network of the cruising community before even leaving. In Richards Bay Nick and Jan, cruising with their two cats Mischa and Tigger, had helped us load *Bosun Bird* onto the flat-bed. Once *Yawarra* made it around to Cape Town, we were able to repay them with some hospitality and the use of our car; they were bound in the same direction as we were, but a few months ahead, and would become good friends. We also spent time with Cory and Willem on the Dutch yacht *Terra Nova*. They arrived in Port Owen from Patagonia, lent us many of their charts for us to copy, and served to keep our spirits up when those Cape storms had us fret-ting at the prospect of even worse weather in South America.

For respite from our boat work, we would go for weekend brunches to the laid-back Sunset Grill, on the enormous and empty sandy beach overlooking St. Helena Bay, and, just before selling off our car, we took a three-day drive around the neighbouring near-desert to see the spectacular early-spring wildflower displays. On Friday evenings we would go for a careful beer or two at the yacht club; with no more paycheques coming in, we needed to get into our long-forgotten and not regretted frugal cruising mode of expenditure. One freezing winter's night the club committee orga-nized a hilarious "revue," of the kind that used to take place in decades long past on cruise liners or in small English villages. It was alternately amusing and touching, and—with only white faces and British accents, here in deepest Africa—a little surreal.

The spring flowers were a sign that we should not be dallying much longer.

∿ In late August 2005, we made our last round of farewells, began cutting our remaining ties to land (I did not mourn abandoning my cellphone and its maddening call tone), and, over cream cakes and strong coffee, started to download the weather fax in the Velddrif Internet café. The ideal scenario: as a moderate front, with its typical northwesterly winds and rain, approached we would top up our water tanks, make a hurried taxi run to nearby Saldanha Bay to formally exit the country, and move *Bosun Bird* to the river mouth. As the front passed, the winds should switch to the west, then southwest, and the skies should brighten. We'd need four or five days of this to reach the next safe harbour, up the coast, in Namibia.

Jenny was quiet these days. I decided to say nothing. For our last week we talked in trivialities. Perhaps enterprises such as this succeed—like marriages—as much because of what is not said as what is said.

3

Rolling Down to *Rio*

IT WAS ONE OF THE BIGGEST STORMS OF THE WINTER: for several days the lighthouse at Cape Point was reporting sustained winds over fifty knots, and there was a warning of heavy seas all the way from the Orange River, on South Africa's border with Namibia, to Cape Agulhas. A weather buoy off the Cape of Good Hope was indicating combined sea and swell of twenty-three metres. In the marina at Port Owen the northwesterly gale made the halyards of the twenty or so yachts flog and tinkle, while incessant rain made the walkways slippery. It was not a day to be out at sea, but the forecast called for the wind steadily to clock to the west over the next forty-eight hours, then southwest and for the skies to clear. It was time to check out.

The port captain at the ore-loading port of Saldanha, who had nominal responsibility for Port Owen, was the same burly, blue-uniformed Afrikaner who had cleared us out of South Africa in March 1988, when we were sailing around the world on *Tarka the Otter*. He did not remember us, but he dusted off the record book for the month in question, and there we were.

He was a stickler for rules, as many of the bureaucrats who survived this country's transition to democracy seem to be. The apartheid regime was strong on regulation if nothing else. He scrutinized our papers then spoke in a slow, clipped accent, "We have a problem." He ran a stubby finger under the relevant line in the rule book, translating from Afrikaans. "You have departed South African waters."

"No, we want to leave now..."

"Your boat was in Richards Bay, yiss?"

"That's right, but..."

"And how did it get here?"

"We put it on a truck, and..."

"So it left South African waters, yiss?"

I could see what was coming and gaped helplessly.

"It says here that any time a vessel leaves our waters," and he put the book in front of me, "you must have the authorization of both customs and immigration, and the same when you re-enter..." He rested his case, looking at me unblinkingly.

"You haf not done this."

My diplomatic skills were exercised. After an hour or more of negotiation, flattery, and eating of humble pie, and no more than a formal slap on the wrist, we were on our way back to Port Owen with the precious clearance papers and exit stamps in our passports. And the port captain had conveniently forgotten to tell us how long we had actually to get out: almost certainly the legal

maximum was twenty-four hours, but if the storm lasted longer
and we waited, we would now be able to plead ignorance.

I was supposed to return my red diplomatic passport to the
Canadian Consulate General for it to be destroyed, as my diplomatic assignment was at an end. But the prospect of another
bureaucratic nightmare when we turned up in Namibia with
brand-new, regular, Canadian passports, showing no evidence
of our having been anywhere, was one I did not wish to face.
Fortunately my successor forgot to insist.

$\approx$ On the evening of Monday, September 5, 2005, we cast off our
heavy mooring lines in the marina for the last time. We made the
tight right-hand turn out of the marina and into the Berg River, and
motored a mile down to the holding dock, close to where the fishing boats tie up, to await the next morning's tide. As the sun set we
watched what had become a familiar sight over our two years in
South Africa: hundreds—thousands perhaps—of cormorants flying
inland in great skeins, from the open water of St. Helena Bay and
the twin breakwaters to their overnight roosting grounds upriver.
For ten or fifteen minutes the whooshing of their wings was all you
could hear.

It wasn't too late to turn back, I suppose. But I said nothing, and
neither did Jenny. We kept our conversation neutral and practical. I stayed awake all night, and I could tell from her breathing that
Jenny did, too.

Next morning was bright and sunny. I walked down to the
beach to see what the swells looked like: nothing too unmanage-
able, I forced myself to think and say. We slipped our lines and,
with a strong ebb tide, motored the last mile downriver, past the
poetically named wooden fishing boats with which we'd become
so familiar over the past two years: *Silver Katonkel, Stormkop,
Loerisfontein.* By coincidence it was exactly twenty years since
we had set off from British Columbia on what was to become a

circumnavigation of the world on *Tarka the Otter*. We sped out
through the breakwaters, lined with hundreds of birds drying their
wings, and set a course to take us clear of the North Blinder reef.
There was no one around to see us off. But we were both happy
with that.

The general plan was to sail some distance up the coast of South
Africa and Namibia. We'd perhaps stop at one of the only two
refuges on Namibia's infamous Skeleton Coast, then haul out to the
northwest and the British island of St. Helena and track across the
top of the high—west and slightly south—to make our landfall on
South America near Rio de Janeiro. But just as in wartime few battle
plans survive first contact with the enemy, so it is with sailing. It
is best only to have estimated destinations and not even consider
estimated times of arrival.

Barely had the low skyline sunk below the horizon than heavy
rolling set in. The swells were still a good five metres and the boom
often grazed the rushing waters as we lurched from one side to the
other and skidded diagonally down the face of the waves. But on
Jenny's insistence I had taken the precaution of dosing up heavily
on Stugeron, the only seasickness remedy that works for me (apart
from sitting under a palm tree). Unlike off the coasts of Washington
and Oregon twenty years earlier, I was now able to contribute to the
handling of the vessel.

The first night out we settled into our regular watch rhythm:
Jenny would start cooking supper on the gimballed stove at about
18:00. After she had cleaned up, I would put on my lifejacket. We
had a rule that not only should both of us wear safety harnesses and
tethers at all times in the cockpit or on deck, but at night we should
also wear lifejackets. Realistically there was very little hope of one
of us being able to turn the vessel around, return and pick up the
other should the other go over, but wearing a lifejacket—with its
miniature flashing strobe light—would at least marginally increase
the chance of survival. Starting at 19:30, we would then alternate

Rolling up the west coast of South Africa.

watches throughout the night: three hours on, three hours off until 07:30, with the duty crew remaining in the cockpit all the time. Every effort was made not to disturb the person sleeping below, but another strict rule was that the "on" member would always wake up the "off" for sail changes, and that sail would be reduced whenever the desirability of this first occurred to either of us. And it was also acceptable for the person below to be asked to call up, on the VHF radio, vessels whose configuration of lights appeared to indicate they might be on a collision course.

In the daytime, Jenny would take most of the morning off, while I took the afternoon, although there were usually small boat maintenance jobs that would eat into these periods. Each day at sea came to an end about 17:30 when we would record our position in the logbook and on the chart and calculate the distance run over

the preceding twenty-four hours. The timing of this little ceremony was a hangover from the days we depended on celestial
navigation: only when we had completed a running fix combining
morning, noon, and late afternoon lines of position could we make
a reasonable estimate of our position. GPS, of course, allows for
instantaneous position readouts at any time of day.

The wind was strong and the sea cold the first night, and it
stayed that way. All the way up this coast the Benguela current,
surging up north from Antarctica, makes things a lot cooler (and
foggier) than you would expect at these latitudes. The cockpit was
rarely dry, and we made maximum use of our new red (and expensive) foul weather gear. As the hours went by we began to learn the
quirks of our new boat: the kind of behavioural oddities that don't
always become evident in coastal sailing. There was an annoying but not dangerous habit of cold water, which had surged onto
the lee deck as we heeled and rolled, gathering like a wave, rushing
aft, and then slopping into the cockpit. And when we surfed down
the waves at speeds exceeding five knots, the freewheeling propeller whirred alarmingly, to the extent of making the rudder itself
quiver. It was months before I learned the simple trick of putting
the shaft in gear and in reverse, which locked the propeller.

We'd inherited with the boat an antiquated and cumbersomely
designed self-steering wind vane called a Wind Pilot. Unlike more
modern designs, such as the Aries or Monitor, which use the non-
intuitive but very powerful servo-pendulum principle to keep the
boat aligned at a pre-selected angle to the wind, without external
power sources, our vane had a fifty-by-twenty-centimetre "sail"
that rotated around a vertical shaft. This turned a large cog that was
directly linked to another cog of the same size—no gearing—that
drove an auxiliary rudder mounted astern of the main rudder. The
main rudder would be locked in neutral, amidships, when the vane
was in use. The principle was a simple one, and the system had the
important advantage of giving us a spare rudder, but it was much

less forgiving and less powerful than the servo-pendulum vanes. You needed to expend a lot of effort trimming the sails and making infinitesimal adjustments to the lashing on the main rudder in order to get the boat sailing herself before you could hand over to the vane. Fortunately *Bosun Bird* was very easy to balance and it is always a good thing to trim the sails properly, but for the first nights we hand-steered as we moved up the steep learning curve of the Wind Pilot.

Unlike most cruising boats, ours did not carry an electronic autopilot: a device into which you dial a compass course and then let it push the tiller or rotate the wheel endlessly back and forth to keep the boat on course. This was for several reasons. First, auto-pilots use a lot of electricity, and this is always at a premium on a small boat such as ours. Second, our experience was that the single commonest equipment-related complaint of cruisers was auto-pilot failure, to the point at which many boats now carry three or four (a very expensive response) and popular cruising destinations are clogged with vessels immobilized because their autopilots have failed. And, finally, autopilots can lead your boat into trouble. They are not sensitive to changes in wind direction and will continue to point in the pre-determined direction even if doing so now means the boat's sails are set up all wrong. Wind-powered vanes make you a better sailor, but autopilots have the reverse effect.

As we rolled north, we saw a lot of ships. For me such encoun-ters are one of the most nerve-wracking aspects of offshore sailing. It takes time and some experience to work out, from a ship's array of lights, whether or not she is on a collision course with you; by no means can one rely on the other vessel keeping a good lookout and/ or spotting you on their radar. The old saw that power gives way to sail should for all practical purposes be disregarded, unless you want it on your epitaph.

One night as we rolled and lurched violently in the still heavy swell I made out what looked like a large and brilliantly lit oil rig, but it was rolling, too, and seemed to be moving slowly our way. Among the mass of dazzling white lights I could make out neither a red nor a green light, which might have given me some indication as to the strange craft's course. I checked our own masthead light was burning properly, went below and dialed in Channel 16 on our VHF radio.

"Southbound vessel off Lambert's Bay. This is sailboat *Bosun Bird*, bound north. Southbound vessel off Lambert's Bay, this is sailboat *Bosun Bird*, bound north. Over."

A South African accent answered quite promptly, but it took some to-ing and fro-ing on the bridge before the helmsman could confirm to me that he could see the tiny red light on our swaying masthead, and make a slight course change that would be sure to take him well clear of us. The vessel, it turned out, was a "crawler": a large flat barge of a kind that moves endlessly up and down these shallow waters, trailing beneath it enormous vacuum hoses that graze the bottom. Crawlers suck up hundreds of tons of gravel every hour, which is automatically sifted—for diamonds. I recalled the unusual notations on the charts for this coast. There are few natural harbours anyway, but even if you were tempted close inshore on a calm day, landing is strictly forbidden for a stretch of over two hundred miles. This is the *Speergebeit*, a forbidden zone closed to all but a few carefully screened and selected diamond prospectors, and reputedly the largest private closed-off section of land in the world.

One bonus of the cold current was extraordinarily abundant bird life. Until we were over halfway to St. Helena we were never without three or four albatrosses wheeling in our wake, a tiny Wilson's Storm Petrel dancing the foam of our bow wave, and Cape Petrels, all of which are considered Antarctic birds. The albatrosses are awe-inspiring to watch: for minutes on end they have no need to beat their giant wings as they soar and dive, keeping a wingtip a bare centimetre or so above the breaking wave crests.

(Jenny thought they were just showing off.) Close to land we were visited by curious Cape fur seals, escorted by dolphins, and, one dark night, a whale startlingly exhaled and drew breath only a few metres away. Even when the stars were in (as they were most of the time) we left a trail of glittering phosphorescence, and some nights there would be strange and sudden flashes of light from beneath the sea, all around.

It seemed rougher than I had ever remembered offshore; colder, too. I supposed we must have had many nights like these when we were circumnavigating with *Tarka*, but the nights I'd chosen to recall were all tropical ones, with the wind astern of the beam, pushing us along gently, the water rustling past. So far, we'd been rolling around so much every night that Jenny hadn't been able to cook anything more than instant ramen meals. If things were this cold and uncomfortable off South Africa, what were the Roaring Forties and Patagonia going to be like?

During the evening of Friday, September 9, our fifth night out, the wind began to build. Soon we were running with just our storm jib flying. For the first time in our sailing careers, and after nearly 30,000 miles at sea, I knew with certainty a full gale was blowing.

As dawn came up, the scene was alternately majestic and frightening: sea and sky were the same gunmetal grey, but the rollers were now breaking with a great roar in four-hundred-metre-long foaming stretches. Every thirty seconds or so our stern would rear up as one of these breakers built then sent us surging forward at an alarming speed, with spray everywhere. The trick, we soon learned, was to let the breaker take us at maybe 10 or 15 degrees off 90 degrees so that we would not pitch straight forward and risk burying our bow in the subsequent trough (called pitchpoling), then straighten up again as we slowed, lest the next wave catch us sideways on (or, broaching). The wind vane cannot anticipate the way a human can, so it was necessary to hand-steer, which required concentration—with one eye constantly over the stern—and some strength.

Some small-boat sailors report that they find sailing in these · conditions exhilarating. I find it an ordeal: the noise is relentless, the motion violent and unpredictable, and, however well built your boat is, there is always the nagging fear that under strains like these something critical could break. At about 06:00 I shouted down below, "I don't think we should try for Lüderitz in these conditions..."

White-faced, Jenny nodded her agreement.

But far quicker than it had come up, the gale faded away. Over the course of half an hour, as we pitched and swayed horribly in the leftover seas, we increased our sail area from just our tiny storm jib to every inch of canvas we possessed. On the horizon, as we came to the top of each wave, was a low line of blackish cliffs, backed by dusty brown hills. The sun came out. To the northeast and through the binoculars we could make out the shape of a red-and-white hooped lighthouse: Dias Point, the gateway to Lüderitz.

As so often happens at sea, the relief of a successful landfall—this time coupled with the return of good weather after a gale—more than cancels out the bad times.

LAAIPLEK TO LÜDERITZ: 440 NAUTICAL MILES (N.M.); 5 DAYS.

〜 Lüderitz is strange: a tiny, German-speaking outpost near the bottom of Africa, with hundreds of kilometres of the Namib Desert as its hinterland, just one road in and out, and no source of fresh water. We'd bypassed it when we came this way last time because it is so often shrouded in fog. But the combination of GPS and up-to-date charts that we now had was, in these well-charted waters, nearly as good as radar; this sounded like an interesting stop.

The town owes its name to a merchant from Bremen who in 1883 bought this then-deserted bay and hinterland from a Nama chieftain called Joseph Fredericks. This action in turn encouraged Germany to claim most of what is now called Namibia, with the exception of Walvis Bay—the only other good harbour on the coast—which had already been taken by the British.

But the complex of shallow bays by which today's town stands had come to the attention of Europeans much earlier. In October 1486 King John II of Portugal appointed Bartolomeu Dias to lead a small expedition with two aims: to see if there was a sea route eastward below Africa that could serve to link Europe with the Spice Islands, and to make contact with the rumoured domain of Prester John, a black Christian king thought to be based somewhere in modern Ethiopia. His tiny fleet consisted of two, fifty-ton caravels and a supply ship, which spent much of 1487 battling down the coast of the continent, through calms, contrary winds, and against the current.

They reached the limit of previous exploration—Cape Cross, now in northern Namibia—in early December 1487. By Christmas Day they were off a low barren headland that hid a complex of bays reaching several kilometres into the desert. Dias called it Angra das Voltas, or Bay of Curves, and decided that this was as good a location as any to leave his supply ship and scout a route around the bottom of the continent, which he sensed could not be far now. The main expedition ploughed on. By the time they were at the latitude of the Cape of Good Hope they had been blown far out to sea, and they spent weeks trying to make their easting. It was only when they were on their way back, months later, that Dias sighted the great cape, which he named Cape of Storms in memory of those earlier trials. By July 1488 the two big ships were once more at Angra das Voltas.

Of the nine men left aboard the supply ship, only three were now alive and most of the cargo had gone rotten. Dias erected on the headland, close to where the lighthouse now stands, a two-metre-high stone cross—a *padraõ*—to mark his passage, and left once again for the North. The expedition was back in Lisbon in December 1488.

Alfred Lüderitz bought the place up because it was the only good harbour between the British-owned Walvis Bay and Cape Town, and it offered a foothold for him to supply the Dutch and German farmers who were homesteading ever farther north from the cape. But the town boomed for an altogether unexpected reason: diamonds, discovered near there in 1908, long after a disillusioned Lüderitz had drowned in the Orange River.

〜 With the harbourmaster directing us by VHF radio in a thick Afrikaans accent, we motored past two wide bays then turned to starboard into the well-protected inlet at whose head the town lies, its angular buildings and steepled Lutheran churches look-ing tenuous on the steep rock shores. We tied up to a high, rickety, timber wharf, squeezing in between two diamond-dredging boats. A customs official wandered down.

"It's Sunday," he called down. "We're closed."

"So what do we do?"

"Ach, you can go ashore and check in tomorrow," he finally agreed. "But don't get me into trouble...keep your head down."

We paid a call on the yacht club, at the head of the wharf. The barman told us that the harbour bottom was very poor holding. But we were welcome to use one of the two or three moorings laid down by the club. Two young men enjoyed roaring out in a speed-boat to check it out for us, and when they gave us the thumbs-up we motored over and fished for the heavy line attached to the buoy.

On our port side lay *Patience*, and ahead of us *Atlantic Spray*: both ten-metre diamond boats of wooden construction, their purpose given away by the thirty-metre-long, twenty-centimetre-diameter yellow plastic hoses lying like giant sea snakes on the surface behind them. Every season, after the spring gales have swept

Diamond dredger, Lüderitz, Namibia.

through the shallow waters of the Namibian coast, stirring up the bottom, these smaller, often home-built, versions of the giant moving platform we had encountered far offshore venture out, each one to its favourite secret spot a mile or two off the beach. A diver goes over into the frigid water to manoeuvre the hose over the bottom, sucking up gravel that is then sifted on deck. The business is dangerous on account of unpredictable weather and powerful currents. It's also highly competitive, drawing in more than its fair share of colourful rednecks looking to make a fast fortune.

We hoisted our brand-new Namibian flag, with its distinctive sun in one corner, to the starboard spreader as tradition demands, pumped up the rubber dinghy and rowed ashore to stretch our legs for the first time in nearly a week.

The yacht club was a replica of our home yacht club at Port Owen: not too many people actually sail these waters, but a lot like to spend time propping up the bar. The talk was quite similar, too. An old Boer looked over at us over his beer: "Welcome to Southwest..." he said, toasting us.

It didn't take him long to get around to talking about the Old Days. "Shoulda been here then. Before that bugger Sam got his hands on the place. We're going the way of Zim now, you'll see..."

We weren't surprised to see, looking around, that there were no black members or basters (as the local variant of the "Cape Coloureds" are known).

While Namibia's transition from being a de facto dependency of apartheid South Africa to becoming a fully fledged and multiracial democracy had been relatively painless under the leadership of avuncular Sam Nujoma, the racial divisions and inequalities still evident in South Africa lingered here. There was much fear among the white community that the government in Windhoek was about to launch a populist land grab of the kind that had plunged nearby Zimbabwe into turmoil. It was often pointed out that the slightly eccentric Nujoma, who had just retired after two presidential terms, was Robert Mugabe's best friend, even naming a street in the sleepy capital after him.

But while compulsory purchase orders had been made on some large landholdings, everything was thus far being done in a seemly fashion and in compliance with the law. And a number of the more serious accusations made against landowners—that workers were sometimes kept in a state of feudalism, unable to buy land or save money even after generations of service—had been shown to be true. At the extreme end of the scale, the Canadian honorary consul in Windhoek had once told me that he had gone to visit a neighbour of his, to be greeted by a picture of Adolf Hitler over the fireplace and the challenging comment "Greatest man who ever lived..."

The barman passed over to us the club's ancient logbook of visiting yachts. There had been surprisingly few, maybe half a dozen a year. As we read the entries their crews had made, illustrated with drawings or fading photographs, it seemed to us that many had called in because of serious equipment failure incurred in heavy weather after leaving Cape Town.

Leafing back twenty or thirty pages, we came across entries from yachts we had last seen in Cape Town on our circumnavigation in 1987. Here was Dave Dexter on his Vancouver-registered catamaran *Pearl*, here Dutchman Tom Pronk aboard *Kaap Bol*, and here the old Aussie rust-bucket *Malulu* that we'd first encountered in Tahiti in 1986. The most recent entry was from our friends, Nick and Jan, on *Yawarra*, who'd stopped here about six months earlier and who, by now, were in Brazil.

⮀ Disappointingly the geyser at the yacht club wasn't working, so we had to make do with cold showers. And, this being a Sunday, there wasn't much open in town: just JJ's Takeaway. But it was a pleasure that evening to finish reading the potboiler I hadn't had time to finish on the voyage, an untaxing story of heavy seas, whaling, and corset-ripping sex in South African waters, called *Cape of Storms*. It was all the more enjoyable in the knowledge that we didn't need to go to sea again for a few more days at least. It's paradoxical, but many of my happiest sailing memories are of the first night in port, after a passage.

Next, after checking in properly, we took a taxi out into the desert behind Lüderitz, to the old diamond-mining town of Kolmannskoppe. This small settlement, which was started in 1908, was once the richest town in the world. In those days diamonds could be found simply by crawling around on all fours on the desert floor. The glory days were already over by the time the First World War broke out in 1914 and the last permanent inhabitant left in 1956, but the dry desert air means the town is well preserved.

Heavily built, two-storey managers' houses, of a kind you might expect to find in Tunbridge Wells, stand half-engulfed by advancing sand dunes, their glassless windows now staring emptily. Inside, fine tiles and painted wallpaper survive, but there are hornets' nests up in the gables. Bathtubs are half-full of sand, and you have to crouch through many of the doorways, where the dunes have found their way into what once must have been elegant Edwardian drawing rooms. In one of the bunkrooms of the workers' quarters is a life-sized amateur charcoal drawing of a busty blonde, with a coloured-in-yellow dress, and the legend: "Miss Colmans Kop 1921."

The central building in the settlement is the large, heavily built Kasino or clubhouse. There is a creaky stage still set for amateur theatricals, a two-lane bowling alley, a gymnasium equipped with leather-bound vaulting horses, parallel bars, and hanging rings. The walls are covered with black and white pictures of the managerial staff, posed like football teams, and of athletic-looking, blonde-haired, young men with bare torsos performing in the gym. In some of the later photographs, from 1914 and 1915, you can sense the distant turmoil of the Great War. A few of the men now sport uniforms, and there are cast pictures of patriotic pageants on the Kasino stage, of formal balls held under the glaring eye of a giant imperial eagle.

Another day we rented a car and drove out to the imposing Dias Point lighthouse, reached along a boardwalk. Nearby is a three-metre-high slate replica of the original *padraõ* left here by Dias. It's a lonely spot. Although the sea was calm the day we visited, you could feel a chill coming off the water, and it was not hard to imagine how wild this must be when a northwesterly gale is blowing in all its fury, not to mention how desolate and hopeless a spot it must have seemed to Dias. To this day, fresh water is brought in from hundreds of kilometres inland. It was humbling to think that while we had fretted over our charts and GPS readings, wondering if Lüderitz might be a little "iffy," Dias had come this way totally blind. He had no charts at all, no idea where he was going; he was up against winds that were unrelentingly contrary, with an understandably mutinous crew. And his vessels could hardly do better than 90 degrees to the wind.

Nearby are other reminders of the past of Lüderitz. In the shadow of the lighthouse is Shearwater Bay, named after a Royal Navy surveying vessel of the early nineteenth century, where the Russian grand fleet took on coal en route to its annihilation at the hands of the Japanese at Tsushima in 1905. On its wide sweeping beach are great rendering tanks and boilers from the years this was an important whaling station, now rusting and half-buried by the sand like Kolmanskoppe. In town there was talk that Shearwater will be the site of the terminus of a new, 1 billion USD, Trans-Kalahari Railway. The locals smiled and nodded politely, but you sensed they didn't really believe in it.

Penguins mooed like cows, and flamingoes edged their way delicately across the tidal flats as the setting sun turned the hills behind Lüderitz a soft glowing brown.

We stocked up, and a week after arriving, on September 17, were on our way once again, the course northwest: away from the land and out into the South Atlantic.

⌁ On *Tarka the Otter*, the passage from the Cape of Good Hope to the island of St. Helena had been one of the favourites of our entire circumnavigation: a brisk start followed by gentle winds, some swimming when becalmed, ever warmer seas. But that was at the end of summer. Now we were at the tail end of a boisterous winter. Over the next two weeks we saw the sun only sporadically and wore our foul-weather gear most of the time; only when we were a mere sixty miles out from St. Helena did a bosun bird spell off those Antarctic denizens. Day after day the wind blew at an uncomfortable twenty-five knots, building swells that again had us rolling heavily and dumping occasional dollops of cold water into the cockpit. Heading almost dead downwind meant we had constantly to tend the self-steering gear—which involved leaning far out over the transom, the most mobile part of the vessel.

Monday, September 26, was a typical log entry:

The wind got up yesterday evening and the crew deposited her dinner on the cabin floor; but she was able to scrape it up again and eat it. We used the lee cloths on our bunks for the first time. At 07:00 we put a third reef in the mainsail as it was too exciting for the crew. On the net, Alistair reported that the South Atlantic high is at 1030mb, which may be why we are getting so much wind; so much for the gentle trades.

Position at 17:04: 19 degrees, 47 minutes south, 8 degrees, 24 minutes east; Distance made good in 24 hours: 118 N.M.; Total distance made good: 929 N.M.

Most nights we saw the lights of ships. Few would answer their radios when we called them up, and they seemed slow-moving, which led us to conclude they were fishing boats, Korean or Taiwanese, not noted for their adherence to international maritime regulations.

The highlight of every day was when we would mark up our position with a small cross on the chart: an enormous one with St. Helena at the top, Tristan da Cunha in the middle, and—at the bottom, the remotest island in the world, Bouvetoya. Low points were getting up for those night watches, usually just as you had found a position in which you could doze off without rolling off your bunk.

"Ahoy below," Jenny would call. "It's half past one. Time for you to come and get cold..."

By now we hadn't listened to the news or heard a cellphone tone for a month. Escapism? Maybe, but in some ways all this—the

wind, the stars, the rushing ocean, seabirds, the emptiness—
seemed to us just as real and meaningful as the horrors of Iraq,
which had been filling the newspapers as we left South Africa. It
was how the world had always been and, until the end of time,
nothing out here would probably change.

One of the better books I read on this passage was the inspir-
ing if half-mad *Kon Tiki Expedition*. In contemplative mode, Thor
Heyerdahl writes:

> Coal-black seas towered up on all sides and a glittering myriad of
> tropical stars drew a faint reflection from plankton in the water. The
> world was simple; stars and darkness. Whether it was 1947 A D or B C
> suddenly seemed of no significance...

Thirteen days out the captain claimed the prize for the first
sighting of land (no Spanish ounce of gold, as Ahab promised for
the first sighting of Moby Dick, but the prospect of a Big Mac in
Brazil): the rugged sheer outline of St. Helena. But we were still
thirty-seven miles away, and there was no prospect of making the
open roadstead off Jamestown, in the lee of the blustery south-
easter, before dark. We deliberately slowed down and, as night
fell, inched our way closer. There were one or two lights visible.
Occasionally one would become suddenly bright then fade—a car
out for a Friday-night party somewhere, catching us in his head-
lights from twenty miles away. With cloud settling low on the
island, it took on a sinister prospect.

We sailed below the looming black mass of the seven-hundred-
metre-high mountain called The Barn and rounded the island's
northern tip—Sugar Loaf Point, marked with a feeble white light—
at 01:40. But when we came into the lee of Rupert's Hill and
strained to see the longed-for lights of Jamestown we were disappointed. There were perhaps a dozen weak sodium lights strung
out on the shore, a single flashing light warning of a reef, a dense

black mass filling most of our field of vision to the south. There was no moon.

The place seemed lonely, tenuous, and we hadn't even landed yet. The nearest human habitation is more than seven hundred nautical miles away: Ascension Island.

For most of the night we nervously sailed slowly back and forth three miles offshore, anxious not to get blown away from the shelter of the island, but fearful lest we get too close to the unlit coast. I knew that in the dark, high coastlines can often seem nearer than they really are; but we try never to close the land at night unless we absolutely have to.

It was with relief that we got underway again at dawn and motored to our anchorage, in the lee of the towering brown cliffs of Munden Point, to the west of the tiny settlement. When we'd weighed anchor in March 1988, we had never imagined we would see this place again.

LÜDERITZ TO ST. HELENA: 1,366 N.M.; 14 DAYS.

⌁ There's always a feeling of satisfaction as the anchor chain clatters out after a long passage, but, strangely, we are usually reluctant to rush ashore. After so long at sea, in our eight-metre-long world and with no other company than our own, land—with its people who have to be talked to, paperwork to be filled in, phone calls to be made—does not always beckon strongly. We hoisted a multipurpose British red ensign left from our last voyage, above our yellow Quarantine flag (to be lowered once we were certified as plague-free by a government doctor) and, after an hour or so, called up Radio St. Helena on our VHF. The startled duty deejay—who was no doubt dozing as Dolly Parton's Greatest Hits beamed out without interruption—called the harbour-master by telephone, and we were given our instructions.

We were the only yacht off Jamestown. Back on our last visit, which was at the most popular time of year, there were half a dozen

The anchorage off Jamestown, St. Helena.

boats in, and we recalled having an argument with the skipper of one of them when he anchored too close.

"*Resurgam*," I now said to Jenny after a long pause.

"What?"

"That was the name of his boat. Remember? He was a writer, his name was Webb Chiles. He had that trophy girlfriend, a blonde who used to do sit-ups on the foredeck and..."

"...said how beautiful the view was from Rio's *favelas*," Jenny chimed in, finishing my thought. "Didn't you fancy her?"

Remembering the names of the many boats we had met in the eighties, and matching them to those of their owners was a game we often played—and which I usually won.

Jamestown, the one and only significant settlement on St. Helena, did not look to have changed much in eighteen years. The few, run-down, Georgian-era buildings along the short road that is cut under the cliffs to the east of the small settlement, and the eighteenth-century wall blocking the entrance to the gully in which the town lies, were as before. But there were a lot more cars parked on the seafront. There is one for every two of the island's 5,000 inhabitants, we later learned.

One innovation had been made to help the two dozen or so cruising yachts that call here every year. The entire northern coastline of the island is subject to enormous waves, known as The Rollers, that sweep in with little warning and in otherwise settled conditions. They are thought to be generated by distant storms in the North Atlantic and the phenomenon may last for days at a time. In these conditions, landing is impossible, and any cars left carelessly on the front are almost submerged by the breakers. Even in normal conditions there can be a rise and fall of two or three metres at the small stone wharf, where an iron framework has been rigged with half a dozen heavy manila ropes hanging from it right at the water's edge. The idea is that you back your dinghy in and, at the top of the swell, grab one of the ropes and step ashore, letting the dinghy fall away behind you. But this is a skill that takes mastery, especially when alone or short-handed. Mercifully, private enterprise has now stepped in. For one pound sterling a day, per person, a local launch will come and fetch you, deposit you safely, and take you back out to your boat whenever you wish.

The convenience of this service does not take away a thrill as you set foot on the stone flags. Every single person to have ever come to St. Helena, from Napoleon and Wellington to members of the British royal family, has made this same delicate manoeuvre (and a good number have fallen in).

We were given a warm welcome at the customs office, in the unique St. Helena accent and vocabulary (a strange combination of England's West Country, Afrikaans, and Malay), and directed along the harbour wall, across the moat, and through a grand gate in the town wall to The Castle, where all the government offices are located. There was a steep landing fee of twenty-five pounds sterling to pay, and we also had to demonstrate we had medical insurance that would allow for an evacuation from St. Helena (even though, there being no airport, we would in fact probably have to evacuate ourselves).

The Castle lies at the seaward end of an almost perfectly preserved Georgian High Street, featuring the 250-year-old Consulate Hotel, Wellington House, a covered market, and a rotunda-like building known as The Canister. The blue-and-white-painted H.M. Prison (two cells) adjoins St. James's church, which is the oldest Anglican church in the southern hemisphere.

Every day on the radio, "Crime Report" is a regular feature. "A speeding ticket was issued yesterday," the police reporter might start in a ponderous thick burr, before clearing his throat. "There have been reports of littering at the Jamestown bus-stop. Young people are asked to take their rubbish with them or place it in the bins provided. Keep Jamestown clean and safe."

In spite of the limited capacity of the prison and the extremely low crime rate there are a dozen prison officers. Government is by far the largest employer here.

Most things are run from The Castle. Outside, a parking space was reserved and marked "Gov." Like the Falkland Islands, St. Helena is ruled in near-feudal style by a governor. There was disappointment that the current incumbent, an ambassador-rank official of Britain's Foreign and Commonwealth Office, had declined to wear the traditional white uniform and plumed hat to which he was entitled.

There were two shops: Thorpes and a Spar, both of which stocked South African and British imports. Although much of the island's interior is fertile, landholdings are tiny, and the shopkeepers told us that growers find it difficult to compete with imports. Potatoes grown near Lambert's Bay in South Africa, a few miles from our port of departure, were half the price of the local variety.

Pending the construction of an airport (due for 2010, but no one believed this would really happen; it did not), the lifeline to the outside world is the Royal Mail Ship *St. Helena*, the last remaining vessel so designated in the world. She carries up to 140 passengers and a goodish load of containers, and calls about ten times a year, providing a service to Ascension, Walvis Bay, and Cape Town, with one or two trips a year to the UK. Most islanders wishing to travel to Britain now take her to Ascension and then catch the weekly RAF plane to Brize Norton.

Our stay coincided with a call by the *St. Helena*. We watched containers being skillfully off-loaded onto hundred-year-old barges, one at a time, then off-loaded again onto the wharf: impressive in the three-metre swell. But the main attraction of the day was watching those outgoing passengers who, rather than brave the slippery steps and hanging ropes, opted for the Skylift. This was a small white metal cage with two seats inside and a large hook on top. Two at a time, to the accompanying mirth of most of the town, passengers would climb in. A crane would hoist the cage up into the air and down onto the barge, they would process in a stately manner out to sea like Egyptian pharaohs, and the same operation would be repeated for the actual boarding. It looked much more terrifying than taking the steps.

Many island natives (called Saints) have never left home. In fact it was only a year or two ago that they were given the right of abode in the UK. I wonder in how many places, today, you would still find people who have never strayed more than six kilometres from their home (the maximum possible distance here), who have never seen an aircraft, a train, or a traffic light?

One woman we spoke to on the quayside had been once to Cape Town, for two days. "...but I spent all of my time—when I wasn't worrying about being robbed—just people-watching, wondering where everyone could be going. I couldn't see why they seemed to be hurrying so."

Another habitué of the quay was a deeply tanned and toothless fellow in his eighties, a radio aficionado. "Oh yes," he said showing off a little, "Victoria is the capital of British Columbia, and Paul Martin is your Prime Minister...Mr. Chrétien was the last one. No, I've never been off the island. And you know what? I never want to."

In spite of the tiny scale of the place—from barely a mile offshore you can see from one extremity of the island to the other—the hills are rugged and the valleys between them so deep that just getting from one district to another can take hours.

"That's right," the Thorpes shopkeeper told us one morning, in mock seriousness. "Did you know that the cars here don't actually have third and fourth gear? It's never flat enough to need them, you see."

All around, especially along the coastline, is evidence of the role St. Helena once played as a coaling station and for re-victualling ships holding the empire together, standing, as it does, on the direct sailing route from the Cape of Good Hope to the English Channel. There are crumbling fortifications at every conceivable landing place, as well as a fortress high on a crag called High Knoll that was refurbished as late as the 1850s with (according to a plaque on the wall) the aim of providing the population with "safe refuge in case of invasion" (by whom?).

When Charles Darwin was here in 1836, at the conclusion of his five years aboard HMS *Beagle*, he remarked a little sourly, "...the first circumstance which strikes one is the number of roads and forts: the labour bestowed on the public works seems out of all proportion to its extent or value."

Many of these fortifications were constructed or beefed up on account of St. Helena's most famous one-time resident, Napoleon, who was imprisoned here after his defeat at Waterloo until his death in 1821. But one suspects the islanders are a little tired of hearing about him. On that note, and still in acerbic mood, Darwin added: "...after the volumes of eloquence which have poured forth on this subject, it is dangerous for me even to mention Napoleon's tomb."

Mr. Harris took us in his taxi to The Briars, the small country house overlooking Jamestown where the emperor spent his first month or so. A nicely polished brass plate gives equal pride of place to another temporary resident of The Briars who had stayed here a night or two several years previously: Arthur Wellesley, later the Duke of Wellington. Perhaps Napoleon did not appreciate this irony.

On a cool and misty plateau in the centre of the island is his longer-term home, Longwood, outside which the tricolour flies and which is maintained by the French government. Here is the large billiard table on which Napoleon spread out his campaign maps while dictating his memoirs to his faithful secretary, idly rolling an ivory ball from one side to another; the deep iron bathtub in which he spent hours reading and soothing his ulcers; the peepholes he cut in the shutters to observe his guards and—of course—the bed in which he died. A small brass plaque screwed into the floor marks the exact spot of the bed at the time of the emperor's death; many visitors leave flowers.

Jean-Pierre, our young French guide at Longwood, was an employee of the French government. He was overdressed, suave, fluent in English, and we sensed he felt out-of-place among the rustic Saints. He had no time for Sir Hudson Lowe, the then-governor and Napoleon's de facto gaoler, who inhabited the more salubrious and grand Plantation House. "He was an unpleasant man," Jean-Pierre commented thoughtfully. "Vindictive. But that doesn't mean you should believe those stories that circulate. He did not have the emperor poisoned."

Jean-Pierre walked over to the wall and fingered the dark-green wallpaper. "It is true that they found arsenic in his hair when they exhumed him from here, to take him to Les Invalides. But now they think it was from the glue they used for the wallpaper, reacting with the damp."

Meanwhile, over at Plantation House, the present governor was not receiving. But we did meet the five other beings with whom he shared his grounds: Jonathan, David, Myrtle, Fredericka, and Speedy. They are all very large Seychelles tortoises. Jonathan was brought here in 1880, at which time he was recorded as being "mature." In the tortoise world, this means over fifty, which now makes him over 170. While he wasn't exactly sprinting around the lawn, he did move at least thirty metres over the two hours or so we were in the area. The green paint on his carapace was the same shade as on the garden fencing, which suggests that once he had made an escape bid.

Joshua Slocum stayed a few days at Plantation House, in April 1898, toward the end of his single-handed circumnavigation of the world: "Most royally was the crew of the *Spray* entertained," he wrote, gushing over a large fruitcake baked for him by Lady Sterndale, the governor's wife. He stayed in a room that the butler assured him was haunted. Slocum hoped he would encounter the ghost of Napoleon, "but I saw only furniture."

We went for several long walks in the hills, found a Boer POW camp and cemetery, poked our noses into rural churches, and chatted with the locals, who have an old-style courtesy we had only encountered in one other place: Ireland. The place was small enough that after a couple of days you were nodding on the High Street to familiar faces.

Country and Western was by far the favourite music and the island's two radio stations played little else. I recalled that in 1988, top of the playlist was Benny Hill's "Ernie: The Fastest Milkman in the West," along with "St. Helena Blues," composed and played by the sole prisoner in the Jamestown lock-up. Things had not changed much. This week's memorable Number One, repeated every twenty minutes or so, performed by The Notorious Cherry Bombs, went:

I've learned she can resist me
By the way she always disses me
And comes to bed at night with that cold cream on

Sometimes I might feel frisky,
But these days it's just too risky

With the refrain:

It's hard to kiss the lips at night
That chew your ass out all day long

We wandered along the coastline. Many of the paths linking the old strong-points were dangerously crumbly, but it was evocative to explore ruins that really were ruins and had not been tastefully restored for tourists. At Thompson's (a corruption of Tombstone) Valley it took us two hours to scramble down to a Martello Tower and a lone battery ninety metres above the crashing surf. There was no sign of the modern world, and it was easy to put yourself in the shoes of the lonely sentries who spent months at a time here, bored, looking out to sea, watching for ships coming to rescue Napoleon.

With no other yachts in, the traditional yachtie hangout, Anne's Place, was quiet. We left an entry in her logbook and retrieved the volume including March 1988, with a half-page written by the crew of *Tarka the Otter*. Reluctantly, but we had no choice, we traded some of the not-so-bad paperbacks and a July copy of *The Economist* that we had read en route from Namibia, for Maeve Binchy and Rosamunde Pilcher.

We were shocked to hear one day from Anne that a yacht bound for St. Helena from Cape Town, the *Nautigal*, had just been reported to have foundered in heavy weather with the loss of two of her three crew, only ten miles out of Cape Town. Winter was still biting in the cape.

It was a busy twelve days in St. Helena, but the next wide open space on the chart—2,170 nautical miles to Rio de Janeiro—beckoned. On Thursday, October 13, we hauled up our anchor. Like Joshua Slocum we were sad to leave this unusual and remote place, the more so in that Brazil seemed so far away. Slocum wrote in his log, "...I watched the beacon light at Plantation House, the governor's parting signal for the *Spray*, till the island faded in the darkness astern and became one with the night, and by midnight the light itself had disappeared below the horizon."

I was inclined to feel similarly lonely. But Jenny was unaffected, blithely humming—as she put the coffee on—the other catchy hit on the local playlist: "Don't you wish your girlfriend was hot like me..."

⌒ Soon we were back into the old rhythm, one day merging into the next, our only calendar the daily run of a hundred miles or so. It was another fast and windy passage, but, unlike on the way to St. Helena, we did have some long periods of blue sky and warm weather, this even though were sailing south from St. Helena's 15 degrees of latitude to Rio's 22.

The steady weather meant we could listen to the CD portable player at night (*Evita* in preparation for Argentina), and once a day to the news on the BBC's African service. We also started to pick up Brazilian AM radio stations from 1,500 miles out, but only late at night when it was all phone-in talk-shows. By far the most powerful signal was Radio Globo, which had a distinctive jingle produced in an echo chamber. I would annoy Jenny by waking her up with my rendition of it, complete with an authentic Rio accent, when it was her time to come on watch: "*Gajyo Globo–o–o...Às cuarto e meia da manhã!*"

Often, though, we would spend the three-hour night watches simply sitting in silence. I'm sometimes asked by non-sailors whether those long hours alone in the cockpit, with only the stars for company have led me—or Jenny—to any great revelations. In modern life, perhaps only monks and nuns ever sit in enforced stillness for comparable periods. But I have never experienced a Moment of Truth. Some of the time I would usually spend worrying about the latest weather forecast, or an as yet unsolved problem with the engine, or the next landfall. Or I would spend hours simply remembering: school and university days, friends not seen in forty years. I did not arrive at any deep conviction of a Creator or a Plan out there; quite the contrary, the more hours I spent contemplating the night sky, the less I felt I understood, and the more insignificant life on Earth seemed.

There was something I did learn, although it is in most ways obvious and commonplace. When we completed our circumnavigation on *Tarka*—one dark night a thousand miles off the coast of Mexico—I felt suddenly that I understood the size of our planet (small, even though it had taken us four years to go around). There's also something more instructive, not to say satisfying, about travelling around the globe and returning to your starting point, entirely under your own propulsion, rather than in a 747. On your own and with no sophisticated instruments or technology, you have proved to yourself a deep truth—the spherical nature of the world—that was still doubted as recently as 450 years ago.

We fished but caught nothing; instead we had to reel in the line a couple of times when oceanic birds displayed interest in the lure. Several mornings we awoke to find flying fish stranded on deck, one a good thirty centimetres long. Watching them shoot out of the front of a wave and zoom over the surface for fifty metres or more, we appreciated why the French name for their deadly anti-ship missiles, *exocet*, was so apt.

The only landmarks on this voyage were the oceanic islands of Martin Vaz and Trindade, Brazilian possessions but over 750 miles offshore. Volume One of the *British Admiralty Pilot* describes the 750-metre-high Trindade discouragingly as "...a rugged and arid mass of rock of volcanic origin...The coast is steep and almost entirely fringed by reefs of coraline formation and ledges of rock on which the sea breaks with great violence. Goats and swine have been landed on the island at various times and are reported to have multiplied." The island now has a small military detachment, which was reported not to welcome visitors; Martin Vaz is uninhabited. We passed twenty-five miles south of the islands and had them in view for most of one day.

Then, still two hundred miles or so out from the mainland, we skirted a large area of offshore oil drilling. It was eerie at night, with enormous gas flares reflecting off the cloud bases and creating an apocalyptic mood. More practically, there were lots of ships around, some of them at anchor, so we had to keep a particularly good watch.

After Trindade the dependable trade winds (southeast and east) faded and we had days of strong northwesters, which meant we were hard on the wind, the sails sheeted in tightly, *Bosun Bird* heeling. Things got wet, especially in the constant squalls, which made for sudden Chinese fire drills in the middle of the night as we rushed to take sail down or put it up again once the squalls had passed.

The unsettled weather culminated in a very sudden and strong blow—Force 8 or higher, a phenomenon known here as an *abrolhos*—twenty-four hours out from Brazil. This had us surging along downwind, at six knots, with one square metre of sail up, spray from the wavetops whipping into us from astern, and the occasional large dollop crashing aboard. The phrase "white-knuckle

At anchor, Rio de Janeiro, Brazil.

sailing" applies literally in these conditions as you wrestle with the tiller; at least the water was warm.

The same afternoon, November 4, the distinctive outline of Cabo Frio came into view, and the final seventy miles west along the Brazilian coast to the entrance of Guanabara Bay were much more tranquil. By dawn, we were off Ilha Rasa (Smooth Island) and the entrance to the bay.

Entering Rio after twenty-two days at sea was an experience we'd been anticipating for nearly two years. Behind us the rising sun created all sorts of spectacular effects on the unsettled eastern sky, while in front there steadily grew the famous outline of the Sugarloaf with, behind it, the sharper peak that is the Corcovado, its huge statue of Christ illuminated a pale blue. Then the sun hit the skyscrapers and the luxury hotels on Copacabana and Ipanema beaches.

Unfortunately, the entry was not as relaxed as it might have been. As the wind died off Ilha do Pai, we cranked up the engine and set a course to join the main shipping lane inward. Within a few minutes, there was a pleasant smell of sandalwood.

"I can smell the land," I called out happily to Jenny, who was below.

"I don't think that's the land," she said after a long pause.

"What?"

"It's coming from the engine..."

I reached inside the cabin to switch off. For the next hour, we rolled uneasily in the swell, a mile offshore, as I wrestled to push back into place the water pump shaft, which had worked loose and drilled an impressively neat hole in the wooden engine cover. Following this, the crew was designated to stay below and watch the shaft attentively as we negotiated the final entry to the harbour.

By mid-morning we were motoring through the narrow and shallow channel between Punta de Saõ Joaõ and the colonial-era fortress island of Ilha Laje, at the very foot of the Sugarloaf. We turned left and anchored in six metres, in Urca Bay. We were back in South America.

ST. HELENA TO RIO DE JANEIRO: 2,169 N.M.; 22 DAYS.

Three Fronts, *a* **Pampero,** *and a* **Zonda**

RIO MEANT TWO THINGS TO US: SEX AND CRIME.

We'd stopped here for two days of honeymoon, en route from
Britain to Argentina in 1978. Heavily laden down with the wedding
presents that had come too late to be included in our sea shipment,
we had found our way to the "medium rent" area of Copacabana.
It was not on the beach with the swanky Meridien and others, but
not so far back as to be adjoining the *favelas*. We should have been
alerted by the large round bed and the pair of lights outside the
door—one red, the other green—but it was only when we asked
the price and were given an hourly room rate did it start to dawn
on us. This was a love hotel.

With all the comings and goings at night, we had needed to catch up on our sleep on the beach. This was a bad idea. On our first morning, with our towels and most of our clothes wadded into pillow-like bundles, we made for a safely crowded area and settled down. Ten minutes later I received a polite tap on my shoulder and a voice asked me for a light. I sat up, mumbled an answer in fractured Portuguese...and my pillow was gone. An elderly couple close by shrugged sympathetically. We had to get back on the bus in bathing suits only, and beg to be excused the bus fare.

We remembered these episodes, especially the mugging, as we now eyed the shoreline. Referring to our daily routines in both Cape Town and Bogotá, Jenny reminded me, "We have to get back into security mode."

There were several good signs: a half-dozen unattended but well-kept sailboats swinging at anchor, whose skippers must be confident of coming down here on the weekend to find their expensive possession still attached to the bottom; a military installation at the head of the little bay; rigid and inflatable dinghies stacked up against the seawall. And the neighbourhood was clearly upper-middle class.

Just in case, we stripped the deck and cockpit of anything easily removable and installed our lockable washboards in the companionway. After a luxurious shower in precious fresh water carried all the way from St. Helena, we pumped up the dinghy, rowed ashore and asked a rotund and respectable-looking man, holding an Antarctica beer in a small foam cooler, if this was a safe place.

"Yes, more or less...but you are in Rio. You should lock the inflatable, and don't leave those oars around."

I remembered now the Carioca accent—he pronounced the name of his city as Ghee-o.

It's not easy to secure a pair of two-metre, white-pine oars, so we resigned ourselves to carrying them wherever we went in Rio. To their credit, polite bus drivers didn't bat an eyelid as we forced our way through their turnstiles, and the usherette in the posh cinema we visited one afternoon even helped us prop them up by a vacant seat.

Our first expedition was to the huge Iate Clube do Rio de Janeiro, which occupies prime foreshore at the head of Botafogo Bay. Although our present anchorage under the Sugarloaf was scenic enough and didn't seem too unsafe, we thought we'd be even more secure if we could perhaps rent one of the yacht club buoys, and go to and from the shore through their installations. Some hope. At the front desk, the uniformed receptionist didn't actually sniff, but you could tell he wanted to.

"You are most welcome, Sir. Visitors may use the facilities of the Club with a signed introduction from three members in good standing and following consideration of your formal application by the Committee. Would you care for a form?"

Later, we found this attitude toward foreign cruising sailors to be typical in Brazil. In this country sailing is an activity for the mega-rich, and yacht clubs are meant as stages for sailors, their wives, girlfriends, and large entourages. Cruising yachts, with weed-stained waterlines, clumsy-looking self-steering gear, laundry hanging from the rigging, and hirsute crew lower the tone. In the case of the Rio club, we learned there had also been several "unfortunate incidents" at the end of the once famous Cape to Rio yacht race, with international sailors overdoing the champagne; the race now went to Salvador instead.

Darwin spent several months in a rented cottage in Botafogo Bay, as the *Beagle* made its leisurely way to Patagonia in 1832. It was his first extended period of living ashore in the tropics, and he marvelled at the abundant lush life everywhere around him: "In England any person fond of natural history enjoys in his walks a great advantage, by always having something to attract his attention; but in these fertile climates, teeming with life, the attractions are so numerous, that he is scarcely able to walk at all."

It was difficult to imagine there could ever have been cottages in Botafogo. An eight-lane boulevard crammed with frenetic honking traffic belching diesel fumes rings the bay, while inland high-rises almost block the view of the dramatic Corcovado mountain. We hadn't heard a car horn since Cape Town.

The first objective was to secure some money, without which we could not even get on a bus. After we had found a branch of the one bank that would accept Bank of Montreal bank cards in their ATMs, there was a further puzzling half-hour trying all the ATMs in the bank until we found the one that was actually geared up for foreign exchange. By now we were wilting, footsore, and short-tempered. Everyone seemed in a hurry; most people weren't actually rude but they seemed impatient with us. It was going to take us some time to readjust to shore life, even in laid-back Latin America. Dispirited, we trudged back to the sanctuary of *Bosun Bird*, our jobs only half-done.

Foreign yachts arriving in a new country are in most places treated exactly as 200,000-tonne supertankers are. When we braced ourselves to sally out again, it took us all day. First you must locate the appropriate set of immigration officials, in this case in an unlit office in an echoing warehouse in the docks that, on the rare occasions cruise ships call, is used as a disembarkation terminal. Then to customs, where a temporary import license for the boat must be obtained (the boat gets a longer stay than the individual in Brazil, which is mystifying but typical). Here the underworked and overqualified customs officer, who had only processed thirty-three yachts in the first eleven months of 2005, was keen to practise his English, so it was two hours before we could break away, all the time clutching our oars.

Next to Health, located behind an unmarked steel door and up a staircase at Warehouse 18, reached via a workers' bus that runs the length of the docks. We were asked if we felt all right and were given a fine-looking "certificate of pratique," which entitled us to take down the yellow Q flag we had hoisted on entering Guanabara

Bay. Finally, with three voluminous sets of papers now in hand, to the port captaincy, a branch of the navy. Most ports have such a presence, and at each, you must check in and out, obtaining clearance for the next destination.

As we left the port captain's, I leafed through the most recent of our stamped papers. "Look," I said to Jenny. "I'm down as Master and Commander. Just like Russell Crowe..."

Jenny was simply "crew," and on one form "cook." She was not impressed.

Joshua Slocum called in at Rio on his way south, in 1895, but he is unusually sparse in his commentary, noting only that, "...as I had decided to give the *Spray* a yawl rig for the tempestuous waters of Patagonia, I here placed on the stern a semicircular brace to support a jigger mast..."

I don't know what a jigger mast is, but we did have a long list of jobs to be accomplished before the next leg. Some of these were routine for every stop: climbing the mast to check the fittings, lights, and antennae at the top; checking the hull underwater; replenishing the water and diesel; restocking the galley. Then there would be repairs or modifications to be effected. In Rio we had a whisker pole (a lightweight aluminum pole, used for holding the stay-sail out when running before the wind) made up to our specifications, chased down otherwise hard-to-obtain stainless steel fittings and bought four hundred metres of line in preparation for mooring in the south. Bizarrely, the camping/outdoors shops where one could usually find rope doubled as pet shops, which made for many delays as Jenny paused to stroke kittens and poke her finger into budgie cages. To locate the small Argentine flag that we would need to fly once we were south of the River Plate, we were sent to a supplier of military uniforms, in the dock area. As Master and Commander, I was briefly tempted to buy the uniform of a full admiral in the Brazilian navy, but our budget would not run that far.

With so much to do, we had relatively little time for sightseeing. But we did ride the cable car to the top of the Sugarloaf (for the third time) and caught a movie. We also ate out, but the common wisdom was that we needed to be back on board, with the dinghy chained and locked to the boat, by dark: this inhibited our night life. Although we grew tired of carrying the oars onto buses, into department stores and restaurants, we had nothing stolen. Jenny survived a halfhearted mugging attempt by four youths in the area known as Flamengo; perhaps they were deterred by the captain making motions to assemble one of his oars as a club.

There was vicarious evening entertainment. Right by where we were anchored, under the Sugarloaf, was a popular bar at which, every evening, large groups would congregate. People would buy a 1.5-litre bottle of Antarctica, put it into their foam cooler, break out three or four small glasses, and sit on the harbour wall getting progressively drunker as the evening went on. Musical tastes were different here than they were in St. Helena. One Friday night I spent what seemed like hours drifting in and out of sleep as the same bars wafted over the still waters to *Bosun Bird*. I couldn't make out the song until in a burst of confidence the choir lurched into just-recognizable English: "More, much more than thees...I did it my vay..."

~ We read the news (speaking Spanish, it's easy enough to read papers in Portuguese), chatted with the locals at the Garota da Urca pizza shop, and caught up on modern Brazil. Last time we had been here, the country was coming into the final stretch of twenty-one years of military dictatorship, with General Joaõ Figueiredo succeeding Ernesto Geisel. Now the government was thoroughly civilian, with President Luiz Inácio Lula da Silva, commonly known just as Lula, likely to win a second term next year.

Brazil never underwent the horrors of Argentina's and Chile's dirty wars, but several hundred suspected leftists did disappear

between 1964 and 1985, and there would be periodic references
in the media to campaigns for a thorough investigation of those
abuses. Otherwise, the news was much the same as it always had
been: the fortunes of Brazil's soccer team and its chances in the
next World Cup; gang-led crime in the *favelas* of Rio and allegations
of right-wing vigilante groups having ties to the police; political corruption. The grandfatherly looking Lula and his party were
the subject of a raft of corruption allegations that filled the headlines most days, but the public had become bored with it all. Sure
enough, we later read that Lula duly romped home to a second
presidential term.

Two Rio institutions were no more. Ronald Biggs was a bit player
in the spectacular 1963 robbery of the night train from London
to Glasgow, which netted 2.6 million pounds—a fortune at the
time—and became part of criminal folklore as The Great Train
Robbery. Biggs escaped from Wandsworth Prison and fled to Rio in
the knowledge that the UK had no extradition treaty with Brazil.
Just to be sure, he married a Brazilian stripper called Raimunda de
Castro and had a child with her: Brazilian law accorded extra rights
to the parents of Brazilian-born children. Various farcical attempts
were made to force him back to Britain, but in the meantime he
enjoyed the high life, charging English tourists a few pounds to
have tea with him in Copacabana and recording two tunes for
a documentary on the Sex Pistols punk rock group. In 2001 he
surprised everyone by saying he was prepared to return to Britain.
The tabloid *The Sun* paid for his passage home, but any hopes he
may have held that he would be given a pardon were dashed when
he was locked up to serve the remaining twenty-eight years of his
sentence.

And only a year or two previously, the woman who had year
after year won the accolade of the sexiest airport announcer in the
world, working out of Galeaõ international airport, had retired. The
arresting, softly sensual manner in which she would announce that

Varig's flight 206 to Manaus was now ready for boarding or that
Aerolíneas Argentinas' noon flight to Buenos Aires was delayed for
technical reasons had soothed the tempers of millions of travellers
and won her fans worldwide. They were not in the least disappointed when a Rio investigative journalist reported in the late
1990s that she was a rather dumpy spinster in her late sixties.

⌖ It was now spring, even early summer in the southern hemisphere, but we were disappointed at the number of fronts pushing
through Brazil, with their origins in powerful systems far to the
south. Every two or three days there was heavy rain and whitecaps
in the bay. Fortunately, we only needed a short break in the weather
for our next leg: sixty miles west, to the bay of Angra dos Reis.

This is an awkward distance. At an average speed of just over four
knots, given reasonable wind and no adverse current, to accom-
plish this in daylight we would have to leave at dawn and risk
arriving after dark. Better to leave in the early evening, sail overnight, and then have all of the next day in reserve should the wind
and current not co-operate.

On this occasion, Murphy's Law was operational. Leaving
around 16:00 we edged out under the Sugarloaf, into a heavy swell
and a strong adverse current between the peak and the old fortress
on the island, and turned right, parallel to the coast. The wind was
twenty-five knots from astern, whipping up the sea off Copacabana
and Ipanema into a brownish froth. With two, then three, reefs in
the main we raced along, soon losing the bright lights of the famous
waterfront and passing in front of the distinctive square-topped
Gavia ("topsail") mountain that Darwin climbed. The GPS told us
we also had a knot of current in our favour, which meant that by
02:00 we were already close to arriving. We had to spend several
uneasy hours tacking back and forth in the dark off Ilha Grande, at
the eastern entrance to the bay.

In colonial Paraty, Brazil.

Although our GPS was giving us a constant readout of our position, our confidence was not enhanced by the fact that two key lighthouses had failed to appear. As if to compensate, there was an unexpected large and brightly lit oil terminal, with several attendant ships offshore, in a location that our chart showed to be uninhabited swamp. Ruefully, we agreed with each other that we should have bought, at the yacht chandlery in Rio, a new chart for this area: ours was a smudged photocopy of a British chart dating back to 1960.

We spent the next ten days cruising the spectacular islands and bays of this region, sailing only very short distances and anchoring every night in a different cove, each with dense tropical jungle tumbling from hundreds of metres to the shore itself, mirror-flat calms, and warm swimming. Occasionally a fishing boat would pull in late at night, and on the weekend there were some more powerboats and yachts around, as the Saõ Paulo crowd materialized. Our final stop was off the beautiful old colonial town of Paraty, once the seaward terminus of the road from Ouro Preto and Diamantina, at which the Portuguese galleons were loaded. The town is so close to the water and so low that the streets flood at high tide (an efficient means of clearing them out), and the old centre has been declared car-free.

Opposite Paraty, we made use of the so-called International Yacht Club, an abandoned white house by a small and isolated beach, with a spring channelled into a hose, which has over the years come to be used as an informal gathering spot for yachties. Here we met two of the very few foreign sailboats we had so far encountered: *Feng Shui*, French-flagged, twenty years out from France and just back after wintering in Buenos Aires; and *Marie Galante*, from Puerto Madryn, Argentina. There was also a tiny, home-built, wooden, six-metre catamaran, crewed by a young black Brazilian couple living on almost nothing. They'd sailed here all the way from Bahia, hundreds of miles up the coast, so the vessel must have been more seaworthy than it looked.

The French had originally intended to carry on farther south to the Beagle Channel, as we did. "But everyone we knew had a problem...they all came back. It was too rough for any yacht, it didn't sound like fun. *Ce n'était pas pour nous.*"

This wasn't encouraging: the French were obviously veterans, their steel-built yacht looked solid. Pascal was wiry, deeply tanned, and wore his thinning hair in a ponytail; his wife went topless when on board. I fleetingly recalled an embarrassing moment from our 1980s circumnavigation, when an Australian couple invited us over for a drink and suggested—when we arrived—that we strip off like them.

Our new Argentine friends were much more positive about the journey. "We insist: you must come and see us at Madryn. You will love it..."

"But what's the anchorage like?"

"Well, to be honest, there is no anchorage, you just drop the hook off the pier...most of the time it's fine."

"And when the wind goes easterly?"

"Well, yes. You have a problem...But it's only twenty-five miles across the bay. Then you are in a lee again."

The Ilha Grande area merited weeks of exploration, but it was November 22: summer was approaching and it was time to be off again. It was a long and slow sail southwest along the coast for forty-seven miles to Ilha dos Porcos (the Isle of Pigs), made all the more frustrating by the breakage of the cast aluminum fitting at the end of our brand new whisker pole. Then another twenty-five miles to the Newport or Cowes of Brazil: the town of Ilhabela, on the east side of a narrow strait separating the high and lush Ilha de Saõ Sebastiaõ from the mainland.

RIO DE JANEIRO TO ILHABELA: 197 N.M.

~ At Ilhabela, two of the three major yacht clubs that fill all of the available shoreline were like Rio's. With the Iate Clube da Ilhabela sharing its entrance with a Vuarnet boutique we sensed it wasn't even worth asking. And some Brazilian sailors warned us that the Iate Clube de Santos (which had very elegant gold and black flags fluttering on its moorings) was just "out of the question," touching their noses and tipping them upward to signify snobbery. But at the scruffier Clube Pinda, we were kindly guided to a free mooring and given the use of the club facilities (including hot showers) for a week—which is more typical of international practice. When we asked where we could buy diesel, José, the captain of *Caretta*, told us not to go to either of the two big yacht clubs—where the price was double the usual commercial price—and instead loaded up our empty jerry jugs into his car and drove us halfway around the island to a normal gas station.

We checked out formally from Brazil at the nearby oil terminus of Saõ Sebastiaõ, reached by a ferry from the big island. We breezily assured the suspicious immigration official that we would be off "immediately," even though—as it turned out—we had to wait several days for the right weather conditions (hoping no official would ask to see our passports, with their prominent exit stamps).

After the usual nervous scrutiny of Windguru and other Internet weather aids, Jenny wrote in the log on November 26, the eve of our departure:

> ...the weather looks as if it will be OK for the first two or three days, but we'll probably get unfavourable winds by the middle of the week. We may as well go.

On a sparkling morning we passed the rugged Ilha dos Alcatrazes (Booby Island) on the approaches to the busy port of Santos. Brown Boobies are tropical birds but we knew that we were now moving out of the tropics and back into cooler—and stormier—waters. And a day or so later, with only 250 miles behind us, at 27 degrees 30 minutes south, we sighted a truly southern giant seabird. Jenny verified in the bird book that it was a Yellow-nosed Albatross, "length 80 cm, habitat open sea from Brazil to Argentina, breeds on Tristan da Cunha."

The next eight hundred miles, to Mar del Plata in Argentina, threw more bad weather at us than we had experienced in four years and 36,000 miles offshore in the eighties, circumnavigating the globe.

A note of uneasiness first creeps into the log on November 30:

> The weather is still fine, with the wind at NE Force 3 to 4, but the pressure is falling and it looks as though a front is coming...

That night the wind died away completely, and then it began ever so gently to whisper from the south. By 06:00 it was blowing twenty-five to thirty knots, the seas were grey and building, and *Bosun Bird* was pounding under a triple-reefed mainsail and a heavily furled genoa. We were making painfully little progress, so, for the first time on this voyage, we hove to: the reefed-down main sheeted in hard, our stay-sail backed to windward, and the tiller lashed to leeward. Just as we'd rehearsed back in South Africa, we were effectively parked: the bows angled at the correct 60 degrees to the wind and oncoming seas, rising and falling gently. Down below the lessening in the noise was dramatic and sleeping was surprisingly restful.

Albatrosses soared and dived around us, seeming never to beat their wings, and for fifteen minutes a school of a dozen dolphins leapt simultaneously from the front of oncoming breaking waves, circled back beneath us, and put on repeat shows. It was one of those magic times when, though the noise of the wind in the rigging was like a nagging and inescapable fear, we knew we were doing something unique and unrepeatable, something we would never be able fully to explain to others back on land.

On the second morning after we had hove to, a Friday, we made radio contact with Nick and Jan, snug on board *Yawarra* in the comfort of the Yacht Club Argentino marina at Mar del Plata (known to cruisers as Mar Del). Jan was crackly and distant: "We're just back from checking the Internet forecast for you," she began. "For your position, the wind is supposed to move back into the north on Saturday and Sunday, but on Monday it will switch again, thirty-five knots from the south."

"What's your weather now?" asked Jenny.

"It blew hard in the night and we had to get up and readjust our lines, but it looks as though it's starting to ease now. Why don't you try for Uruguay, La Paloma, or even Punta del Este?"

Asking Jan to hold, we pulled the chart over and I measured the distance to La Paloma using dividers. Well over two hundred miles, and the wind hadn't even started to go favourable yet; we'd never make it; and La Paloma's entrance sounded iffy in bad weather.

"I think we're just going to have to plug on..."

"Good luck then," said Jan after a long pause.

On Saturday the wind duly began to edge around from south, first to east, then to the northeast. We made 114 miles that day, but by evening—although still favourable in direction—it was blowing over the forecast thirty-five knots, and we were surfing down the waves at seven knots, carrying only our tiny storm jib.

In local parlance, this wind, which came out of a bright, utterly cloudless, blue sky, is known as a zonda. All night we hand-steered, fearing that otherwise we would broach as we careered down the front of breakers, the rudder momentarily losing traction as the stern rose up into the air. By Sunday afternoon the gale was down, but so was the pressure. Even from the cockpit I could see the steep downward line that the nib of our barograph was tracing in ink: 1014 millibars to 1006 in twelve hours. Another blow was coming.

And so it went on. Three more fronts swept across our track: great tails extending northward from powerful depressions rolling eastward through the Drake Passage. For two of them we had to heave to again, all the while keeping an anxious eye open for passing ships and small, often unlit, fishing boats that were almost invisible in the heavy swell. There were times when our evening ritual of marking up our position on the chart showed—depressingly—that we had gone backward; we spent three successive nights gloomily contemplating the glow in the sky from the Brazilian city of Rio Grande. Nick and Jan fretted on our behalf: *Yawarra* was much heavier and longer than *Bosun Bird*, and hence much faster, but they guessed how violently we were being thrown around.

Gradually we worked our way past the Brazil/Uruguay border and into the mouth of the River Plate. At night we could now simultaneously see the looms of Montevideo, Punta del Este, and—more distant—Buenos Aires.

"D'you remember the last time we saw those lights?" I asked Jenny.

She came out into the cockpit and joined me. A long silence, then, "July 1981. Twenty-four years ago. We caught an early morning flight to Mexico City, then on to Vancouver...it was still dark when we left."

Somewhere to starboard we had passed the spot where Joshua Slocum accidentally put the *Spray* on the beach. In a rare understatement (perhaps he was embarrassed) he remarks "this was annoying." He nearly drowned when his dory was swamped three times as he tried to lay out kedge anchors to seaward. Slocum had to evade the attempts of an aggressive gaucho to lasso him before he was able to float the vessel again.

We were also in the waters where in December 1939 a small squadron of British warships—the *Exeter, Ajax,* and *Achilles*—forced the German pocket battleship *Admiral Graf Spee* into Montevideo, where her captain scuttled her rather than venture out again. It was the first significant allied naval victory of the war. I recalled as a boy, on a Saturday night in the darkened school gymnasium, watching the guts-and-glory movie *The Battle of the River Plate.* The town of Ajax, Ontario, is named after one of the British ships, and some of its streets after members of her crew.

We were tempted, after the pounding we had taken, to turn right. As late as the 1980s Montevideo and Buenos Aires were almost obligatory stops for southbound yachts: Slocum, H.W. Tilman aboard *Mischief,* the Baileys on *Auralyn II.* But the detour into the vast muddy estuary of the Plate is a long one, the channel to BA through miles of sandbanks dangerous and winding. Meanwhile, Mar del Plata, farther south but barely off the direct route, has a good artificial harbour. We plugged on.

Unfortunately, there is one phenomenon that does not show up in weather forecasts, and that we'd been worrying about for months.

We were now in the zone infamous for short-lived but very fierce squalls known as pamperos that—blowing off the pampas and into the estuary—can reach seventy knots for an hour. We had read that signs of an imminent pampero included a long, dark, cigar-shaped cloud and a phenomenon known as the *Baba del Diablo* (Devil's Dribble): gossamer cobwebs, and moths and other small insects congregating in the rigging (blown in front of the squall). One such wind in the nineteenth century, combined with a spring tide, blew so much water before it that it briefly dried out the wide stretch of shallow water between Buenos Aires and Montevideo, and a horse and carriage were able to ride across. In our time at St. George's we'd experienced three or four bad ones, one of which blew down the palm trees that shaded the school swimming pool.

Sure enough, on the morning of Monday, December 5, and past the point at which it was easy to turn to BA, there were cobwebs in the rigging, insects wedged in crevices or in the blocks, and small land birds were fluttering tiredly around us. The blue canvas dodger that protects the companionway was covered with tiny globules of dew, and there was a sinister halo around the morning sun. We held our breath. Nothing happened. Then, late in the evening, tall, anvil-shaped clouds formed. A dramatic but short-lived thunderstorm came up. The wind shifted 180 degrees in ten minutes: perhaps it was a pampero after all, but a modest one.

For the last two days we had favourable winds, and we pressed on as fast as we could so as to make Mar del Plata before sunset on our sixteenth day at sea. Fleetingly, I recalled that off to starboard must be the mouth of the Samborrombón River, which we'd explored by kayak all those years ago, but there was little time for nostalgia. Every fifteen minutes or so, I'd call out to Jenny, "Boat speed?"

"Five point two....five....four point eight....five."

"Distance remaining?"

"One hundred and twenty-two."

"Course to steer?"

"235 magnetic."

We had the familiar experience of the engine misbehaving at the worst possible moment. Just after we had surfed in between the artificial breakwaters forming Mar Del's harbour and were searching in the gloom for one of the two complimentary mooring buoys supposedly stationed outside the yacht club marina, the water pump began spraying sea water all over the inside of the engine compartment, including—dangerously—the alternator. Rags tied roughly around it, plus some adrenaline-fuelled pumping of the bilge, stabilized matters. But then Jenny, tired after our day of pushing *Bosun Bird* to the maximum so as to make port before dark, failed in three successive attempts to grab the mooring buoy with our boat hook. On the third she lost her grip on the boat hook, which drifted off into the darkness.

"I've let go...," came the plaintive admission.

Angry silence from the captain as I pushed the tiller over and started to turn another circle.

"Well...what are you waiting for? Down on your stomach; get your arm over the side...coming around again, on the port side..."

"Port...port...HARD PORT!" Jenny yelled back as we closed in. Then a muffled, "Got it!"

It had been a stressful passage. Unusually, I had been able to read only one book: Trollope's *The Eustace Diamonds*. This was sufficiently slow-moving and ponderous for me to be able to read two or three pages, rush to tend to the sails, and then pick it up again in only the approximately right place, without losing the plot. There was also usually too much going on at night for us to want to listen to music on our portable CD player. We slept well that first night in port.

ILHABELA TO MAR DEL PLATA: 1,125 N.M.; 16 DAYS.

〜 "*Hola! Soy Luis. Bienvenidos a Mar del Plata!*" was the cheery morning cry, followed by a polite knock on the hull.

We hurriedly got up, pulled on shorts and T-shirts, cranked up the (still leaking) engine, cast off, and followed Luis in his 1930s wooden launch through the narrow entrance to the marina of the Yacht Club Argentino, its swing bridge obligingly in the open position. There were more welcomes, this time in English, as other cruisers helped us to manoeuvre nose-first into the tight space allotted to us and asked us the ritual questions:

"Where was your last port?"

"How many days?"

"How was the weather?"

"When you're ready, why don't you come on over?"

It was fun at last to meet a significant number of other cruisers, if only so we could reassure ourselves that what we were doing was not complete lunacy. We'd just missed one wave of southbound cruisers (among them *Yawarra*); worryingly, some had had to wait for nearly a month before they had judged the weather conditions favourable. But there were several boats on their way north, with a wealth of stories to frighten and fascinate us.

Tom and Vicky, British and in their fifties, were the owners of a beautiful, highly varnished, wooden vessel called *Sunstone*, currently looking not-so-seaworthy on account of a large green inflatable Christmas tree suspended in their rigging. They had sailed across the North Atlantic from England, through the Panama Canal, on to New Zealand and up to British Columbia (where they had spent many months sailing in our favourite haunts). Then they'd edged all the way down the west coast of the Americas to the Beagle Channel before heading up to Mar Del. They were serious racing sailors, veterans of a Sydney to Hobart race.

"But you know what," said Tom in his very English accent, one day over coffee in the cockpit, "Patagonia was the toughest cruising we've done anywhere, bar none."

We must have looked worried.

"Don't worry," Vicky added. "If you've got this far you must be doing something right."

Tied up next to them was an equally beautiful boat of more modern design: the eighteen-metre, blue-hulled *Sarau*, crewed by former boatyard owners Malcolm and Joan from New Zealand. *Sarau*, as we would later learn, was constructed of kevlar and boasted, among other modern conveniences, a washing machine, heated towel rails, and a power-flush head. Malcolm, with his thick white hair and an equally thick white moustache, looked like a middle-aged Ted Turner; Joan dressed like a grande dame and entertained lavishly, with semi-formal drinks parties on board most evenings. They had spent the winter in the South and were lyrical: they spoke of still, cold days among the glaciers, of cruising for weeks without seeing another human being, of condors and guanacos. But they'd had their difficult times, as well. On their way north Malcolm had succumbed to a severe infection, leaving Joan, who was a lot tougher than she looked, to single-hand the vessel all the way up. Fortunately *Sarau* was so automated that this was not as arduous as it might have been on a smaller or more basic boat.

Then there was Rob, a fifty-year-old, sunburned, Australian bachelor with a long ponytail, aboard *Gannet*. He was an ex-para-trooper with the Australian armed forces and had been on an exchange for a year with Canadian paratroopers in Canada; his ship's library was full of books about the exploits of the SAS in Iraq, along with a few Tom Clancys and Clive Cusslers.

Rob was quite famous. Approaching Cape Horn from the west a year earlier, he had been overtaken by a storm of frightening proportions. *Gannet* was rolled and dismasted.

"Yeah," said Rob. "It was a pretty bad scene, I reckon. I had a panic attack. Not ashamed to admit it; more scared than I ever was as a para. No two ways about it: I thought I was for the fuckin' chop…"

Once the seas had subsided to manageable proportions he was able to cut away most of the wreckage on deck, painstakingly dry out his engine and batteries, and continue his voyage under power.

In touch with the Chilean navy by radio he was advised formally to declare an emergency.

"No fucking way was I gonna do that. I knew they'd make me go to Puerto Williams, where I reckoned it'd be really difficult to get any work done on the boat. And I knew they wouldn't let me fuckin' go without certifying the boat..."

"So what'd you do?"

Rob shrugged. "Wasn't too much choice. Decided to carry on around the Horn, then turn back into the Beagle and make for Ushuaia, on the Argentine side...I had lots of fuel. But I can tell you, powering around the Horn in a sailboat with no mast, all that shit on deck, and no sleep for five days, it was no joy ride..."

We were all duly impressed. There was a silence. Then, sipping from his beer, he went on, "Going south, I suppose? You must be fuckin' crazy. I wouldn't go back for a million bucks. It's Brazil for me, and a few of those girls in tangas."

Rob was the social secretary of the Mar del Plata cruising community. Always on the lookout for available young women, he knew every bar and barman in town. He wasn't always success-ful. "It was at the Sheraton bar one evening," he said in his lazy Australian accent. "There was this señorita next to me, a real cracker, you know what I mean? Anyway, we get talking, and things are going pretty well. After a couple of drinks she takes off for the head. I'm fancying my chances by now, but just in case, I check the form with the barman. I mean...I don't think she is, but she might be a hooker, know what I mean? So he looks at me for a mo, and I reckon he hasn't understood. Then he leans over and says, dead serious like: 'Señor, esa Señorita es un Señor.' I couldn't fuckin' believe it! But when she came back, you know what I did? I checked out her throat. Sure enough, she'd got an Adam's apple...Fuck me!"

Rob's sometimes reluctant best friend was a shy English single-hander in his sixties called Roger. His boat was a fifty-year-old, Nicholson-designed, wooden boat called a SCOD (South Coast

One Design). At twenty-six feet, *Herschel* was one of only three boats smaller than ours that we were to encounter offshore in two years. Rob would periodically haul Roger off to trawl the red-light districts of the port area, but the truth was that the earnest and modest Roger was only concerned with replacing some distressingly leaky underwater planking on his boat before heading off on the very long haul to Cape Town. Roger had left once before, only to be forced to turn back, several hundred miles out, when *Herschel* began taking on an unsustainable amount of water through one side. He had to manage the sail back in such a way that the plank in question remained, as long as possible, above the waterline. *Herschel* was now propped up on dry land while Roger disconsolately picked at the guilty planking.

On our first evening in the marina, Rob persuaded us all to accompany him to a slap-up dinner at a restaurant called The Lexington. The place sounded classy and expensive, and our fears were confirmed when we saw the décor: discreet wooden panelling, English-style racing prints on the wall, tuxedoed waiters, and full silver service. We felt out of place, even in our best cruisers' togs, but we need not have feared. Rob had negotiated an incredibly cheap deal for a three-course steak dinner with unlimited wine. Afterward, in the taxi back to the port at 2:00 A.M., I asked how he'd managed it. Turning round from the front seat, he said, "Hadn't yer figured it out, mate? It's the Mar del Plata mafia, it's a money-laundering racket. The more foreigners they get in there, the better. Makes it all look less suspicious, like..."

Later, for Christmas Eve, Rob negotiated another special deal for a cruisers' table at a nearby fish restaurant, complete with an Argentine musical trio called Gama that performed accented cover versions of "What a Wonderful World" and "Man, I Feel Like a Woman." When we finally left at 2:00 A.M., Rob was deep in conversation with another señorita, spandex-clad—and with no Adam's apple.

⤳ Like those Brazilian yacht clubs, the Yacht Club Argentino (whose headquarters is in Buenos Aires) has a long pedigree and a distinguished membership, but it also warmly welcomes long-distance cruisers. The morning we arrived, there was already a Canadian flag flying from the cross-trees of the club's flagstaff, along with the ensigns of all the other foreign visitors. Luis supplied us with forms and advice to help us through the arrival bureaucracy, showed us the showers and club restaurant, and gave us a map of town.

As we headed up the hill to start our paper trail, I noticed the name of the road on which the club stood: Navegante Vito Dumas. Therein lies a story.

Born in 1900 in Palermo, Buenos Aires, Vito Dumas grew up in the pampas but made a local name for himself with five attempts to swim across the River Plate, none of which were successful. Thinking the English Channel might be easier, he tried his luck there in 1931, failed again, and decided to make the best of a bad job and return from France to Argentina by sailboat. Adventuring of this kind was hardly known in South America at the time, and he sailed into BA to a hero's welcome after 121 days at sea, including several stranded on a sandbank off the Brazilian coast.

Ten years later, in June 1942, he set off again, in a thirty-one-foot double-ended Colin Archer ketch called *Lehg II*; the name was reportedly derived from the initials of his mistress. His aim was to be the first man to sail solo around the world south of the three great capes: Horn, Good Hope, and Leeuwin. Making stops in Cape Town, Wellington, and Valparaíso, he was successful in his objective. His feat went largely unnoticed in a world at war, but he became an instant national hero in Argentina, where his name is still revered, and especially in Mar del Plata, where he finished his voyage.

Dumas recorded his exploits in a book called *Los Cuarenta Bramadores: La Vuelta al Mundo Por la Ruta Imposible*, available in

English as *Alone Through the Roaring Forties*. It is a good read, and there is no doubt Dumas was a superb natural and innovative sailor. It is largely due to the tactics he employed in heavy weather in the southern Indian Ocean, which he recounts in his book, that offshore sailors now prefer whenever possible to run before heavy weather, with sail up, than face the consequences of lying ahull, vulnerable, with all sails down.

But Dumas was no modest Alec Rose or Bernard Moitessier, both of whom preferred the solitude of the ocean to life ashore, setting off and returning with the minimum of fuss and understating their achievements. The title of his book is a giveaway: 85 per cent of his voyage was actually north of the Roaring Forties, and this was by no means The Impossible Route. The direction in which he sailed, east-about with the prevailing winds, was the obvious and easiest one, employed by all of the trading clippers through the nineteenth and into the twentieth centuries.

And Dumas' achievement was a very specific one: a particular direction, a particular route, and alone. He makes no mention of the fact that in 1934 the Norwegian Al Hansen had sailed solo around Cape Horn the real wrong way (East to West), that Conor O'Brien had in 1923 (albeit not alone) sailed the same route he (Dumas) was now attempting. And he ignores the much longer voyage of Slocum, apparently because the American sailed through Magellan rather than around the Horn, even though Magellan is considered harder for a sail-only vessel.

Dumas does not tell us how they came to know about his plans, but he recounts that the day he left the national newspapers all had his voyage as their headline. Slocum would have cringed. Later, leaving Cape Town, he writes: "Nobody, nobody until now has ventured into the desolate regions where I am about to sail"; nearing Australia: "I have almost crossed the Indian Ocean. Something nobody has ever done alone..."; on arrival back in Argentina: "I had done the impossible." Dumas was a hero, of that there is no doubt,

but a rather grandiose, self-conscious one (in the Argentine stereo-
type, it might be said unkindly).

At the Yacht Club Argentino, where his later green-painted sloop
Sirio still lies, mention of the Great Man brought a strangely ambig-
uous response. I never hear a bad word said against him, but when I
asked Luis about Dumas he suddenly became shifty.

"*Oye, don Nicolás*...they say that to mention his name brings bad
luck. We don't like to talk about him...Someone told me that there's
a play by Shakespeare like that: you mustn't say its name."

I wondered if today's Argentine sailors, while recognizing what
Dumas achieved, are a little embarrassed by the fact he was also
a shameless showman, someone who deliberately set out to do
"something great" and then lived off his laurels. The widely distrib-
uted pictures of him in a Sou'wester, apparently braving a Southern
Ocean storm, were posed in a studio after the fact.

~ In Mar del Plata our waiting game began again. Our previous
leg had been much harder than we had expected, and we were sure
that the next—1,200 miles, clean through the Roaring Forties and
almost to Cape Horn—would be tougher still. We knew that somewhere we would be hit with really heavy weather, but we wanted
to set off with the best possible window: ideally, three days of
projected favourable winds, followed by an adverse wind change
bringing no more than thirty knots.

For the time being, such a prospect looked remote. We decided
to take a few days off in Buenos Aires.

You could tell by the slightly puzzled looks we got at the train
station ticket booth that not many people went by train these days.

"But sir," said an old uniformed clerk, who was almost invisible
behind the heavy grille of the booth, "why don't you go by bus? It's
quicker and it's only a bit more expensive."

With salesmen like these I could see why Ferrocarriles
Argentinos were not making much money. But we had so many

happy memories of long train rides across the pampas that we
went anyway.

The trains had had a new paint job. The old brown exterior was
now a snappier red, white, and blue. But these looked suspiciously
like the same carriages: cheap vinyl seats in the original muddy
colour, windows that were either jammed open or jammed closed,
ceiling fans that didn't work. And it was the same ride: long vistas
of flat cropped meadows divided by rows of poplars; small one-
square and one-storey towns with the place names still picked out
in white relief on a wooden black board; men and boys on horseback trotting the dusty lanes that run parallel to the train tracks.

Coming into BA, there was a suddenly familiar smell, too, some
unique combination of diesel fumes, sun-baked shit on the raised
train embankments, and the redolent aroma rising from the black
and oil-polluted waters of the Riachuelo, the foul creek around
which the old quarter of La Boca is built. At Avellaneda we joined the
main line into Plaza Constitución and were on the suburban track
Jenny had taken twice a day for nearly three years. It took her a few
minutes, but soon she was recalling the sequence of stations. "Bernal,
Hudson, Sarandí...and there's the waterworks, the polo ground..."

At the ever more frequent stops vendors got on. The routine was
the same. "Ladies and gentlemen, a very good day to you all. It is my
great privilege to be able to offer to you today an item of the highest quality, this fine leather wallet, not yet available in the stores, at
a fraction of the price you would normally expect to pay."

A shifty-eyed salesman in a shiny suit would display the wallet,
with its multiple pockets, credit-card holders, hidden compart-
ments. There would be a bored silence; no one made eye contact.

"But most esteemed ladies and gentlemen, that is not all. For
every purchase I am willing to offer this fine stainless steel comb,
the last word in modern fashion, at absolutely no extra cost."

One or two faint expressions of interest, an almost impercepti-
ble flickering of the eyes.

"And I have not finished yet. What superior gentleman wishes to be without a cigarette lighter as he goes about his daily business? Ladies and gentleman, for absolutely no extra cost and at great sacrifice to my suppliers, this wallet, this modish comb, and this lighter...all for the original and laughably low price...Where in today's world can you obtain a fairer deal?"

By the end of the patter a surprisingly high number of commuters would have signed up.

In the great echoing downtown station there were the old sellers of *alfajores* (a unique and very rich Argentine biscuit), hawkers of *Clarín* newspaper, and as we took the stairs down into the Subte, a familiar rush of warm air blew up toward us, smelling of dust and lubricating oil. For some reason I suddenly remembered one of the last times I had been here, with Abba's "Chiquitita" coming tinnily from the tannoys on every corner. There's supposedly a scientific explanation for it: smells are far more stimulating to the human memory than visual or aural prompts.

We went out to St. George's one evening. It was early in the school summer vacation and Mike and his wife, Alejandra, greeted us lazily at the gate of the Second Master's house that was now theirs. Mike had joined us in our last year in Argentina from Huddersfield (England) and was one of two expat teachers from that period still at St. George's.

Mike had barely changed: suntanned, a few more wrinkles, but the same North of England accent. Over a Quilmes beer in the front garden, he filled us in on a quarter of a century's worth of school gossip. "Remember Flores? We used to call him Flowers. Tall thin kid, Cutts House. A real rogue. Well he's now on the board of governors: much more responsible than you would have ever thought. Rick? Wasn't he one of the school house staff with you? Well, there's a bit of a story there. He always was a bit bolshie, you probably remember. Tried to take me on once too many...left in a bit of a hurry. And you remember Horacio, the chem lab assistant? Little guy with a moustache? Well he's still here, but very ill: looks like cancer."

We wandered around the eucalyptus-smelling campus in the gathering twilight. The school was doing well (there had been times in the turbulent late seventies when it looked as though it was going under), but, now that there was a fast and direct highway into Buenos Aires, it took almost no boarding students, which had changed its character considerably.

Mike and Alejandra told us of some hard times they had been through. First there was the *corralito*, when the government had confiscated dollar deposits in banks. "We lost almost everything... got back maybe 30 per cent on the dollar. The bastards..." Mike shook his head.

Then there had been a real-estate scam in which, looking to invest in one of the now popular "countries" (gated residential estates), Mike and Alejandra had lost most of the rest of their money. But things were more stable now and they were looking forward to a quiet retirement.

"We'll stay on...Nothing to go back to in UK. We've had our ups and downs, but coming here was the best decision I ever made... Fetch us another beer, luv."

As we caught the pale-blue 580 bus to central Quilmes, for the last train back into BA, I realized that Mike had not asked me or Jenny a single question about what we were doing now, or what we had done since leaving the school. It was true, I reflected, that we hadn't been particularly close friends: perhaps over the years I'd exaggerated in my own mind the companionship, the high jinks I thought we'd had in those days.

I wasn't sure if I envied the sameness, the stability, the sense of comfort that Mike and his wife seemed to enjoy, while Jenny and I had in the intervening period changed nationality, lived in five different countries, embarked on new careers, met then lost a hundred friends. Or had I somehow been hoping that they would envy us?

Going back was all rather unsettling. Not that St. George's was smaller or less beautiful than we remembered—it was neither. Perhaps it was because it gave us a glimpse of what might have been had we not chosen a forking path back in 1981, a look into a kind of parallel existence. Whether it was a better or a worse existence I couldn't decide.

In spite of the recent hard times, BA was buzzing. The decrepit dock-land at Dársena Norte, where we had queued with a bottle of Scotch to renew our residence permits, was now a plush office and marina development, with fancy restaurants lining the waterfront. Florida was as jammed as ever with fashionably dressed shoppers; the green Harrods sign was still there, but the store looked to be closing down, a sign of rapidly diminishing British influence. At night on Corrientes all the movie theatres offered *trasnoches* (all-night showings), and, when we came out from *King Kong* at 2:00 A.M. the street was still brightly lit and crowded. We went for a pizza at Los Inmortales, near the Teatro Colón: it had gone a little up-market and the signed photos of tango stars, such as Carlos Gardel, had been removed for safe-keeping.

The Plaza Británica, with its tall clock tower presented long ago by the British community is now known pointedly as the Plaza de la Fuerza Aérea (Airforce Square). There is a dignified memorial, in pink granite, to the Argentine dead in the Falklands/Malvinas conflict, guarded around the clock. Nearby, in the Plaza de Mayo, the mothers of the dead and disappeared from the seventies still— movingly—marched. But with an explicitly sympathetic government now in place, it looked as though they would soon suspend what may have been the longest continuous protest in the world.

We talked to many people about the war in the South Atlantic. Almost no one thought that the Argentine invasion had been a good idea. "It was stupid...Taking on *los ingleses* and *la Thatcher*? Crazy."

But no one thought Argentina should renounce its claim to the islands. There was a feeling by many that Argentine veterans of the war had been treated very shabbily; some made the comparison with Vietnam vets. Their heroism—particularly that of air-force pilots who had flown desperate do-or-die missions again and again, even though their commander, Brigadier General Lami Dozo, was the member of the junta most reluctant to go to war—was not recognized by a series of administrations that were only too happy to forget the whole saga. The media were now taking up stories of war-survivors committing suicide or dying in penury. Every monument to the conflict had fresh flowers on it.

Argentina was also taking a fresh look at Evita. There is an Evita museum in BA, and many branch offices of the ruling party are named after her. The granite Duarte vault in Recoleta Cemetery, on the must-see list of every tourist, is also often bedecked with flowers, and there are plaques recalling her grand-sounding but—on close examination—vague calls to arms: "I shall return, and I will be millions!"

Some historians have described Peronism, as practised by Juan Domingo and Evita Perón, as nothing but fascism with a Latin American face. Certainly its original dogma seems to borrow much from National Socialism, and Perón made no secret of his admiration for Mussolini. But just as the Party of the Institutional Revolution (PRI) in Mexico did for so long and so successfully, Peronism has evolved with the times. Carlos Menem was Peronist, like the Kirchners, although most would struggle to place them in the same political box. As for Evita, there is now ungrudging recognition that she played a role in winning the vote for Argentine women and that her charities—though inefficiently run—were sincerely motivated and surprisingly effective. I wondered if her rehabilitation may also be due to the fact that, since the eighties, we have become much more used to the idea of stars as politicians, and vice-versa, and to strong women playing unofficial but legitimate roles in political life.

We wandered around the Evita museum, located in one of the grand, neo-gothic, suburban houses that she had taken over as a hostel for abandoned women. I recalled that once when visiting a family living in the slum *villa miseria* near St. George's (the school had an enlightened program of assistance to the local orphanage), I had seen in the bedroom what looked like a shrine to the Virgin Mary. Except that the picture beneath which the candles burned was one of Evita. In those days, an indication of sympathy with Evita would be enough to have suited and sunglass-wearing men in a Ford Falcon take you away, perhaps never to be seen again.

⌇ Back at the marina in Mar del Plata there were finally some southbound yachts. Antoine Duguet, a dashing yet modest young Frenchman from Brittany, was single-handing his *Moustique*, a 6.4-metre racing sloop of a class known as the Mini Transats. These light boats, with tall rigs, are seaworthy in their way but half of the boat is open cockpit, and in waters such as those we were now approaching it seemed to us it was vital to have somewhere to hide from the heavy weather. Antoine, seeing kindred spirits in fellow small-boat owners such as ourselves, showed us around enthusiastically.

"I've pumped foam into every corner. Even if I'm swamped, she'll still float. But you know what the most important advantage of *Moustique* is? She goes fast, really fast."

Hand-steering, Antoine could surf at twelve knots, three times faster than we normally sailed—which in turn meant he needed to be exposed to the possibility of heavy weather for less time. The snag here was that the boat would not easily self-steer.

"I often have to steer eighteen or twenty hours by hand. If she's steady I'll rush down below to heat up some soup. It's tough but you know what? I'm young."

Antoine had a cheery optimism that we were sure would get him through tough times. He had almost no money, but had spent a year in Buenos Aires building up his kitty by selling homemade jewellery. We huddled below decks with him one morning, poring over our respective sets of charts as Antoine plied us with maté. He had a number of charts of the Patagonian coast that had been helpfully marked up for him by local fishermen, and we had a larger range of the waters around Tierra del Fuego. We consolidated and took one enormous roll to be photocopied.

There was yet another single-hander: Julian, aboard his all-yellow Peterson 26 sloop, called *Harrier of Down*. Julian, jowly, lugubrious-looking, and by his own admission out of shape, was a former lecturer in architecture at the University of Strathclyde. He was recreating Darwin's voyage on the *Beagle* (hence the ship name's reference to Down House, Darwin's residence for the last forty years of his life).

"I'm over seventy now, you know," he drawled over a glass of wine in *Bosun Bird*'s cabin. "It was now or never. Bloody wife took all my money when I divorced here. That's why *Harrier*'s so small. You might have heard of my mother, Anne. Anne Mustoe. She's made some epic bicycle journeys, written about them in books. Bestsellers as a matter of fact. Brave lady, though I say so myself. I'm hoping to do the same."

Julian had his own website that (prematurely, we thought) described him as a "circumnavigator." There was something fishy about how he had come by his boat, but we would only learn the details of this much later.

Making up the flotilla were Cor and Petra from Holland, aboard their large heavy *Simon de Danser*, and Mark on *Zanzibar*. Cor and Petra were very cautious, even more so than we were. Every day (or twice a day) when they returned from the Internet café on the corner with their latest assessment of the weather outlook, they would dampen our own more optimistic analysis by pointing out some feature on the surface analysis that we had failed to spot.

The beach and casino, Mar del Plata, Argentina.

Mark—lean, tanned, German—was at the other extreme. He'd made one sally south already and—with a small paying crew of young backpackers—had nearly reached Puerto Madryn, three hundred miles on. There he had experienced major engine problems and, knowing there was no way he could tie up, let alone haul out there, he'd turned back. Now he hoisted his three-cylinder Volvo out of the boat completely for a thorough going-over. With more paying crew awaiting him in Puerto Natales, well into the Chilean channels, he was impatient to be off again and was determined to take a direct offshore course to the Strait of Le Maire. We had already decided that the seas would be likely to be lower close inshore, even though this meant taking a longer dogleg.

While we all waited, there were jobs to keep us busy. We tested out the fourth reef in our mainsail; made several trips to Sr. Gallardo,

the ironmonger, to have our broken whisker pole fixed; had our
storm sails re-stitched by Oscar, the local sailmaker; and spent days
out in the industrial suburbs of Mar del Plata tracking down
O-rings and oil seals for the engine. As fluent Spanish speakers we
were much in demand when friends needed to make similar
missions. But in the cruising world everything seems to even out:
most of them were more practically minded than we were and
could offer useful advice to us.

Mar del Plata, our base, is the largest holiday resort in South
America: its sandy beaches are almost obscured by row upon row
of semi-permanent tents that families from BA typically rent for
the entire summer season. From late December through February,
theatre and revue troupes decamp with their shows from the capital to Mar Del, and the country's top soccer teams hold pre-season
training camps open to the public. Every day the newspapers carry
special supplements featuring starlets seen on the beaches, and
radio and TV presenters report in the daytime from the beaches, in
the evening from the city's huge and opulent casino.

But tucked away in a corner of the fishing port, we were out of
all this. The bark of sea lions encamped on the breakwater was a
call from the far south, references in the papers to the passing of
the summer season were tentative niggling reminders that if we
did not leave soon then we would be sailing into autumn south of
50 degrees. At night when the breeze blew off the ocean it was cool
enough to make you shiver.

~ Wednesday, January 4, 2006. We'd been at Mar Del three weeks
and not once had our ideal weather window opened. We had yet
another look at the charts, made another trip to the Internet café.
The wind was northerly this morning, but on Friday it was due to
turn against us again. We decided we should have enough time to
reach Quequén (ke-KENN), about seventy miles along the coast. It
wasn't much but we knew that unless we set off soon the temp-

tations of marina living might become too much for us, not to speak of Cor and Petra's always reasonable but also dissuasive gloom.

We walked down to the *prefectura naval* (port captain's), did the necessary paperwork to clear out, paid our bills at the yacht club, and by noon we were motoring out into the South Atlantic once more.

It was a quiet overnight sail to the west-southwest, with the low coastline of the Province of Buenos Aires—here mainly small seaside resorts like Miramar, among the sand dunes and pine trees—to starboard. By dawn we could see the powerful Quequén lighthouse and were edging our way carefully into shallower water and the narrow harbour entrance. Like Mar del Plata's, this is between two artificial breakwaters, but here complicated by out-flowing current meeting the incoming ocean swell. We couldn't make out the green light that was supposed to mark the head of the westernmost breakwater and, as it got lighter, we realized why. The breakwater itself was being extended by four hundred metres and the light was obscured by trucks and mounds of rubble. It was just as well we had decided not to break our rule and enter by night.

Quequén is an industrial grain-loading port on one side of the river, with the better-known resort of Necochea on the other. First we motored over to the Club Naútico de Necochea, on the port bank. There were two or three scruffy-looking sailboats on moorings off the small club building, but through the binoculars the place looked abandoned. As we got closer we could see that the sailboats were lopsided; enormous fur seals had somehow climbed aboard, and the same were also in occupation of the beach and sailing club. Although our chart ended here, we carried on carefully upriver, motoring at four knots against a three-knot current and with an eye on the depth sounder.

We passed a row of huge grain elevators adjoining a high-walled commercial wharf and up ahead, where the river turned to the right, made out some characteristically orange-painted fishing boats. At least we'd be able to tie alongside one of them while we figured out what to do next.

A friendly fisherman waved us in and took the lines we threw for him.

"I'm just heading out for the day," he said. "But you're welcome to tie up and wait for the tide."

"Is it best if we carry on upriver?"

"Yes," he said, waving upstream and past a ruined highway bridge both of whose ends looked to have collapsed into the river only yesterday. "There's enough depth to carry on upstream, at least to the other yacht club. There was a big tide yesterday and the river nearly dried out, but it's the first time it's happened in years..."

Later, the fisherman, Antonio, gave us his card: "40 years of experience," it read; "High Seas Fishing and Cocktail Parties." The fishing was lately a bit unreliable, he explained, so he'd diversified. But it was a lot of work cleaning the boat up every evening and trying to get rid of the fish heads, oil, and bad smells before the holiday-making set came aboard on summer evenings.

MAR DEL PLATA TO QUEQUÉN: 76 N.M.; 1 DAY.

≈ From the Vito Dumas Yacht Club, a small whitewashed concrete cube with a floating dinghy dock, a bespectacled young man in a rowing boat set off earnestly, as soon as he saw us coming. Every few seconds he would drop an oar to wave furiously at us, losing control of his boat. We slowed down, in case he wasn't just waving from friendliness: in flowing fresh water the depth sounder is not always reliable. Sure enough, as he drew us closer, he beckoned for us to head back a little way and tie up to a mooring in midstream, marked by a plastic juice bottle and with two old rusting hulks half-beached on the bank opposite.

Once we were settled, this same young man, Daniel, showed us around the club: a cold shower, a tractor-pulled contraption for pulling sailboats in and out, and a bar.

Anchored off the Vito Dumas Yacht Club, Quequén, Argentina.

"As far as I know," he said excitedly, "we've only ever had five or six foreign yachts. The last one was three years ago, and called *Chinese Moon*. Perhaps you know it?"

Amazingly, we did. *China Moon* (as she was really called) was a junk-rigged catamaran, which for a year had been tied up next to us in Port Owen, South Africa.

This wasn't the Iate Clube do Rio or even the Yacht Club Argentino of Mar del Plata, but Daniel, Boris, Gaby, and other members of the Vito Dumas put those posh Brazilian sailing clubs to shame with their hospitality. Almost every time we went ashore there would be someone on hand to run us into town with their car, even if they weren't going that way, to help us fill up on fuel, to show us the way to the Prefectura, to invite us for a maté in the spare club house.

One member, Jerry, had just finished home-building a squat, square, steel, sailing dinghy, and we spent an afternoon helping him launch it with the help of two bicycle wheels and his under-powered black and yellow taxi. It floated lopsided, which had him mystified, but this didn't deter him from immediately setting off, with the help of a smoking Seagull outboard engine, on a maiden voyage downriver. We were dismayed when the engine coughed to a stop and Jerry, with his jagged metal edges, drifted fast downstream within a few inches of *Bosun Bird*, quite out of control, but he was taking it all calmly. Three hours later he was passing us again in the other direction, this time being towed by a black inflatable marked Prefectura Naval.

As predicted, the wind turned into the south and blew hard. For a day or so we felt smug: we had made a few miles, and we weren't getting pounded. Nick and Jan on *Yawarra* had just turned into the Beagle Channel, and we could hear their sense of triumph over the ssb radio.

"It's a glorious sunny morning," Jan said. "We can see snow-capped mountains, the sea is mirror calm, and Nick's grinning from ear to ear."

But they'd paid their dues. A severe gale crossing the Gulf of St. George had reduced them to running under bare poles at six knots. In the same blow, one of the other boats they were sailing with had broken its spinnaker pole, and on a third a crewmember had broken his arm. We started to feel a little less smug.

Back to the old routine of checking the weather, eyeing the calendar, and having almost daily crises of indecision. The Interquén Internet café had six or seven small cubicles, each adorned with old movie posters. The one we seemed always to be assigned was *The Day After*, showing New York being engulfed by massive waves under a glowering sky. Discouragingly, the log entry for Saturday, January 7, was to be repeated several times over, during the next week, with only minor variations:

At the Internet café, Quequén, Argentina.

We spent the rest of our time double-checking charts and tide tables for the next leg, visualizing what would happen in a rollover and securing lockers and loose items accordingly, and tinkering as usual with the engine.

Quequén wasn't scenic, but there was a cheap and cheerful beach with several churros stands: hot-dog lengths of deep-fried batter stuffed with delicious dulce de leche and sprinkled with sugar. The other local delicacy was shellfish. There were many varieties, but at the Rincón del Pescador the menu was strangely defensive, with legends under each dish such as: "Neither hard nor rubbery"; "Without a bitter taste"; "No sand, no bones."

Many of the quiet, dusty, and grain-strewn roads were clogged with large trucks from all corners of the pampas, waiting to offload their grain for export. Some had messages painted above their rear number plates. One I copied down was:

Si su hija sufre y llora, es por este chófer Señora
("If your daughter is suffering and weeping, it's 'cause of this driver, lady")

⌒ Thursday, January 12. We made three visits to the Interquén and decided that things looked as good as they were likely to get. We made plans to leave on the next morning's ebb tide. I'd been sleeping lightly for a long while now, but that night was particularly restless.

From here we would be turning unequivocally south, into the Roaring Forties. The next land we hoped to touch would be Fireland, Tierra del Fuego.

— 5

Bright and *Fierce* and *Fickle* is the *South*

A RADIO NET, run by a former cruising sailor called Wolfgang from his hobby farm in the Chilean Andes near Villarica, was our lifeline from Quequén onward. Every morning at 08:00 we would wait for Wolfgang's characteristic whistle, then, in German-accented English: "This is *Wilde Mathilde* for the Patagonian Cruisers' Net. Are there any emergencies? Come now."

Wilde Mathilde was the name of Wolfgang's old boat, although he had long ago given up the sea. In response to his roll call, we'd check in, hear what other boats were doing from here all the way south and into Chile, and—on this stretch—talk to Les.

Les, a British yachtsman on board *Islander*, was cruising in the
Falklands. He was far more adept than we were at reading the
varied weather information available to us, and frequently came up
on the SSB just to give a dedicated forecast for the stretch of water
we were approaching. Les was also patient when, on account of a
faulty microphone contact and/or a loose fibre optic cable behind
the set, Jenny kept going off the air for minutes at a time.

We got to know other yachts and their owners over the radio
without ever meeting them. Ron, an American on board *Restless*,
sounded—as Les put it one day when we knew Ron wasn't
listening—like a relaxed Barry White. In fact, I started to imagine
him as very large and black. Ron was never flustered and always
had a coffee in front of him. One morning the conversation went
as follows.

"*Restless, Restless, Wilde Mathilde*."

A longish pause.

"*Wilde Mathilde, Restless*. How're ya doin', Wolfgang?"

"Good, good. Ron, tell us your position and weather conditions."

"Well, Wolfgang, I gotta say we had an interesting day
yesterday...Just hold on while I fetch that coffee...The engine died on
me outside the bay here at the western tip of South Georgia. Lotsa
ice, lotsa wind, night comin' on, know what I mean? Not a copacetic
situation. Any way, I sailed 'er in, got the hook down, and now I'm
relaxin', enjoying the view; coupla penguins on the beach..."

"And the engine, Ron..."

"Oh yeah, well I reckon she's completely seized up. Sounds like a
broken piston rod. Could be kinda interestin' getting outa here..."

One morning Ron laconically recounted how he needed to delay
his departure from Port Stanley so as to tow out to sea an oarsman
hoping to row around Antarctica (the rower lasted twenty-four
hours before requesting that the Royal Navy bring him back in).
And from Ron, we learned that Antoine aboard his tiny *Moustique*,

had made it safely to the Beagle: they had shared an anchorage near the very tip of Tierra del Fuego.

Another boat that we would hear for months on an almost daily basis was *Dreamaway*, with Graham and Avril on board. The very British-sounding Avril, whom we would not meet face-to-face for nearly another year, did all the radio work, except on one morning when, after reporting that *Dreamaway* was entering the Golfo de Penas and encountering heavy seas, she interrupted Wolfgang's sympathetic reply to say she would have to pass the mike to Graham: "I need to go out and be sick."

⁓ On our third day and 150 miles out, Les warned that by afternoon we could expect thirty-five knots from the southwest (gale force). In the now familiar routine we hove to for a few hours, rising and falling in the building swells, the rigging shrieking. In a lull we sailed on, but by 22:00 the wind was up again, stronger if anything, and it blew hard all night. By evening on the fourth day we had moved only a further twelve miles in the right direction.

Day five and the wind was back in the north, blowing us onward. Albatrosses were now with us all the time, and at night we could hear the occasional moo of a Jackass Penguin. Jenny wrote in the log:

> Les says it will stay northerly at 25 to 30 knots all day today, but then southwest at 30 plus; we are wondering if there is any shelter we can make for.

There wasn't. Gradually we got used to the cycle of the wind blowing hard from the north as the pressure dropped steadily, a front coming through, then a rise in pressure as the wind moved into the southwest or south. The steeper the rise or fall, the stronger the winds. On Wednesday, January 18, we noted the barograph had dived eighteen millibars in twenty-four hours and Jenny recorded:

> More strong northerlies in the night, with lightning. Around
> midnight it peaked at Force 9 and we ran on under bare poles
> (in part because the stay-sail sheet had shaken out of its block).
> I started to develop blisters from hand-steering. The front came
> through in the morning but wasn't as strong as we had expected...

Running downwind with no sails up at all was not as stressful
as we had feared when planning for winds and seas like this. With
the sails firmly stowed, sheets in tight, *Bosun Bird* steered well, her
stern rising gently to every following crest, briefly accelerating
to perhaps five knots from four. Protected in the trough for a few
seconds, she would gather her breath, then the wind would be on
the stern once more and we would be off. But we were glad we had
plenty of sea room: it would have been impossible to sail against
this wind.

Unexpectedly, I felt buoyant. Running under bare poles is one of
those mythical tactics discussed in yacht clubrooms in awed tones,
much as weekend ramblers might talk of the Hillary Step on the
upper slopes of Everest. Here we were, heading for Cape Horn, deep
in the Roaring Forties, and it actually seemed quite manageable.

But January 20 was one of those days when lots of small things
seem to go wrong at the same time. The snap-shackle on the starboard running backstay broke, meaning we had immediately to
drop the stay-sail, hacksaw the old shackle off, and install a new one.
Then, in a period of motoring, the alternator belt unaccountably
developed slack, which in turn led to overheating of the alternator;
finally, there was an unfamiliar grinding noise from the engine.

Next morning, we began our crossing of the Gulf of St. George,
where *Yawarra* had hit her heaviest weather. Early on, the wind
was light and we were able to run, but I was determined to find out
the source of the grinding noise from the engine. Repeatedly we
unpacked and repacked the cockpit lockers, to see if something had
shifted and was just causing unusual vibration. At last, by touching

various parts of the boat with the engine on, I discovered the cause. Two bolts holding one of four reverse-L-shaped support mounts that connect the body of the engine to the hull had sheared off, so that in effect the engine was only supported on three corners. The fact that the engine was no longer properly secured to the boat probably accounted for the slack alternator belt, as well.

Jenny had steered throughout the several hours I had taken to determine this. Expectantly, sensing I had come to some conclusion, she looked in from the cockpit and asked, "Well?"

"The good news is that I've figured it out."

"And the bad?"

"The bolts have sheared flush with the engine casing. And there's only an inch, there, between the casing and the engine bed. To get at the bolts we'll need to shift the whole engine forward...and I'll need mains power to drill out the remains of the bolts."

Jenny, who by her own admission is no mechanical genius, looked at me briefly and then went back to steering, without saying a word.

The wind built. By 03:00 on January 22 we were again running under bare poles but were almost across the gulf. At dawn, far away on the starboard horizon, we saw a faint smudge of land: it was Cabo Blanco, north of Puerto Deseado. We hand-steered for most of the day, put in a good run of over one hundred miles, but at midnight the usual switch came: we were hove to once more.

We didn't say much to each other. I fretted. We were a sailing boat and for now we could well do without the engine. We had plenty of water on board, and we could easily spend another month at sea if that was what it took. But I knew the Beagle Channel would be either hard upwind sailing or calm, and that at our destination— Puerto Williams—there would be little assistance available.

Before it was too late, we decided to turn back the twenty miles or so to Puerto Deseado, the only more-or-less accessible port on this entire coast, and fix those engine bolts. I asked Jenny to get a new chart out.

"It looks a bit tricky," she said, smoothing the large and slightly blurred photocopy into manageable dimensions. "Quite narrow, a submerged reef on one side that uncovers at low tide..."

"Strength of current?"

"Wait a minute, let me get the Admiralty Pilot out...Yes, five to six knots at springs, three to four at neaps...slack lasts only five minutes. And it says severe squalls, which arrive without warning, are common."

Even a four-knot contrary current would be far too much for our sick engine to fight against. But we didn't want to rush in, out of control, when the current turned in our favour either. Ideally, we would head into the narrows at the very beginning of the flood (ingoing, or rising) tide, when we would have some assistance from the current, but not too much, and most of the hazards would be visible, above water.

This meant a very uncomfortable night at anchor in the more-or-less open ocean off the small town, waiting for the right time. We took turns to sit in the cockpit with a flickering hurricane lamp, gazing at the white lights on shore, the blackness to seaward. At 23:00, when we had dropped our anchor in eight metres south of an invisible rock called Roca Foca, Jenny wrote, "Wind force 3; anchorage OK." But three hours later the wind was up to twenty-five knots from the northeast—the direction of the open Atlantic.

In the dark a tug suddenly appeared behind us and, dazzling us with its searchlight, its captain shouted through a loud-hailer, in mixed English and Spanish, "*Hola! Bienvenidos! Hay algún problema?* I am tug. I can tow you if you please..."

We shouted back a thank you but declined. The tug would go too fast for us, the tow might break and then we would be in a far worse state than before, adrift in the fast-flowing, narrow river in the dark. Better, if it came to it, to cast off and head out to sea again. He turned away with a cheerful "*Hasta mañana!*"

By dawn the situation was serious, our bows plunging into every oncoming wave and the anchor straining. We would have to go in on the high-water slack and not wait for low water seven hours later. Jenny climbed forward, encumbered by her foul weather gear and with her heavy rubber gloves on, while I switched the engine on.

"Forwards!" she shouted over the wind and spray, reinforcing her cry with a hand signal.

"It's not coming..." she eventually yelled. "You've got to get the strain off the chain..."

We traded places. The anchor line was bar-taut. With Jenny holding the throttle fully open, and by waiting for each lurch to the trough of the wave and the marginal slackening of the line, I was able to haul it in, metre by metre.

"Free!" I shouted as I sensed the anchor was beginning to lift from the bottom. "Let's go!"

With the bows peeling away, there was no time to engage our forty metres of chain onto the windlass and crank it in: by sheer adrenaline, I hauled it all in by hand, returned panting to the cockpit, and sent Jenny below to guide us along the carefully plotted GPS path we had drawn for ourselves through the narrows. With a tiny shred of genoa flying and the frail vibrating engine just ticking over, we sped in, with jagged rocks to starboard and the low long sandbank that is Chaffers Island to port. Jenny sat below and called out to me how far we were deviating from path: "Port, port, starboard...dead on...port, port..."

I was in no mood to appreciate them, but we were welcomed in by a gambolling school of the rare and beautiful Commerson's dolphins and flotillas of penguins. Somewhere we passed over the location of Roca Beagle and hoped that the inexplicable legend on the chart—a handwritten "Blown Away"—referred to the rock, not just to its marker beacon.

We have rarely been as relieved as we were finally to pick up one of the two pink buoys off the local sailing club. To add to our euphoria, there on the other buoy was Mark and his little white and black *Zanzibar*, and a friendly wave to greet us.

QUEQUÉN TO PUERTO DESEADO: 719 N.M.; 10 DAYS.

〜 The location now known as Puerto Deseado was possibly visited by Magellan in 1520, probably by Drake (who named it Seal Bay) in 1578, and certainly by the Welsh corsair Thomas Cavendish.

He anchored here on December 16, 1586, with his flagship *Desire* and coined the place's definitive name: Port Desire. Puerto Deseado, which literally means "Desired" or "Longed after Harbour," is an inexact translation into Spanish. One of Cavendish's crew named the exotic and funny-looking swimming birds that lined the shore *pen gwyn*, which is Welsh for "white head."

Six years later, in 1592, the *Desire* was back again, this time under the command of John Davis, already the hero of three expeditions to the Northwest Passage, where Davis Strait bears his name. He stayed here from May to August, having lost contact with Cavendish in his *Leicester Galleon*. On August 6 he filled his hold with the corpses of 14,000 penguins and set off south to try and find Cavendish again, believing him to be in the Strait of Magellan. Three days later the *Desire* and its smaller companion, the *Black Pinnace*, were hit by a severe gale and blown westward; they sighted a group of islands "lying fifty leagues or better from the shore east and northerly from the Strait." This was the first sighting by a European of what are now known as the Falkland Islands. The ship is commemorated once more in the motto of the Falklands: "Desire the Right."

Davis never found Cavendish, but his terrible six-month voyage back to Bearhaven, Ireland, which saw all but fourteen of his crew succumb to scurvy and the maggot-infested penguins, is thought to be the inspiration for Coleridge's *Rime of the Ancient Mariner*.

Four times fifty living men,
(And I heard nor sigh nor groan)
With heavy thump, a lifeless lump,
They dropped down one by one.

One of the survivors of the *Desire*'s expedition wrote: "There was nothing we did not devour, only iron excepted."

Over the next three hundred years Port Desire became a regular calling place for sailing vessels bound for the Strait of Magellan or making a final stop on the continent before heading downwind to the Falklands.

In December 1615 Captains Jacob Le Maire and Willem Schouten, seeking on behalf of the East India Company a new passage to the Pacific south of Magellan, arrived in the *Eendracht* (*Unity*), and the *Hoorn*, named after Schouten's home town. After the long passage from Europe, the tidal river mouth of Port Desire seemed like a good place to careen the *Hoorn* and burn the weed off its bottom. In what in other circumstances might have passed for comedy, the *Hoorn* caught fire and was destroyed completely. The now-crowded *Eendracht* and her crew sailed on in January 1616 and discovered the strait that now bears Le Maire's name; then to the southwest they rounded a rocky headland that they named after the defunct *Hoorn*. This was corrupted into English as Cape Horn, and even more misleadingly into Spanish as Cabo de Hornos; this literally and unromantically translates back into English as Cape of Ovens.

In 1670 John Narborough, in command of the *Sweepstakes* and the *Bachelor*, actually claimed Port Desire for England. And ninety years later Captain John Byron, known in his day as "Foul Weather Jack" on account of his talent for attracting storms and later as the grandfather of the poet (George Gordon, Lord Byron) was another caller, with HMS *Dolphin*.

But the most famous visitor was the *Beagle*, which arrived in Puerto Deseado with Charles Darwin on board in December 1833.

They stayed nearly three weeks. Captain Fitzroy's journal includes an engraving, itself taken from a painting by Conrad Maartens, entitled HMS Beagle *at Port Desire, Christmas Day.*

Much of what Darwin got up to would not today be termed politically correct. One day, he writes in *Voyage of the Beagle:*

> ...a party of officers and myself went to ransack an old Indian grave, which I had found on the summit of a neighbouring hill. Two immense stones, each probably weighing at least a couple of tons, had been placed in front of a ledge of rock about six feet high...

The emptiness and desolation of the Patagonian plains impressed the young naturalist deeply, and he hints at the lively discussions he was by this time having with Fitzroy over the age of Earth, recalling a poem by Shelley:

> There was not a tree, and, excepting the guanaco, which stood on the hill-top a watchful sentinel over its herd, scarcely an animal or a bird. All was stillness and desolation. Yet in passing over these scenes, without one bright object near, an ill-defined but strong sense of pleasure is vividly excited. One asked how many ages the plain had thus lasted, and how many more it was doomed thus to continue.

> None can reply—all seems eternal now
> The wilderness has a mysterious tongue,
> Which teaches awful doubt

Roca Beagle, which we would later learn had been blown up by the Argentine navy (hence the handwritten "Blown Away" on our chart), was so named because the usually ultra-cautious and skilled Fitzroy twice grazed it with the *Beagle's* bottom.

~ Puerto Deseado today is a small town of low buildings on the north side of a mile-wide estuary of bright-blue, glacial run-off. It is surrounded on all sides by hundreds of kilometres of flat, dry, and windswept heathland: classic Patagonia. The only industry is the servicing of a large fleet of red-painted, ilex squid-fishing boats. Once every ten days a freighter calls in with supplies, running between Buenos Aires and Ushuaia, and leaves with frozen squid.

This hasn't always been just a fishing port. The countryside roundabout is gaucho country. One February afternoon during our stay the whole town ground to a halt for the annual parade. The cowboys from all the nearby estancias trotted through town in their baggy black leggings and frilled white shirts, behind a sacred Virgin who was carried solemnly in a glass case on the back of a gleaming red Model-T Ford. From an improvised grandstand an announcer gave comments on their deportment, their costume, their horses, and at the end of the day winners were announced and the red wine began to flow. At university, I'd studied one of the great classics of gaucho literature, *Don Segundo Sombra*, and as these stern dark men with their craggy and scarred faces, sixty-centimetre-long knives thrust into their belts behind them, strutted past unsmilingly, you could guess that not too much had changed in a century. But the disastrous worldwide slump in the price of wool meant that in another generation or so, their like would be gone.

We got to know Deseado well, and by the time we left people were greeting us on the main street and enquiring keenly in shops: "*Cómo va el problemita de las patas?*"

Patas, literally, are paws; I'd first used the term as an approximation, when trying to describe in Spanish our four engine mounts; it stuck.

Our land base for operations was the local Club Naútico. With its bar run by two voluptuous Brazilian sisters (out of place here), it doubled every afternoon as the broadcast centre for Deseado FM

and the local cable TV station. When there wasn't much happening on TV, which was most of the time, the camera was focussed on *Bosun Bird*, bobbing just offshore. On hot afternoons—there are a few in Patagonia in January and February—le tout Deseado would flock to the narrow pebbly beach, and a surprising number of people, given the frigid water, would go swimming.

Antoine, on *Moustique,* had evidently been a big hit with the younger of the two sisters in the bar, who repeatedly showed us the little sketch he had made of his boat on a napkin, which she had then carefully stuck into the yacht club's visitors' book. She would sigh and moon over it, "Oooh, he was so handsome you know...so young...so French. When do you think he will be back?"

We spent much of our time at the cluttered and dark workshop of Coco, the diesel mechanic invariably recommended to us as the best in town. Coco, aristocratic-looking in spite of his normal apparel of blue overalls, was nearly seventy and not in great health. He had three grown-up daughters who lived in BA, "...but they never visit this poor old man. Baah! Women! Who would have daughters?"

In his younger days Coco was one of the top mechanics on the Argentine motor racing circuit, specializing in tuning hot rods (same term in Spanish). He was very impressed when I dropped the name of Andrea Vianini, a crippled racing driver whose son I had happened to teach at St. George's twenty-five years earlier.

"*Pero es uno de los grandes!* One of the greatest of all time! I can't believe it! You have actually met him? Only Fangio was better, the immortal Juan Manuel...If it weren't for the crash..."

Coco rarely appeared at his workshop before noon, by which time there was a line-up to consult him, and much of the afternoon would be spent in companionable maté sessions with anyone who

< *(top) The gaucho parade, Puerto Deseado, Argentina. (bottom) Nick, Coco the mechanic, and Jenny, Puerto Deseado, Argentina.*

happened to show up, squatting around a gas stove in one corner, under a grimy picture of the 1978 River Plate soccer team.

"They were the best ever," Coco assured me emphatically. "Boca Juniors? *Una mierda*...they are shit. That Maradona, a big-balled idiot..."

Occasionally his attention would wander to a 2002 calendar featuring a skimpily clad Miss Dayco Fanbelts, and the talk of football would falter. Coco was easily distracted, but he knew his stuff. He pondered our problem long and hard, made several trips on board to inspect the engine in situ, and for his fine-tuning session, worked with us until 1:00 a.m. He would accept only token payment.

Many others were just as helpful. Miguel, captain of the tugboat *Yamaná* that had come to visit us in the middle of the night, looked like Groucho Marx but was a lot more practical. He was also secretary of the yacht club. He tenderly moved us back and forth while we were engineless, tied to the side of his boat. Santiago, the radio technician, spent two hours cleaning and repairing our ssb radio, and would accept no payment whatsoever. Pedro el Tornero (the "lathe man") realigned our engine and gave us much valuable miscellaneous diesel advice. All the while the dusky Brazilian sisters plied Jenny with *feijoada*, sighed, and asked when Antoine would be back.

Every day the sun shone brightly. And the wind blew hard. As long as the wind had some north in it, we were sheltered by the low cliffs of the north shore in whose lee we lay. But as it shifted to the west then southwest, so it would rise in intensity and the fetch would simultaneously increase. There were days when the wind was forty knots for hours on end. The spray broke over our bows and we strained at the heavy line that (we trusted) was firmly attached to a five-tonne mooring on the bottom; if the line, its attachments, or our cleat failed we would be on the rocks in a matter of seconds. Going ashore in these conditions was out of the question.

Mark, aboard *Zanzibar*, had beaten us here by a day or two. He had chosen the offshore route and had taken a thrashing. His canvas spray dodger was wrecked, stanchions were bent by the force of waves breaking over him, and his crew for the passage, a young and severe Israeli, had hightailed it out of Deseado within minutes of arriving. "He said he never wanted to see the sea again," said Mark philosophically. "I can't really blame him."

But Mark's adventures were not yet over. After a few days, he set off again, bound for Punta Arenas on the Strait of Magellan. We had a farewell coffee with him at our favourite *confitería*, the Santa Cruz, and thought we would not be seeing him again, at least for a while. Ten days later, we were amazed to see *Zanzibar* once again entering Deseado, this time under sail: Mark must have lost the use of his engine.

Back at the Santa Cruz and obviously relieved to be alive and to tell his story, he told us the grisly details, "I took the offshore route again. Two nights out it started to blow hard. At some point, I don't know when, I lost the dinghy, which I'd lashed on deck, it just blew away. The solar panels were smashed, the mainsail tore..."

Entering the strait shortly afterward, he was twenty miles in and dodging unlit and unmarked oil drilling platforms when he saw a wall of white water coming toward him: a squall of such intensity that he had no choice but to turn tail and run back to the Atlantic. At the height of the crisis (imagine, all this on your own and in the dark), his engine failed to start.

"Everything was going wrong, just everything. I was really tired by now, I wasn't thinking straight. I needed to rest. The chart showed a good lee east of Cape Virgins, at the eastern entrance of the strait, but we touched bottom on an unmarked shoal. I bent the anchor bringing it up, I'll show you later."

Fearing further unseen damage, Mark then headed up the coast to seek refuge in the Argentine river port of Río Gallegos. But again he grounded, this time severely, and spent hours high and dry.

Radio contact with the authorities in Gallegos resulted in an offer to tow him in, but at a price of 4,000 USD—money Mark did not have. So, it was back to Deseado to recuperate and repair damage.

"But I'm not going south again," Mark concluded. "Panama has got to be easier than this."

In the meantime Mark's boat was leaking and needed to be taken out of the water. Groucho and the crew of the *Yamaná* rallied round and, after making a few telephone calls (Puerto Deseado is that kind of small town), they had lined up a crane and a flatbed truck. We spent the day helping. It was chaotic in that only one other boat had ever been hauled out of the water at Deseado, and memories of how it should be done were hazy. Initial attempts to lift *Zanzibar* from the old wooden wharf by the club failed when it was realized that the crane's arm was not long enough and it would simply tip into the sea if a five-tonne load were put on it. But by evening, the task complete, we were all enjoying cold beers at the Club Naútico, and the next day Mark organized a traditional Argentine *asado* to thank everyone who had participated.

A bubbly and tightly permed Argentine lady of a certain age, who introduced herself as Peluche (Teddy Bear), kept appearing at the yacht club or accosting us in the street, "Have you seen our *amiguito*, our little friend Julian?" she would coyly ask with a little giggle. "I just can't wait for him to get here..."

The skipper of *Harrier*, during his time spent living and working in BA, had evidently been a big hit. Peluche had never met him but all her high society friends had told her all about him. When Julian's distinctive yellow yacht did eventually sail in and take up the buoy Mark had conveniently vacated, we hastened to tell him Teddy Bear was looking for him.

"Mmmm...is that so?" Julian answered, instantly looking haunted.

He eventually sailed away leaving Peluche presumably distraught and ourselves mystified.

≈ In between these episodes and daily visits to Coco's workshop, we did the sights of Puerto Deseado. Among these is a grandiose railway station that would not have been out of place in a large city. But the line from Deseado runs inland for about 230 kilometres, to an even smaller location called Las Heras, and then stops. This had been one of several infrastructure projects dreamed up at the very end of the nineteenth century when it was feared that the continued emptiness and underdevelopment of Patagonia might lead some European power (or, worse, arch-enemy Chile) to stake a territorial claim. The hope was that a network of new lines would encourage settlers and stimulate the wool business; this although the population of Puerto Deseado at that time, we are told, consisted of exactly five families.

The money ran out, a new administration came into office in BA, and when the Welsh colony in nearby Chubut voted to remain Argentine rather that offer themselves up to Chile, fears of foreign occupation no longer seemed so urgent. For seventy years two steam locomotives kept up a sporadic service up and down to Las Heras, but this was abandoned in 1978. The station and its small museum are now maintained by a dwindling band of elderly gentlemen who used to work on the line; one, wheelchair-bound, showed us around.

"Our ambition is that they reopen the line," he said. "We are all lovers of the railway. But now we are so few."

Another tiny museum contains artifacts retrieved from HMS *Swift*. The *Swift* was a Falklands-based warship that struck a rock and sank in Deseado in 1770. It was close to shore and only three of its hundred-member crew were lost. But the situation was dire. The nearest known help, overland, was Buenos Aires: 2000 kilometres across trackless and unexplored desert, peopled by the unfriendly Tehuelche people. A junior officer, Mr. White, asked for volunteers, and they calmly set off to row back to the Falklands in a small whaler that had survived the wreck. It was four hundred miles, in some of the windiest and roughest waters in the world. Amazingly, they made it to Port Egmont and a rescue expedition was mounted successfully. Mr. White, for his pains, was "permitted" to present himself for the next available promotion. Alas, we do not know if he was successful. The ratings who rowed him to the Falklands remain anonymous and unrecognized.

The *Swift* was forgotten until the 1970s, when an Australian descendant of one of the crew turned up in Deseado, asking if the site of the wreck was known. The answer was a mystified "no," but the interest of several local teenagers was piqued. By deduction and careful study of the charts, they located the wreck in about twenty metres of water in 1982. The items that have been retrieved thus far are in amazingly good condition and include fine Chinese ceramics, hourglasses, and one drinking glass in which was found, intact, a penguin egg.

One of the leaders of the ongoing operation to explore the *Swift* was a local polymath and environmentalist, Marcos Oliva Day. Marcos had founded the Club Náutico, too, and had led a kayak expedition of local youngsters from Deseado to Cape Horn itself. As well as telling us all about the wreck, one evening he took us over in his inflatable launch to visit the distinctive pile of rocks on the south shore that he thought was the Indian grave looted by Darwin. Unfortunately, when we mentioned next day to Groucho, the captain of the *Yamaná*, how much we had enjoyed our expedition, we realized we had stumbled into one of those minefields that bedevil yacht club politics everywhere. After years of running the club, Marcos had just been deposed in the latest committee elections and was now embroiled in a dispute with its new members over who owned the land on which the club stood.

Mark and *Zanzibar* would find themselves involved in this land dispute, too. Barely had his yacht come to its final rest on land, and the crane had trundled off, when Marcos dourly informed him, "Of course, you'll have to move it. This is my land."

Deseado was where we first crossed the track of *In Patagonia* author Bruce Chatwin. Since Chatwin's 1974–75 visit to the Southern Cone and the now-iconic book's appearance in the following year, two related industries have sprung up. First, more and more busloads of tourists appear every year in the most unlikely places, tracking Chatwin. For some reason (perhaps the quality of the translation?) a disproportionate number of these pilgrims are Italian. Second, it has for some time been fashionable to debunk the author, specifically to cast doubt on the factual accuracy of what he wrote. On board we carried what was only the latest in a series of such hatchet-jobs, *La Patagonia de Chatwin*, by Argentine writer Adrián Giménez-Hutton (who happened to be a friend of Marcos).

I wasn't actually that bothered about the literal truth of what Chatwin had said, but it was interesting over the next several months to eye the scene with *In Patagonia* in one hand. Of Deseado he uncontroversially wrote: "...[it] is distinguished for a Salesian College that incorporates every architectural style from the Monastery of St. Gall to a multi-storey car-park; a Gruta de Lourdes; and a railway station in the form and proportion of a big Scottish country house."

I couldn't argue with that, nor with his slightly melancholy contemplation of the local bird life: "Albatrosses and penguins are the last birds I'd want to murder."

⮀ Mid-February, and the days were getting noticeably shorter. We were obsessed by our own customary "awful doubt" over when to leave. The usual agonizing in the Internet café, discussions on the SSB with Wolfgang and our weather guru, Les, and more pondering of the charts: should we steer the rhumb line south for Le Maire, or hug the coast in case of strong westerlies? Finally, and once more feeling queasy with apprehension, we made the decision to leave on the evening tide of Friday, February 17, (oh dear, another

Friday), and to steer a compromise, crescent-shaped course: first SSW, then SSE.

Dull fear was by now becoming a habit, but I never really got used to it. Sometimes it felt like the early stages of seasickness. By this point in the voyage, it was not confidence in our own abilities that was keeping us going (I still lack that) but rather the knowledge that if we turned back now we would just never forgive ourselves, we would always wonder what might have been. What I dread most about old age is the possibility of feeling I should have done more in life, that I should have pushed myself harder. The older I've become, so I've become more—not less—restless; one day, doubtless, this will get us into trouble.

Getting out of Deseado was as fraught as arriving had been. We were on an exceptionally strong mooring, part of which consisted of ship-sized chain. The problem was that at high tide (precisely when we wanted to leave), the boat would lift a portion of this chain off the bottom, the additional weight in turn making it extremely difficult to lift off the line attached to the boat. Adding to our stress level as we struggled with this was the fact that our favourable current was ebbing away and we were having to rush to the VHF radio every two or three minutes to explain to the harbour authorities why we weren't quite ready to go after all.

In desperation, we cut our own line and shot out into the Atlantic dusk, assisted by an outgoing current now running at three or four knots. For an hour we sailed in company with a reefed-down French boat that had briefly been moored alongside us, *Atao*, but it was twice our size and soon overtook us. *Atao* was crewed by Olivier and Cécile de la Rochefoucauld; Olivier, with his name, scarcely needed to work but was in fact a boss in a major French merchant bank. They had five children under the age of six, whom they called *les petits mousses*—the ship's boys. Their main reason for stopping in Deseado had been to have several sackloads of nappies laundered.

And so we crept from the Roaring Forties into the Furious Fifties. Ironically (although we weren't really complaining), we now had more periods of sustained calm than anywhere on the voyage so far. Although we covered eighty miles in our first twenty-four hours, our average soon started slipping and soon we were doing well to be making twenty-five miles a day. For three successive nights we could see out to port the city-like loom of the ilex squid fleet.

It was tempting to resort to the engine to power through these calms, but yet another set of mechanical problems had by now developed. These seemed ultimately to stem from the same alteration made to the engine's cooling system by Richard that had caused our problems entering Rio. I spent most of my off-watches wrench in hand, clad only in my underwear so as to spare my shorts and T-shirt from oil stains, attempting varied remedies. I'd work for two or three hours, sweating profusely and cursing as the boat rolled heavily in oily swells, switch on to test, then curse all over again as the dreaded red light came on that indicated the alternator was not functioning. In the end I thought I had achieved a partial solution, but meanwhile—sigh—another problem emerged as the ambient sea temperature dropped: slow starting. This, I knew, would take longer to fix, but we needed to have it in hand before we began the long journey north again through the Chilean channels.

Thus we crept closer to our nemesis: Le Maire (which appropriately rhymes with nightmare).

I knew well the key entry from the Admiralty Pilot, which warned that when a strong wind blew against a spring tide, then ship-killing conditions, with standing waves of up to eight metres, could occur. There were anchorages to the west, on the very tip of Tierra del Fuego, and to the east on the north shore of the mountainous Staten Island. But none of them were safe to enter in heavy weather, and they could be impossible to leave for days on end. Only in an emergency would we consider them. We needed a fair wind of moderate strength, and we had to arrive at the beginning of the ebb.

The gods of diesel may not have been favouring us lately, but someone else was surely looking after us on the night of Friday, February 24.

With incredulity, we found ourselves approaching our GPS waypoint, at the northern entrance of the strait, at the exact speed that would place us there at the optimum time: 03:49. Less positively, it was a moonless overcast night, with occasional squalls of cold, hail-like drizzle. As we coasted in we could see neither of the key lighthouses that mark the two sides of the strait, let alone land. Instead, phosphorescent wave-crests were breaking all around us, rustling sharply. Every few minutes, although the wind was quite steady and remained astern of us, there would be a flurry of louder breakers, with one wave train suddenly appearing from a new direction to meet the more regular train. These were "whirlpool" effects caused by the current rushing along with us. One or two breakers climbed into the cockpit and gave us cold baths, but there was nothing threatening.

As dawn came up, the wind eased, and, out of the all-encompassing murk, we made out the faint lights of a cruise ship

"Vessel northbound in Le Maire, this is yacht *Bosun Bird*. Vessel northbound in Le Maire, this is yacht *Bosun Bird*."

"*Bosun Bird, Bosun Bird*, this is *Carnival Two*," the surprised watch officer eventually responded in an English accent. "I see you on my radar. Bound for New Island, Falkland Islands. Be safe."

And then the mist started to lift on the starboard side. There, tantalizingly revealed for a few minutes at a time as the clouds swirled in then out, were the steep menacing mountains of the tip of Fireland, and there—we were now past the most threatening point—was Buen Suceso (Happy Event) Bay.

It was a happy moment for *Bosun Bird* and her crew and a reminder of the day we had sailed through here twenty-five years earlier on the Argentine navy's *Bahía Buen Suceso*.

But there was more stress to come. Now the wind almost died and—yes—switched by 180 degrees. The current that had been favouring us started to wane and, we knew, would soon also reverse. All day we tacked anxiously back and forth across the southern entrance of the strait, aware that we could easily get washed back in and blown north again; my queasiness was back. For hours our GPS showed we were making no progress, or maybe half a knot, and we became familiar with a distinctive set of rocks called Sail Rocks.

I grimly recalled for a moment how the *Allen Gardiner*, which had brought Mary Bridges to Harberton in 1871, had been twice blown back through the strait in just such a situation and eventually had to come around into the Beagle Channel via the eastern tip of Staten Island. Lucas Bridges, recalling years later his mother's experience, writes:

> It is difficult to describe the mountainous waves made steeper by the world-famous tide-rip in those Straits, or the nights hove to and battened down, when water pounds on the deck or swills about in the bilge, and the creaking of timbers and spars is accompanied by the roar of the gale in the rigging. And the occasional machine-gun rattle of the storm-sails when, instead of filling, they shake in the wind...

By comparison we'd had a free ride. But for a short while, with the tide turning, Jenny became so despondent that she wondered aloud if we should make for Port Stanley (Falkland Islands) or even run back all the way to South Africa: 5,000 miles through the Fifties and Forties.

Gradually, we began to make headway and inch our way west, the steep and uninhabited shores of Tierra del Fuego's Mitre Peninsula now to the north of us. By midnight, it looked as though we had a chance of making safe haven in Bahía Aguirre, a large indentation in the coastline giving some shelter from the south-westerly gales that blow straight up from the Horn, which was now only eighty miles to windward.

The moment the anchor went down, at 01:30 in Spaniard Harbour, a nook in the northwestern corner of the bay, marked the end of what had been—I now see—the most stressful twenty-four hours in my life. As I sat in the cockpit I realized for the first time that I was trembling. We celebrated, notwithstanding the hour and the miserable night (more rain, wind, no stars visible), with two glasses of wine each.

PUERTO DESEADO TO BAHÍA AGUIRRE (PUERTO ESPAÑOL): 509 N.M.; 8 DAYS.

~ Aguirre was beautiful, wild, and scary. There were many more miles to windward before we would reach the relatively protected waters of the Beagle Channel, and just around that rocky point off our beam there was nothing between us and Antarctica. It felt like we were hanging onto the bottom of the world.

And the place did not have a very happy history.

All of the first white settlers in this part of the world were missionaries, who saw the hardy and aggressive Aboriginal peoples of Tierra del Fuego and its channels as one of the last great challenges remaining for any evangelical worth his salt. One of these was Allen Gardiner who, after retiring from the Royal Navy, had made converts to his muscular Christianity in Zululand, New Guinea, and Bolivia before he tried his luck here. In September 1850 he had himself put ashore with six companions at Banner Cove, Picton Island, where they hoped to establish a mission among the relatives and descendants of the famous Fuegian — Jemmy Button—whom Captain Fitzroy had, years before, taken to England aboard the *Beagle*.

But barely had they landed and the ship that brought them had disappeared over the horizon, than a horrific oversight came to light: they had left all their ammunition, which they would need for hunting and/or for self-defence, aboard the *Ocean Queen*. Within days the party was under siege by the Indians, and they had to retreat to their small boats for safety. Eventually, they fled downwind to Spaniard Harbour, Bahía Aguirre, leaving on a large rock at Banner Cove the painted message "Go to Spaniard Harbour; March 1851" in hope of some rescue party miraculously appearing.

Winter set in. One of the boats was lost in a storm. In an exceptionally high tide, most of their supplies, which they were keeping in a cave, were ruined. All of the party started to show signs of scurvy; all they could find to eat were shellfish, seaweed, and the odd dead seabird. One by one, they died. On August 26 Gardiner's assistant wrote a last testament, but—either hallucinating or casting himself as a latter-day martyr—claimed that he would not change his situation with anyone on Earth. He concluded: "I am happy beyond words."

Gardiner himself wrote his last words on September 5, in a similar state of religious ecstasy. All the bodies were found a year later by a passing ship.

Gardiner's cave can still be seen. As well, there are two or three semi-derelict buildings remaining from an estancia that was last a going concern in the 1970s; a caretaker occasionally visits to repair the fences, and when I ventured ashore two horses rushed over excitedly to take a look at me. The Admiralty Pilot notes that the nearest permanent human settlement is Ushuaia, "five days' hard ride."

We spent nearly a week at Aguirre, waiting for some respite from the fierce westerlies outside. Every morning we would check in to the Patagonian Net for the best weather estimates. It was of some selfish consolation to know that others were daily facing much greater hardships than ourselves. Ron on *Restless* was still wrestling with that wrecked engine in his iced-in bay on South Georgia; he was relaxed enough to tell us that he'd be taking trips ashore to look at the elephant seals before deciding what to do next.

⁓ May 1, 1982. After weeks at sea the British task force that had been dispatched to re-take the Falklands was coming on station. At 04:00 the first offensive operation in the recovery of the islands took place: Operation Blackbuck, a raid by a single Ascension-based Vulcan bomber on the Port Stanley airstrip. Twenty one-thousand-pound bombs were released from a height of ten thousand feet. One hit the runway but that was not enough to deny its use to Argentine Hercules transports and their light Pucará ground-attack fighters.

In a wide arc off the coast of the continent, meanwhile, the Argentine fleet lay waiting in three naval task groups. The south-ernmost, GT3, consisted of the cruiser ARA *General Belgrano* and the destroyers *Piedrabuena* and *Bouchard*; they had sailed out of Ushuaia on April 26. Intelligence suggested to them that the British were committing their fleet to an imminent landing, probably in the vicinity of Port Stanley. The British would never be more vulnerable. But GT3 also had the job of keeping a wary eye open for the Chilean navy, lest the old enemy try to take advantage of the tense situation.

At 15:55 Argentine naval headquarters in Comodoro Rivadavia signalled to their flagship, the carrier *25 de Mayo*: "You have freedom of action. British fleet committed."

But by midnight HQ was wavering. There had been no British air activity since 19:00. A landing looked improbable. More worry-ingly, it wasn't known where the British carriers *Hermes* and *Invincible* were. Rear Admiral Allara on the *25 de* Mayo indicated that in any case he needed twenty-five knots of wind to launch his Super Etendard fighter-bombers; he only had five. A new signal went out from Comodoro: slow down.

At 01:00 the decision was taken to pull right back. GT3 was ordered from position "Luis" to position "Miguel," to the south of the Falklands and east of the Strait of Le Maire. There was fear that up to six British nuclear-powered submarines could be in the area, but at position Miguel the depth of water was less than 120 metres, which would make manoeuvring difficult for the British.

Some time in the long winter night, HMS *Conqueror*—the only submarine in fact present in the region—made contact with GT3. It was suggested, but never proven, that Chile provided the Royal Navy with the small force's position. In later testimony to the House of Commons, British Defence Minister John Nott said:

> This heavily armed surface attack group...was closing on elements of our task force...We knew that the cruiser...had substantial fire power, provided by 15.6 inch guns, with a range of thirteen miles, and Seacat anti-aircraft missiles. Together with its escorting destroyers, which we believe were equipped with Exocet anti-ship missiles, the threat to the task force was such that the commander could ignore it only at his peril.

Commander Wreford-Brown awaited orders from the British task force headquarters at Northwood. They came in the mid-afternoon of May 2: sink the *Belgrano*.

At 16:00 he fired his first torpedo, a Second World War–vintage Mark VIII, from a range of about three miles. It hit the *Belgrano* on the port bow. A second hit in the stern, near the ship's canteen. After ten minutes the ship was listing at 15 degrees to port, after another ten minutes at 21 degrees. Captain Héctor Elías Bonzo found himself totally without power, unable to start his pumps. He had the order "Abandon ship" passed from mouth to mouth.

In an hour, the *Belgrano*, a survivor of Pearl Harbor and the Battle of Leyte Gulf, was gone, at position 55 degrees 24 south, 61 degrees 32 west. This is about 140 miles ESE of Bahía Aguirre.

Three hundred sixty-eight crew of a complement of 1,138 died. The *Piedrabuena* and the *Bouchard* had the unenviable choice of hunting the *Conqueror* or lingering to pick up survivors. They went for the submarine, whose crew underwent a harrowing two hours

The ARA General Belgrano *goes down, May 2, 1982.*

being pinged by enemy sonar and depth-charged before they were able to slip away. The *Conqueror* returned to Faslane and flew a Jolly Roger as it docked; the Argentine fleet retreated to port and never sallied forth again.

Britain's *Sun* newspaper marked the event with the most notorious headline in tabloid history: "*Gotcha*." There was immediate controversy in that the *Belgrano* was at the time of the attack acknowledged by all parties to have been outside the British-declared "exclusion zone," but Bonzo himself later admitted the sinking was a legitimate act of war. Admiral Allara wrote, "We, as professionals, said it was just too bad that we lost the *Belgrano*."

More serious and lasting were allegations that a peace proposal, which supposedly had the support of General Galtieri, had been passed to London by Peruvian mediator President Belaúnde Terry just fourteen hours before British PM Thatcher gave the green light for the attack. The suspicion lingers that Thatcher's intent in sinking the Argentine heavy cruiser was to torpedo any chance of a negotiated end to the standoff.

As the late summer evenings drew in and the sea's surface turned from blue to grey, then to black, I'd find myself wondering what it was like, those last few minutes out there on the *Belgrano*.

≈ At last the break in the weather came. We made an overnight dash forty-five miles to Picton Island, at the very mouth of the Beagle Channel, and a Chilean possession (one of that group of three islands over whose sovereignty Chile and Argentina came to the brink of war in 1978). It was bitingly cold and, as the seaway narrowed, the navigation became delicate. Jenny spent the night below, making endless calculations on the GPS and constantly adjusting our old paper chart (with its pre-GPS latitude and longitude lines) to reality, while I hand-steered and strained to see the shoreline. Just after dawn we were off Gardiner Island, which half-obscures the entrance to Picton's Banner Cove; we followed a blue fishing boat in.

Allen Gardiner's distress message on the rock has long since faded, and there are no longer any aggressive Natives stoning passing boats. Quite the contrary: barely had we anchored and run our lines ashore than the crew of the fishing boat, the *Macarena*, came over. "You like *centolla*? How many?"

In front of us, they pulled the eight, thirty-centimetre legs off each of two enormous and discomfited king crabs, and were pleased to accept our last remaining bottle of Argentine plonk in return. They also told us we should check in by radio to the Chilean navy. We had been spotted by navy radar on nearby Snipe Island and the *Macarena* had been asked to alert us.

Snipe gave us permission to anchor at Picton but warned that having entered Chilean waters we must subsequently proceed not to Ushuaia, on the Argentine shore, but to Chile's Puerto Williams. We had anticipated just such a scenario when leaving Deseado and

Puerto Williams, Navarino Island, Chile.

had formally checked out of Argentina. We knew better than to ask by radio if we could go ashore. Legally speaking the navy official would be bound to say "no"—as we had not cleared in. But the *Macarena* crew agreed that no one would really mind, as long as we said nothing about it.

We thoroughly explored the heavily wooded Gardiner Island as we waited yet again for a break in the westerlies. Up the whitecap-dotted channel and in luminous visibility we could now make out the great, snow-capped mountains of Navarino Island and the range that backs Ushuaia. Some days there seemed to be clouds of mist skipping over the water. These were the infamous williwaws, or rachas, of the far south, hurricane-force gusts that last only a few seconds but that can knock a sailboat flat; we knew we would be living with them for the next nine months.

Reasoning that we were now nearing civilization again, we turned on our radio one night in the hope of picking up Puerto Williams or Ushuaia. To our astonishment, all we could get was live football commentary, in English, from Highbury (London). We waited until the end of the game (Arsenal vs. Real Madrid) and learned that we were listening to The Voice of the Falklands, from Port Stanley.

One more stop, at Puerto Eugenia—a remote estancia on the eastern end of Navarino—and we were entering the narrow confines of the channel proper. Here it was only a couple of miles wide, the mountains of Argentine Tierra del Fuego on the right, a succession of Chilean islands on the left. We were not completely alone. Relations between Argentina and Chile are now ostensibly correct, but Chile maintains a large and vigilant naval presence in the area, and we were politely ordered to report all our movements first to Snipe Island, then to Puerto Williams itself.

⌁ Finally, on Thursday, March 9, to Williams. The southern-most town in the world, the southernmost yacht club, in fact pretty much the southernmost everything. This to the chagrin of Argentines, who have now all but given up claiming such accolades for Ushuaia, which is indisputably several miles north. An efficient but warm welcome from the naval authorities, a little chit-chat with the three other boats in (a Kiwi, a Canadian, and a German)—and it began to sink in.

I recalled a poem I once had to memorize at school. We'd arrived in Tennyson's Bright, Fierce and Fickle South.

BAHÍA AGUIRRE (PUERTO ESPAÑOL) TO PUERTO WILLIAMS: 72 N.M; 5 DAYS.

6

Winter in *Fireland*

YOU MIGHT THINK that having an old warship as your yacht club is unique. In fact the only other sailing club we'd ever belonged to also had one.

The Blue Nile Sailing Club, established 1926, was housed in the now-beached gunboat HMS *Melik* on the banks of the Blue Nile in downtown Khartoum. I'd been posted for three years as the sole Canadian diplomat in Sudan and, with little else to do in the dusty and joyless city, we'd renovated a 1950s-vintage steel Khartoum One Design sailing dinghy, painting it in Canadian colours, and enthusiastically joined the local racing fleet. The *Melik* had been one of several gunboats brought up from Cairo by Lord Kitchener in 1898 to recapture the city from the heir of the Mahdi, the messianic dervish who had killed General Charles Gordon on the steps of his residency a decade earlier and humiliated the British Empire. Its powerful searchlights had terrified the dervishes, and its Maxim guns cut them down in their hundreds. Now it was beached and listing, its ship's bell serving to signal the start and finish of races.

The warship-grey *Micalvi*, to which we were now tied up and which constitutes the clubhouse of the Puerto Williams Sailing Club, lies similarly grounded, in a shallow and well-protected creek just to the west of the small town. It is connected to the shore by a wooden walkway, and yachts can tie up to its outer (port) side or, if they have a shallow enough draft, snuggle in between its starboard side and the shore.

Weighing in at 800 tonnes, the *Micalvi* was built on the Rhine in 1925. It had a brief inglorious career carrying garbage up and down the river before it was chartered by the Chilean navy to bring a cargo of ammunition down from Europe for the battleship *Latorre*. After it had unloaded, the Germans decided they didn't want it back, and for the next fifty years the *Micalvi* plied the Fuegian channels, transporting sealers, gold miners, and loggers, servicing lighthouses and remote Yahgan villages. She became a legend in her time but hit a rock in 1976 and was withdrawn from service.

Francisco Coloane, a Chilean who wrote short stories set in the far South based on his experiences as a young military trainee then sheep-shearer, miner, and jack-of-all-trades, recalls one of the *Micalvi*'s voyages in "The Submerged Iceberg":

The wharf at Punta Arenas, carpeted by snow, thrust into the sea and into the night like a white shadow. On one side the freighter *Micalvi* puffed away, waiting only for an expedition of gold-miners, bound for Lennox and Picton Islands, to come on board. Over the screeching of the winches as they slackened their loading slings

could be heard the voices of the men; many of them were drunk;
wiser than I, they fled from one life to the next with the help
of alcohol...

There were days tied up to the *Micalvi* when it was blowing fifty
knots in the Beagle Channel, just outside, but our wind generator
hardly stirred, so perfect was the shelter behind the old ship. With
our kerosene lamp reflecting softly off the interior woodwork, the
Force 10 heater hissing away gently, and the tape deck playing old
hits by Blondie or Abba, we were as snug as could be.

≈ We'd arrived in the peak season. It was several days before boat
movements allowed us to manoeuvre carefully into the choicest
spot: on the inside, with Chilean/American Charlie Porter's
Gondwana between us and the *Micalvi* and a small wooden motor
launch called *Pampas* on our outer side, almost touching the
shoreline.

Charlie was garrulous, opinionated, and a very experienced
skipper in these waters. He often took groups of scientists up into
the channels for weeks on end, occasionally venturing farther: to
Antarctica, South Georgia. His arch enemy was Ben, another long-
term resident American, who also owned a large sailing boat, the
gaff-rigged wooden ketch *Victory*, on which he would occasionally
take tourists sailing. Yachting etiquette demands that one always be
polite about one's friends' boats, however ugly, inelegant, or poorly
maintained they may be. But Charlie would have none of this.

"The *Victory*? Whatta piece of shit! Ben's a fool; he built her out
of green wood, and she's been leaking ever since. Anyone who goes
out in that old tub is risking their life. He shouldn't be allowed to
advertise."

Ben, who was paralyzed from the waist down as a result of a
diving accident at Easter Island, doubled up as an evangelist. One of
Charlie's favourite pastimes was to stuff bundles of Ben's religious

pamphlets into the external ventilation dorades of the *Victory*, where it was impossible to get them out.

Mr. *Pampas*, meanwhile, was a rather self-important retired naval officer, who ran a small lodging house-cum-restaurant in town. His ambition was to fix *Pampas* up and run a passenger-ferry service on the twenty-mile run to Ushuaia. There was a lot of money to be made as in summer the only way tourists could otherwise travel between the two towns was flying all the way up to Punta Arenas, 120 miles north, then back on another flight of one hundred miles to Ushuaia, this at great expense and inconvenience. But *Pampas*'s old Chevrolet engine had seen better days. Day after day, week after week, Mr. *Pampas*'s mechanic sidekick would clump across our foredeck in his heavy boots, usually tripping over some line or cable and cursing, and set to work on the engine. He would be smoking a cigarette, its burned ash section lengthening in direct proportion to the reek of raw gasoline. Mr. *Pampas* would all the while lean over the wooden balustrade on the walkway.

"Listen," he'd shout out, "clean out the carburetor, like I told you last week. It's always the carburetor..."

"Yes, boss," the sidekick would answer quietly, before taking another drag, scratching his head, and getting back to work on the cooling system.

One day the engine looked finally to be ready. Six young backpackers were hustled down aboard *Pampas*, their packs stowed below in the tiny cuddy-cabin and lifejackets issued. For two hours the mechanic struggled to get the engine to fire. Finally it coughed into life, in a cloud of blue smoke. *Pampas* lurched off, leaving its mooring lines trailing in the water. Forty minutes later, they were back. The engine had failed, just off the navy wharf. It was just as well a navy RIB had been on hand to tow them back in for out in the channel the wind was already up to twenty-five knots, the sea picking up. They never let poor Mr. *Pampas* out again. Charlie was predictably scornful.

⌇ The nights began to lengthen, and we slowly settled in for the winter.

One morning on the Patagonian Cruisers' Net there was some worrying news. Yves, an experienced French yachtsman sailing alone aboard *Agur,* had limped into Puerto Deseado, his mast down, his vessel battered. He had been knocked down and rolled over in a storm off the eastern entrance to the Strait of Magellan. He had lost all contact with the boat he was sailing with—our friend Antoine, aboard his tiny *Moustique*—and feared for the worst.

Later, Yves forwarded us his log. Here are some extracts, translated from the French.

I first met Antoine on January 26 at Puerto Williams, after I had just arrived from Polynesia via Cape Horn. I can still see him as he calls over from his boat, in that young and energetic tone of voice: "Hi there! Is it true you've just come singlehanded around the Horn? Bravo! I'd like to hear all about it when you have five minutes..."

Along with *Astarte,* the three of us decided to sail together to Ushuaia...we decided then to head up into the channels and split up once we reached the Strait of Magellan; I'd turn right to the Atlantic, they'd go left to the Pacific.

Over the next three weeks the three boats made their leisurely way west. Antoine found that there was either no wind at all, or it was blowing fiercely from the wrong direction. *Agur* towed him for much of the time. Antoine and Yves became firm friends. Yves continues:

FEBRUARY 17. Caleta Lagunas. I think Antoine has decided to drop the idea of the Pacific; we can't wait to get back to the Atlantic, the sunshine and Brazil!

MARCH 5. Bahía Santiago, Strait of Magellan. Our departure into
the Atlantic will be delayed a little. It's 09:00, we're still anchored in
Bahía Santiago in a thirty-five knot westerly, with the hellish chop
that goes with it. It's impossible to get the anchor up in these conditions. 11:00: panic! My anchor line parted, it was rubbing so hard
in the fairlead. In these infernal conditions (forty-five to fifty knots,
gusting nearly to sixty), it's impossible to make any headway with
the engine. I could see the beach getting closer, with *Moustique*
looking on helplessly. With my anchor and all the chain already on
the bottom, useless, I threw out my second anchor with a long rode;
it held when I was still two hundred metres from the shore. I put
out a third anchor.

In the afternoon the wind went down to twenty-five knots and
I was able to get the anchor up...We sailed out toward the First
Narrows, with a good thirty knots up our backsides and a contrary
current, which raised the chop to two metres. Finally the current
reversed and we were able to sail in calmer conditions to the large
bay at the eastern entrance of the strait.

Moustique calls me from two or three miles behind, on the VHF.
"The forecast's calling for thirty to forty knots from the northwest,
not so great for heading out into the Atlantic. I'm going to anchor
near Cabo Vírgenes to wait for better weather...see you in Puerto
Deseado!"

MONDAY, MARCH 6. At sea, South Atlantic. I passed Cabo Vírgenes
at 02:00 and set my course for Deseado, three hundred miles north.

TUESDAY, MARCH 7. Wind northwest thirty knots. The barometer
has been in free fall since yesterday and the wind has gone to the
NNW and is rising. I'm under storm jib alone and the barometer is
at 975 millibars, the lowest I have ever seen it. All I can do is turn,
run back and seek shelter behind Cabo Virgenes. But barely have

I gybed around than the wind shifts, too: it's just as easy to go on to Deseado after all. By dawn the wind has gone down to twenty-five or thirty knots and I put up the mainsail, with three reefs. The barometer is still very low, which tells me the wind will soon be back.

WEDNESDAY, MARCH 8. No wind at all this morning and I put the engine on...There's 150 miles to go; I hope I don't have to motor all the way. Barometer still low at 984 millibars, sky overcast, very light wind at five knots from the north. Odd. 17:30: the wind is back, from the SSW. Fantastic. A good thirty knots pushing me from behind to Puerto Deseado.

FRIDAY, MARCH 10. Puerto Deseado. I didn't update the log yesterday; I just couldn't. The night of March 8–9, which began calmly with a beautiful half-moon turned little by little into a terrible nightmare. Thirty knots, then forty...I took all my sails down, we were doing five or six knots. I went below, my eyes fixed on the compass course, with the wind blowing harder and harder, the seas building...fifty knots now, and no sign of it coming to an end. I put my harness on. Another look at the GPS. Oh no! We're nearly broadside on, the autopilot can't hold the course. I rush out; the anemometer was showing over sixty knots apparent wind and, in the complete blackness, it was impossible to see the waves. I put us back on course. But at that moment I heard the deafening roar of an enormous breaker. The next moment there was a terrible impact, and we capsized, or pitchpoled...I don't really know which. For a moment I was head down in the water. Once *Agur* righted herself I could see the mast had snapped.

Yves recovered, restored his boat to a more or less manageable condition and motored the remaining fifty miles to Puerto Deseado, where Mark, from *Zanzibar*, helped him tie up.

THURSDAY, MARCH 16. Just after I'd come back to *Agur* last night, the Prefectura people came over in their orange Zodiac, with a telephone number. It was the French navy. I called them this morning. It was just as I feared. They're looking for Antoine. I just hope my friend is alive somewhere.

THURSDAY, MARCH 23. There's now almost no hope of finding Antoine. *Moustique*'s been seen by a fishing boat, half underwater, the mast broken, nobody on board. An Argentine navy vessel has gone out to bring the wreck back. I can hardly believe it. Antoine, who was all life and happiness. How can this be?

The navy couldn't find *Moustique*. Weeks later, the wreckage of a small fibreglass yacht was sighted from the air, on a beach in the inaccessible Jason Islands, part of the Falkland group. Antoine was never heard of again.

Friends held an informal memorial ceremony on a beach near Ushuaia, for which we sent a short message to be read out. Antoine's parents, devastated, could not bear to have contact with any of us. On *Bosun Bird*, we didn't talk much about it. We knew the risks; the Roaring Forties had let us pass; they hadn't let Antoine. We found ourselves saying to other cruisers: "Well, at least he died doing what he wanted to do."

But as I tried to imagine what Antoine's last moments must have been like, likely swept overboard and watching *Moustique* recede irretrievably, I didn't really think that was much consolation.

≈ Puerto Williams is built along the shoreline of Navarino Island, overlooking the dark but often wind-flecked waters of the Beagle. Thickly wooded hills rise behind it to an altitude of five hundred metres; there the trees give out abruptly but the hills rise again into jagged bare mountains, here crowned by a set of saw-tooth peaks known as the Dientes del Navarino. About half the town's

2,500 people are navy personnel or their families. Their houses, and the official navy buildings, are nearly all smart, white, prefabricated, one-storey affairs. The civilians' homes are more typical of Patagonia: ramshackle wooden-frame houses clad in brightly painted zinc, with old cars, disused fridges, and piles of chopped wood cluttering their sparse, fenced-in gardens. Packs of semi-stray dogs roam everywhere; the village cats prefer to make the most of the few hours of sunshine that Williams receives in winter by basking in front windows.

The town centre is known optimistically as the Centro Comercial. Dominating a large muddy expanse is the bright-yellow-and-green, corrugated-iron-clad Dientes del Navarino restaurant, run by Doña Carmen and her son. Next door is the office of DAP, the airline that links Williams and Punta Arenas with its Twin Otter; there's a post office; a telephone office with four public calling booths, where you can also rent DVDs; and Don Mario's bakery, with fresh rolls every morning at 9:00. Finally, there are two shops selling clothes and plastic toys and Gaby's "Travel Agency," open only in summer, where you can pay to use one of her two computer terminals.

During the course of the winter, the old and abandoned Café Pinguino, on the north side of the square was revamped by a friendly Argentine lady who started what aimed to be Puerto Williams's version of Starbucks: Café Angelus, specializing in exotic coffees and homemade cakes. It was hard going. The workers from the crab-packing plant and the off-duty naval ratings preferred the stark, even bleak Dientes with its fluorescent lighting, its perpetually on TV, and its much cheaper prices. There were dark mutterings of, "How come they let those Argentines buy property here..."

Seventy-five-year-old Doña Carmen at the Dientes, shapeless in her baggy cardigans, her eyes seeming to bulge behind exceptionally thick spectacles, adopted us. One evening, after she'd brought us our steaks, she stayed on to talk, hands on hips.

"Yes, Sir...I started as a cook at the British Club in Valparaíso. Those were the days. One year, in the fifties, I won a prize as the best employee. It was a luxury cruise to Europe. It was grandiose, I'll never forget it!"

Carmen had stayed at the Ritz in Paris, seen Buckingham Palace, travelled on the Tube, but remembered how rationing was still in force at that time. Later, she'd married a naval engineer, Ricardo (Valparaíso is the country's naval headquarters). He specialized in submarines, and when his new vessel was being commissioned in Britain, she travelled there again, this time for eighteen months, all spent in the dreary North Sea port of North Shields.

"North Shields was not romantic, you have to admit. A working town, like Talcahuano. Good people. We used to eat fish in a news-paper. And soft peas. My husband liked the beer. Not like Chilean beer, you know, but not bad all the same."

Carmen and Ricardo came to Puerto Williams when he was posted here early in the 1970s. She bucked local tradition, by which navy wives were not supposed to work, and opened a sandwich shop. Ricardo—she pensively pulled out his old naval identity card one evening and passed it over to us—died of meningitis in 1992. Carmen had never found any reason to go back to the "continent"; now she was one of the oldest residents of Williams. She was sad that the navy was gradually scaling back its presence.

"When the navy was in charge here there was order in the streets; there was never any rubbish; as soon as responsibility for the electricity, gas, and water went to civilians the prices went up.... The day the navy goes, I'll be off, as well."

One morning when we came in for a coffee, there was a sense of high drama in the air. Carmen's grandson was nailing a plank across the inside of one of the two street-front doors. She hurried over, took me by the sleeve and whispered conspiratorially, "You are not going to believe it, Sir; we've had a robbery! Yes, a break-in!"

Thieves, she said, had made off—in the middle of the night—with a whole ham, a small sack of onions, and two Sprites from the refrigerator.

"So what are the *carabineros* doing about it?" we asked, feigning seriousness.

"Bah! They're useless. We all know it was those workers at the new crab plant; there are two or three of them who have a record, you know. But they've got friends in high places. Nothing will happen. You mark my words!"

It wasn't wise to talk modern Chilean politics at the Dientes. The navy—indeed all the armed forces—had prospered under General Pinochet. Even today, this was by far the best-equipped and professional force in Latin America. This was thanks in part to a constitutional provision enacted by Pinochet that guaranteed for the military a percentage of the state's royalties on copper sales, which for the past several years been hugely profitable. Pro-military feelings ran high.

One night we found ourselves trapped in conversation by the very-drunk deputy mayor, as Carmen, apologetically and theatrically, shrugged from a distance. He had been a naval pilot. I mentioned that I knew the navy had De Havilland Twin Otters, said these were Canadian aircraft and that they had a fine reputation around the world for ruggedness. Our friend sputtered enthusiastic agreement, started to tell a long story about how once he had experienced engine failure in mid-flight but had been able to pull off the control panel...then he suddenly stopped and, trying to focus, said angrily, "But you must be a spy to know so much about our aircraft!"

There was respect but not too much enthusiasm for Chile's new president, Michelle Bachelet, even from battling women like Carmen. "We, the Chileans, need a strong man at the helm..." she would conclude firmly.

Not that it was a matter of anti-feminism. British Prime Minister Margaret Thatcher's name would periodically be invoked and toasted, the invariable conclusion being that "she had balls, yes, Sir."

The conversation would then turn to anti-Argentine gossip and jokes, and everyone would liven up. The Dientes's patrons revelled in telling Falklands stories (they insisted on saying Falklands, not Malvinas). Argentine warships, for weeks on end, had hurried up and down the Beagle. "Do you remember how we used to jam their radios with insults and jokes?" one would chortle to another.

In a more serious mood, a partially inebriated sailor confided to us one evening a long and disjointed story, the gist of which was that Chile had secretly assisted the crew members of a British helicopter that had crashed in Chilean Patagonia on a clandestine mission and smuggled them into Argentina to spy on Argentine airfields.

Suspicions lingered. Occasionally a black Argentine gunboat, with ominous missile tubes, would pay a "courtesy" visit to Williams; the crew would be served in the Dientes, but in sepulchral silence. Everyone had their story of the near-war with Argentina in 1978–79. Argentine troops had massed near Harberton, we heard, at the narrowest point of the Beagle Channel, and only five or six kilometres northeast of Williams. In response, extra troops had been flown into Williams and were installed in a well-hidden camp behind the town (whose concrete foundations can still be seen), but it was realized Williams would not hold out long. An escape route was traced out through the mountains behind the town, leading to Bahía Windhond on the south coast, where evacuation would take place. Heavy field guns were installed overlooking the channel. One can still be visited in the woods, its barrel aiming through the now-tall trees toward Ushuaia.

The other favourite topic was football. Chile only has three or four good teams and rarely qualifies for the World Cup, but it has produced some fine players over the years. Marcelo Salas, known as El Matador, had gone on from Chile to be a star for Coco's favourite team, River Plate, but in his dotage was now back again. Everyone supported one of two Santiago teams: Colo-Colo or Universidad Católica. They seemed to be drawn against each other in the league about once a month and most of the town would cram into the Dientes to drink Cristal beer in large quantities and watch the Superclásico; these were the only nights when it warmed up in the restaurant.

The World Cup, which in 2006 was played in Chile's deep midwinter, when the town's few orange street lights came on at 4:00 P.M., attracted surprisingly little interest, largely because our friends couldn't find anyone to support. It was explained to me thus: "Argentina? Out of the question; never. England? They never make it past the first round: not worth the trouble. Brazil? Well, you have to admit they're not bad; but, you know, they always win. Italy? Too much like Argentina..."

I watched the final almost alone in the Dientes, in cold-weather sailing gear as the gloom gathered in the square outside and Carmen's shy grandson slipped in apologetically once every twenty minutes to try to coax a reluctant wood stove into life.

As well as at the Dientes, we spent time up at Ben and Monica's house on the hill, which advertised itself as Williams's cybercafé. Ben, the American Charlie loved to hate, spent his time alternately recruiting—long-distance—clients to come and sail on the *Victory* and locals for his evangelical church. But he didn't push either too hard. In fact, after a couple of close calls in heavy weather, when he had found the *Victory* slow to respond and her engine danger-ously underpowered, he was looking to sell the old vessel and was having it fixed up with that end in mind. On the evangelical front there seemed only to be one other member of the church: a simple young man who was the deacon and whom Ben and Monica paid to do odd jobs. One day he would greet and hug us effusively, the next he would be in some dark temper and would be muttering aloud to himself as he angrily dug trenches and ignored us.

We would discuss sailing and the best times for heading north up the Chilean channels. One day the normally cheerful Monica pensively suggested to Jenny that the only sure way to guarantee good weather was to come to God and Trust in Him. Jenny was taken by surprise. "I'd rather trust in Windguru," she said, referring to our favourite online weather service.

Monica made no further attempt to convert either of us.

⁓ As autumn faded into winter, the trees dropping the last of their yellow and red leaves and the snowline creeping lower every day, the *Micalvi* slipped into hibernation, too. There was a bar in the pine-lined forward cabin, its walls almost covered with flags and other memorabilia of yachts that had passed this way over the past twenty or thirty years, but its already erratic opening hours (never before 22:00) became more unpredictable, and then it closed down completely.

In April the charter yachts made the last of their trips to Cape Horn and back. *Le Boulard* and *Santa María* tied up to the *Micalvi* with extra-heavy lines, and their skippers flew off to spend the southern winter in warm Europe. Sailing superstar Skip Novak's deluxe *Pelagic*, on which a berth will set you back 500 USD a day, called in with a crew of eight over-achieving and overpaid New Zealand lawyers. They complained bitterly that they wanted their money's worth when the skipper suggested that in the light of a forecast of sixty-knot winds it might be better to stay in port. He eventually delivered them in high dudgeon to the airport and set off across the South Atlantic for a refit in Cape Town. Keith on *Solquest*, from Auckland, tied up alongside the *Victory*, gave us his keys and bade us farewell, too: he was off to earn some money driving trucks in New Zealand before coming back in the spring.

Soon we were alone. Some nights we would be awakened by a creaking, grating noise. In other circumstances we would have guessed it was the anchor chain dragging on a rocky bottom. It was thin ice forming on the surface of the bay, cracking against our hull as we shifted and the tide rose and fell.

When a big freeze was forecast, the naval ratings on their rounds would turn off the water supply to the *Micalvi*. Usually they would forget to turn it on again in the morning, so if we wanted to take a shower in one of the two sloping-floored stalls that had been put in for the yachties, we trudged up the hill to the base HQ and had a call put out by the duty officer. After a shower one moonless and icy night, making my way in sheepskin slippers from the deck of the *Micalvi* down the iron ladder that led to the foredeck of *Gondwana* and hence to *Bosun Bird*, I slipped on an iced rung and fell in. I went completely underwater. The shock was so sharp that I was out again it what seemed like less than a second, calling on Jenny to rescue my floating-away slipper with the boat hook. At spring tides the port side of the *Micalvi* submerged and the duckboards on the shower floor would float.

We bought a small electric fan heater that we hot-wired to the mothership. This would keep us warm for spells but there was no escaping the damp: once every couple of weeks, we would spread all our books and other documents out on the bunks and blow-dry them with Jenny's electric hairdryer. The damper they got, the more the books expanded, and even blow-drying didn't fix that.

Every night we listened to Magallanes Radio, the Punta Arenas–based naval radio station. We learned by heart the names of the forecast zones and the order in which they were invariably read. Ours was Isla Picton to Puerto Navarino. Usually by listening to Timbales to Navarino, the next zone to the west, you could get an idea of what would be coming up tomorrow. The prediction for Bahía Nassau to Cabo de Hornos, the stretch of water just south of Isla Navarino, would tell us what conditions the same wind was creating in more open waters. After the forecast came the lighthouse reports: Faro Fairway (in the Strait of Magellan), Faro Evangelistas (off the western entrance to the strait), and Cabo

Raper (north of the Golfo de Penas). We learned the special terms for sea state, from *marejadilla* (light chop) at one extreme to the alarmingly frequent *arbolada* (breaking heavily) and *montañosa* (mountainous) at the other.

One Friday in April we had our first heavy snowfall. The creek was always quiet but now the silence was total, and not a single vehicle passed along the nearby dirt track all day. By dusk nearly ten centimetres of light powder had accumulated in the cockpit, on the dodger roof, even on the stern and bow railings. We brushed the solar panels clear, even though at this time of year we were receiving precious few hours of sunshine.

Once the snow stopped, we decided to set off for a long hike before the next storm, after which most of the interior of the island would become inaccessible for several months. Pedro el taxista picked us up at 10:00 on a bright morning and we loaded our packs into the car. His wife came along for the ride: with her raven-black hair and slightly Asiatic looks, she plausibly claimed Yahgan descent from "Abuela" Cristina Calderón, who is thought to be the last living pure-blooded Yahgan. An hour out, wheels skidding in the undisturbed snow, we stopped to put chains on.

The track west stops at Puerto Navarino, on the northwestern corner of this large rectangular island. Throughout these waters the term "puerto" is used to indicate a good natural anchorage rather than any permanent wharf, installation, or human habitation. But this is actually an *alcamar*, or mayoralty of the sea: one of several such small permanent outposts of the Chilean navy in the South, with a brief to report on anything and everything unusual in the waters and islands that fall within its area of responsibility. The large, two-storey house, painted in brilliant red and white, was inhabited by one keen young officer and his more listless wife.

> *(top)* Bosun Bird *tied up for the winter at Puerto Williams, Navarino Island, Chile. (bottom) The Murray Narrows (foreground), Hoste Island, and the Beagle Channel.*

"The posting," he told us, "is for two years. No, we don't get any breaks. Me and my wife, we're on duty and on call twenty-four hours a day, seven days a week. Problems? No, not really. Of course, there's nothing to spend our money on and I can never be far from the VHF but yes, it's a good life..."

Most days a Chilean navy cutter would be going up and down the Beagle, or perhaps diverting south into the Murray Narrows, at the mouth of which is Puerto Navarino; so there was usually someone to talk to.

The narrows separate Navarino from the next island to the west: Isla Hoste. Chile insisted these were "interior" territorial waters, strictly out of bounds to all foreign-flagged vessels at all times. This posture was clearly aimed, with some spite, at Argentine vessels, for which the narrows represented a useful shortcut from Ushuaia to Cape Horn and out into the Drake Passage. But the navy couldn't make it that explicit—so all of us suffered. The prohibition was galling to yachts and other small boats because the narrows guarded access to one of the region's historically most interesting locations, Wulaia, and was also the safest and most direct route to the Horn.

Jenny surreptitiously stroked a friendly but very ragged tabby cat—the officer's wife confided she was afraid of it—as I outlined our hiking plans, which were laboriously written down in the *alcamar*'s official logbook.

On our first day, it took us five hours to cover only seven kilometres, to Puerto Isorna, overlooking the narrows, with rugged Hoste only half a mile away across the deep, blue-black water. We would try to follow the shoreline, but constantly there were surging, sea-filled gullies blocking our way. We would have to laboriously bushwhack our way up steep hillsides and down again, fearful of straying too far from the sea lest in the thick stunted forest we lose our sense of direction. Tired, we lit a fire and lingered over it after supper, warming our hands and glancing up at the black, star-studded sky, but soon it was too cold and we went to bed. It was strange to be sleeping on land for the first time in nine months. I missed the ever-so-slight motion that *Bosun Bird* would make when one of us turned over energetically.

Next day we followed a faint trail to the south, then east, hoping to cut off a large finger of land. After an initial steep climb the surface became boggy. Gnawed-off tree stumps told us we were in beaver territory. These friendly animals were introduced to Tierra del Fuego in 1946 by the (now) very politically incorrect Argentine Society for the Introduction of Alien Species. They were initially confined to commercial fur farms, but these soon failed and the beavers were released. They have bred in alarming proportions, have swum from island to island, and are poised to colonize the mainland. While tourists find them cute, their effect on Navarino and other islands in the Fuegian archipelago has been devastating: once-dry moorland is now swamp as a result of the beavers' insatiable instinct to dam.

In Puerto Williams there is a bounty on their heads and beaver (*castor*) is served in the tourist season in the two or three hostelries that briefly open up at that time. As patriotic Canadians we thought it inappropriate to sample the national animal. Friends said the brown meat wasn't bad, but no amount of fine sauces and trimmings could hide the fact that basically the beaver is a large rat. They doubted it would catch on.

We also glimpsed cows, who were very startled to see us in the woods, and some alarmingly large pigs. They all run wild and are now third or fourth generation since the last farmers left Wulaia. The pigs love to rut in the rich, black, and shell-filled earth near the shore. Often this earth, especially when it seems to be formed in small rises and depressions, is a sign that this was an old Yahgan encampment. Archaeologists have explored some such middens and have found that they were in use from as long as eight thousand years ago to as recently as the 1930s. They have been able to

detect when there have occurred extended periods of Red Tide
(a naturally occurring marine phenomenon that renders bivalves
poisonous), because the shells of the bivalves that were the normal
staple of the Yahgans' diet are suddenly replaced by the debris of
limpets (less appetizing but safer).

We camped for our second night on such a green and bumpy
meadow in the northwest corner of a large and almost landlocked
inlet called Puerto Inútil. When I looked later at the chart I thought
the term "useless" might be on account of the bay's excessive
depth (thirty to sixty metres). But in these parts such designations
are often a warning that locations that look safe on paper may be
liable to ferocious williwaws: it's as well to take the nomenclature
seriously.

Again, the going had been slow and tiring: eight hours for only
ten kilometres. Once more, we went to bed early. I found myself
thinking of the hundreds of generations of Yahgans who had lived
and died in this cold inhospitable location and of the very last
survivor of them all—old Cristina, now living as a curiosity at the
rough end of Williams and charging tourists 50 USD to take her
picture. It also occurred to me that the only human beings between
us and Antarctica were the lighthouse keepers at Cape Horn, now
exactly 1 degree (sixty miles) south of us.

The next day's walk looked to be short and easy, but we spent
the morning climbing in and out of steep and dark ravines, barely
seeing the sun. Late in the afternoon, on a small rocky beach, we
stumbled on two fishermen placidly sitting on a large log. There
was no boat anywhere in sight and the nearest habitation was
where we had just come from: three days' walk away. They were
polite but not forthcoming.

"*Nos estamos descansando.* We are resting," was all they would
(redundantly) say.

Very late that night, as we were camped by the stream at Caleta
José, I heard a boat engine. Certainly, the men had been cattle

rustling—in fact they probably had a dead cow hidden in the trees just behind where we had met them—and now they were being picked up.

The fourth day out, the route turned south and the sun was out all day. Ahead of us now, beyond the snow-dusted, conical peak of Mount Scott King were the deep blue, foam-flecked waters of Bahía Nassau and the islands of the Wollaston Group: Grevy, Bayly, Wollaston, Hermite, Herschel, Deceit, and—smallest but most famous of them all—Horn. To our right, across the calmer surface of Ponsonby Sound, were the jagged peaks and deeply indented coastline of Hoste.

The best protection on Hoste is called Bahía Orange. Long since uninhabited and now devoid of any signs that it ever was lived in, Orange still serves as a reference point from which tidal ranges for much of southwestern Chile are measured, and it was briefly one of the most important scientific centres in the hemisphere.

In 1879 the International Meteorological Conference, meeting in Rome, had taken note of the fact that much of the polar exploration conducted in recent years had been executed in a haphazard sensationalist manner "that serves only to excite the curiosity of the public without any benefit to science." It was resolved to organize a set of serious, co-ordinated, and simultaneous expeditions to an agreed-upon set of polar destinations, whose thrust would be the development of physical and meteorological knowledge with a secondary emphasis on the natural sciences. A particular focus would be observation of the passage of Venus in front of the sun on December 6, 1882. Twelve locations were chosen in the northern hemisphere and two in the southern: Bahía Orange and South Georgia. The French government was assigned the former.

A 1700-tonne hybrid steam and sail vessel, the *Romanche*, was outfitted; it was commanded by Captain Louis-Ferdinand Martial. The expedition reached Fuegian waters in September 1882 and, basing itself in a set of prefabricated wooden huts on the foreshore

Yahgan children, photographed by the crew of the Romanche.

at Orange, remained the entire year. Forays were made all the way up and down the Beagle Channel and to Magellan. A major obsession of Martial, so his logs reveal, was the ships' perennially insufficient supply of Bordeaux wine; but vast amounts of meteorological and hydrographical data were collected. Dozens of new inlets and bays were explored, many of them now bearing the names of the vessel and her crew. Most important, a meticulous photographic record was made of the last of the Yahgans, whom Martial even then recognized could not be long for this world. Haunting sepia photographs show them posing near-naked on deck, or on the beaches of Ponsonby Sound. None of them smile in a recognizably Western manner. Even the little girls, with their thick, black, helmet-shaped hair, seem to have a habit of raising their heads a little and looking down their noses with hauteur at the photographer: the last defiant glance of a people about to disappear forever.

≈ Darwin's voyage on HMS *Beagle* was not that ship's first venture to these waters. The famous ship (which, contrary to popular supposition, was named after a kind of shark, not a small, fox-hunting dog) and HMS *Adventure*, commanded respectively by Captains Robert Pringle Stokes and Philip Parker King, had initially been dispatched by the British Admiralty in May 1826 to survey the coast of South America from Montevideo to Chiloé (chill-oh-WAY). The Lords of the Admiralty appeared to have had no inkling of how long this would take, nor how difficult it would be.

The challenges drove Pringle Stokes to a horrible botched suicide in his cabin in mid-winter in a lonely bay on the Strait of Magellan. After both ships had then sailed north to re-victual in Montevideo and Rio, they received the news that the twenty-three-year-old Robert Fitzroy would—as of December 1828—take up the vacancy left by Pringle Stokes's death.

In January 1829 the *Beagle*, the *Adventure*, and the much smaller *Adelaide* sailed south from the River Plate once more, with King in overall command. Fitzroy was assigned to explore the western half of the Strait of Magellan. He and his crew had many adventures but he revelled in the dramatic scenery and weather; the huge stretches of water now named Seno Skyring and Seno Otway commemorate his lieutenants and mark this period of the *Beagle*'s travels. For the next southern winter, they chose to recuperate near Chiloé, up on the west coast of Chile. During the rough passage north, heavy seas tore away the large whaler used by Fitzroy for day-to-day exploration, but the forests of Chiloé provided ample timber for a replacement.

In November 1829—the *Beagle*'s third season in the South, Fitzroy's second—exploration resumed. The work was often frustrating:

NOVEMBER 27. ...A promising morning tempted me to try to obtain observations and a round of angles near Cape Pillar. To land near it in much swell was not easy upon such steep and slippery rocks; at last we got inshore in a cove, and hauled the instruments up the rocks by lines, but could get no further, on account of the precipices; I, therefore, gave up that attempt and went outside the Cape, to look for a better place; but every part seemed similar, and, as the weather was getting foggy, it was useless to persevere.

NOVEMBER 28 & 29. Gloomy days, with much wind and rain, and the gusts coming so violently over the mountains, that we were unable to do any work, out of the ship.

By late January 1830 the *Beagle* was at anchor in a cove on London Island, near Cape Desolation. The new whaleboat, commanded by Mr. Murray, was dispatched for some inshore exploration. The weather grew bad again and a worried Fitzroy wrote in his log, "...the williwaws were so violent, that our small cutter, lying astern of the ship, was fairly capsized...the ship herself careened, as if under a press of sail, sending all loose things to leeward with a general crash."

But worse had happened to Murray. As he sheltered from the storm, his whaler had been stolen by Yahgans. Using branches, vegetation, and scraps of canvas, Murray and his crew constructed a rudimentary coracle. They had to wait five days before the weather moderated sufficiently; it was then an exhausting twenty-four-hour paddle into the light breeze before they made it safely back to the *Beagle*. Fitzroy brusquely welcomed the men back and set off in immediate and furious pursuit of the presumed miscreants.

The English kept finding signs of the whaler, and they kept taking hostages against its return. But just as soon as one or two sullen men had been brought aboard for rudimentary questioning, two or three more would slip over the side, swim ashore, and make off into the near-impenetrable undergrowth. After days and weeks of such farcical goings on, Fitzroy was left with no whaler and four bewildered young Yahgans on board. He couldn't decide what to do with the children: who their parents were and where they might now be, he had no idea. But this was only the beginning of one of the strangest of stories in the history of exploration.

The children eventually acquired the names Boat Memory, York Minster (after a prominent rocky headland of this name, near where he was seized), Fuegia Basket (after Murray's coracle), and Jemmy Button (on account of a pearl button given to a man who appeared to be his father). *Faute de mieux*, at the end of the voyage, Fitzroy took them back to England with him, where they were a sensation. Boat Memory died of smallpox, but the other three thrived, picked up some English, and met Queen Adelaide.

Fitzroy seems never to have intended to abduct the children. While the *Beagle* was refitting in Devonport for yet another season in the South, this time to be enriched with the nomination by the admiralty to her crew of the naturalist Charles Darwin, the young and ardently Christian captain took pains to stress to his superiors and to anyone who intended to listen that he was looking after the two boys and the girl at his own expense. He would return them to their homes at the earliest opportunity. By now Fitzroy had understood, too, that having these three young people on board could help him learn the language of the Indians among whom he had thus far spent three mainly uncomprehending winters.

So it was that Darwin was able to contemplate Fuegians long before he ever saw the shores of South America, on the long journey southward in 1832. Of Jemmy Button he writes, "He was merry and often laughed. And was remarkably sympathetic with anyone in pain: when the water was rough, I was often a little sea-sick and he used to come to me and say, in a plaintive voice, 'Poor, poor fellow!'"

Darwin was particularly interested to discover how the three youngsters, brought up in circumstances so different from those known by anyone else on board, might be abnormal:

Their sight was remarkably acute; it is well known that sailors, from long practice, can make out a distant object much better than a landsman; but both York and Jemmy were much superior to any sailor on board...They were quite conscious of this power; and Jemmy, when he had any little quarrel with the officer on watch, would say "Me see ship, me not tell."

Fitzroy's first priority on returning to southern waters was to resettle his charges. The *Beagle* was moored in Goree Roads, a stretch of relatively protected water between Navarino Island and Picton, and four ships' boats were outfitted. On January 23, 1833, Darwin goes on:

Jemmy was now in a district well known to him, and guided the boats to a quite pretty cove named Woollya, surrounded by islets, every one of which and every point had its proper native name...The cove was bordered by some acres of good sloping land, not covered (as elsewhere) by peat or by forest trees. Captain Fitzroy originally intended...to have taken York Minster and Fuegia to their own tribe on the west coast; but as they expressed a wish to remain here, and as the spot was singularly favourable, Captain Fitzroy determined to settle here the whole party, including Matthews, the missionary.

Wulaia (as it is now spelled) still has its open meadow and the cove is pretty indeed. The occasional vessel must still call in: there are dilapidated, white-painted, navigational markers on rocks in the bay. Restless colonies of black and white cormorants occupy some of the larger rocks. But dominating the scene on the brown-grassed meadow is a gaunt, pale-brown shell of a building, two stories high, roofed in rusting corrugated iron. The glass in many of its windows is broken. It looks like the house on the hill, behind the Bates Motel in *Psycho*.

The old radio station, Wulaia, Navarino Island, Chile.

This was built as a radio station in 1932, so as to be able to support the first regular flights that were then (in summer) beginning to fly between Punta Arenas and the Antarctic Peninsula. But there'd been a farm here since 1896. It was founded by two gold prospectors who'd been sent to Navarino by Lucas Bridges. They found no gold; in fact Bridges hints in his book that he knew they wouldn't—he just wanted to keep them away from his own lands. Like so many of the mining community, they were from Yugoslavia: Antonio Vrsalovic Ostoic and Luis Mladineo. Both the farm and the radio station have now been abandoned for nearly fifty years.

It started to rain as we trudged up to the house. Carefully avoiding rotting floorboards, we poked around for half an hour. It was obvious the place was still used. One of the rooms was completely blackened and must have been used to smoke ham. In another were deep piles of fresh oily sheep's wool and a few old cooking pots. Upstairs, on the northwestern corner of the house, there was a room with a table, a rickety bench, a few more dishes, and a stove with a pile of dry wood beside it.

As the rain pattered down on the tin roof and the clouds lowered, we settled in. The stove leaked badly and the room was always full of smoke, but for a few hours a day it was light enough to read. I finished *La Patagonia de Chatwin* then spent hours poring over the classified ads of the old newspapers we'd brought for fire-lighting. Chile's is a conservative society but some of the personals in *La Prensa Austral* made for racy reading. We slept on the bare floorboards in a completely empty neighbouring room.

When the rain slackened we would venture out: to forage for firewood, to fetch water, or to wander around the foundations of the old farm buildings and explore the mussel-strewn foreshore. I found a soaked old pair of leather gloves and we dried them out. There were spots where rhubarb had once been planted and we gathered some stalks to stew. But the wild pigs seemed to like rhubarb, too, and they'd already trampled over the choice plants.

A small stream emerges from the trees behind the farm and runs into the bay; there's a little wooden bridge with a rail, although you could almost jump the span. The stream is called the Río Matanza, Slaughter River.

When our food ran out, we climbed up the steep hills behind and emerged onto the moorland to find nearly a metre of snow had fallen while it was drizzling far below. It was heavy, wet going, all the way back. We came to the road at a place called Lum, where a solitary old lady, Abuelita María, welcomed us as if she'd been waiting for us all week.

María had several dogs and a black cat called Nino. She'd come here fifteen years earlier from Chiloé. She'd lived until about four years ago at Wulaia, in the room we'd camped out in; she hoped we'd been comfortable. María fed us bread rolls with homemade *calafate* and rhubarb jam, as our jackets steamed in front of her wood stove, and she said she was thinking of going back.

One day, she said, she'd found a dead body on the beach at Wulaia. "Its feet had already rotted away," she said pensively.

~ Hundreds of Yahgans had arrived at Wulaia in their canoes once news spread that the white men were back. Darwin was fascinated to observe that the Yahgans seemed indifferent to the return of Jemmy, Fuegia, and York Minster. He recounts Jemmy finding his mother again: "The meeting was less interesting than that between a horse, turned out in a field, when he joins an old companion. There was no demonstration of affection: they simply stared for a short time at each other and the mother immediately went to look after her canoe..."

The expedition's catechist, or lay preacher, Matthews, was left behind by the *Beagle*'s crew in the hope that, with the help of the three young Yahgans (who had ostensibly converted to Christianity in the meantime) a small mission colony could be established. But it all went wrong.

> From the time of our leaving, a regular system of plunder commenced; fresh parties of the natives kept arriving; York and Jemmy lost many things, and Matthews almost everything which had not been concealed underground...night and day he was surrounded by the natives, who tried to tire him out by making an incessant noise close to his head...I think we arrived just in time to save his life.

Matthews was taken back on board and the three anglicized Fuegians were left to their own devices at Wulaia. But it was not the last of Jemmy.

Nearly twenty years later, after the disaster that befell Allen Gardiner and his dramatic martyrdom at Spaniard Harbour on

Tierra del Fuego, the Reverend George Despard took up Gardiner's idea of establishing a missionary colony at Keppel Island in the Falklands. The idea was to bring Fuegians there, in small groups, to be converted and learn basic farming and housekeeping skills; then they'd be repatriated to their home islands again.

The Yahgan community at Wulaia was selected as the most propitious community to target, in the hope that Jemmy and his friends might still be there. The first attempt at contact took place in 1855, twenty-two years after the *Beagle*'s last visit, five after Gardiner's martyrdom. Jemmy was alive and well, if almost wild again, but not interested in coming aboard the mission society's vessel, the *Allen Gardiner*. A second expedition in 1856, which included Lucas Bridges's father, was more successful. A small group of Yahgans was persuaded to return to Keppel; they lived there for four years, and the young Thomas in turn began to pick up the rudiments of Yahgan.

It was now time for the next phase: the establishment of a mission at Wulaia itself. In late 1859 the *Allen Gardiner* set off from Keppel once more, under the command of Captain Fell; aboard were three domesticated Yahgan families, several other English crew, and Garland Philips, like Matthews a catechist.

Only one person survived to tell the tale of what happened next: Alfred Cole, the ship's cook.

Things had started to go badly as soon as the small Yahgan contingent got ready to disembark in Wulaia Cove. One of the crew complained that items belonging to him and others had gone missing. There was a fracas; one of the Yahgans, whom the crew knew as Squire Muggins (his real name was Schwaimugunjiz) nearly strangled the captain in his anger at the accusation, even though it turned out to be true.

But matters calmed down. After a week the crew of the *Gardiner* had built a small rudimentary church by the banks of the little Río Matanza (which already bore this name, on account of a long-ago feud between two rival bands of Yahgans), planted vegetables, and re-established what they thought were amicable relations. On Sunday, November 6, 1859, preparations began for the first-ever Christian church service in these lands. All the crew went ashore, leaving only Cole to mind the ship.

Cole watched the party enter the church, heard the first line of the hymn. There were three hundred Natives milling around the outside of the little shack.

As if on a signal, the massacre began. In a few minutes seven white men were bludgeoned to death in the church. Philips, the catechist, was struck down on the beach as he tried to flee back to the boat. Slaughter River briefly ran red again. Panic-stricken, Cole jumped into the ship's dinghy and rowed to an island in the bay (now marked as Cole Island), where he dashed ashore and fled into the woods.

For days he hid out, but he was eventually captured. Strangely he was not killed. He lived as a captive for three months until one day a rescue vessel, the *Nancy*, sent by the Reverend Despard steamed into the bay. Jemmy, anxious now to ingratiate himself once more, agreed to sail with ship to Port Stanley and participate in an inquiry into the massacre.

Jemmy told the judge that raiding Onas, from the Big Island, were to blame, but Cole's version was accepted. Jemmy was not punished. He returned to Wulaia and lived to a great age, becoming a curiosity for visiting ships. No further attempts to colonize Wulaia were made by the white men; instead Lucas Bridges chose Ushuaia, for what was to be a much happier missionary venture.

$\diagdown 7$

More Anxieties and Hardships

"THE GREAT THING ABOUT JULIO as a mechanic," the ever-helpful Charlie said, "is that when he's finished taking apart and putting together your engine, you're sure to end up with some extra parts."

Now Julio wasn't really that bad. He hadn't much education, but he was strong and willing. He had a complete set of false teeth, which he would take out before starting work on the engine; he was mortified one day when I asked to take his picture and he didn't have his teeth with him. And Julio was pretty much the only person in Puerto Williams who knew anything about diesel engines smaller than those used to power navy destroyers. He had

Julio.

a small Yanmar in pieces in his garden and swore that last year he'd rebuilt another yacht's engine, and that they'd made it to Puerto Montt "*sin ningún problema.*" Just to be sure, we had David from *Catch the Wind* and Keith from *Solquest* confirm his diagnosis. The lack of power we had been experiencing, and the excessive blue exhaust smoke, meant we possibly had a problem with one of the two fuel injectors, and certainly could do with a "valve job."

For weeks Julio came and went, and various heavy parts shuttled back and forth to Punta Arenas by (expensive) air freight on DAP's Twin Otter. We lived with the engine compartment open and miscellaneous fuel lines, washers, and other parts lying on oily newspaper on the chart table and galley washboard. I was worried that that someone from the navy would find out, because any time after the boat was disabled you were supposed to get a certificate from them saying you were seaworthy again—and they could be demanding. Julio really wanted to take the whole engine out, haul it off to his backyard to keep the Yanmar company in the rain, snow, and mud, and install a new set of pistons. But long and expensive telephone conversations with Norm and Al, two helpful Bukh gurus who lived in a shed somewhere near Southampton in England, suggested that if things were that bad we would be better off getting a new engine.

We knew that we had a couple of other problems, too. Diesels hate cold weather: the steel block gets cold, the oil becomes thick, the batteries used to start the engine lose a lot of their power, and with the first few turns of the engine all you are doing is introducing near-frozen seawater into its cooling channels.

David was a young English delivery skipper who was spending half of every year shifting eccentric and generally obnoxious millionaires' mega-yachts around the Mediterranean, the other half cruising in Chile and Argentina with his local girlfriend, Catalina. Like most seasoned delivery captains, David was used to dealing with dire practical problems with no immediate remedy at hand; he was just back from a jaunt around the Horn, during which the engine oil pump and *Catch the Wind*'s wheel steering had simultaneously failed, with the wind at forty knots and night coming on. Now he taught us one nerve-wracking but practical trick that dazzled even the imperturbable Julio: by waving a small gas-powered blowtorch over a diesel's air intake when starting, you could substantially increase the air temperature and hasten the firing process. The problem was that the intake was perilously close to the fuel lines.

To help things further, we doubled the diameter of the cables from the starter batteries to ensure that every amp of available power now reached the starter-generator, and we added an electrically powered glow-plug.

Beto and Yésica.

We took advantage of the engine being in many pieces to return to the perennial problem of our misaligned water pump whose shaft liked to exit the engine at awkward times. Here a young and serious naval rating called Mauricio came to our help, surreptitiously turning a new shaft on his lathe at work and making after-hours visits to *Bosun Bird*. We repaid Mauricio with weekly English lessons, in which we would reenact basic situations—at the airport, at the travel agents'—at Mauricio's home, a comfortable and well-heated, prefabricated, navy-supplied bungalow on the hill.

Mauricio was from Concepción, a medium-sized city south of Santiago. It is adjoined by Chile's main industrial and naval port, Talcahuano. When Mauricio, son of a working-class family, finished high school with so-so grades, joining the navy was an obvious choice.

"They have treated me well," he said. "Now I have a profession and here at Williams it's a good place to make money; there's nothing to spend it on. It's boring, sure, and it's too expensive for the family to come visiting, but they'll be sending us to Valparaíso next, and that's a lot closer to home..."

He lived with his young and pale wife, Yésica (*la Yésica* as he casually called her, as if she were an inanimate object), and three-year-old Beto. Once or twice, when we came to give lessons and Mauricio was late arriving, La Yésica confided that she was finding winter in Puerto Williams less than thrilling; she did not appreciate being left alone all day to deal with the chubby and very naughty Beto while Mauricio disappeared to the lathe shed down on the waterfront, or had nighttime guard duty. In fact, I had the feeling that Mauricio sometimes invited us around for a break from horrendous Beto and the often cheerless Yésica.

One evening we invited the family around for dinner on board. Beto greatly amused himself by pressing every button and pulling every switch in sight, nearly dropped a pair of binoculars overboard, and generally had a hilarious time. Mauricio, in spite of his humble background, was keen, always open to new ideas: as well as learning English he had made himself into one of Williams's computer experts. But La Yésica seemed listless, incurious, even though this was the first time she had ever been on a boat of any sort; she was a very fussy eater and left all her pasta.

In July the nights seemed really long and colder than ever. So as to dispel the torpor that descended on the little town at this time, the elders organized a grand two-week-long talent show called *Futuro 2006*. Jenny had gone to England for a respite from the winter, so I was alone. Every night, beginning about nine, I would listen to the local radio station—Jemmy Button FM 102.5, run from a half-container on a corner near the Simón & Simón store—to check that the proceedings had indeed started. I'd pull my rubber boots and warmest clothing on, climb up on to the deck of the *Micalvi*, and set off in the starlight and the snow on the fifteen-minute walk to the high-school gym.

Here, in a hot dark fug, the town would be assembled on folding chairs and the basketball bleachers. If you arrived on time you were treated to the full overture: the evocative music and a fuzzy DVD clip of *March of the Penguins* interspliced with highlights of last year's show and a few recordings of star performers from this year. Over the stage hung a banner informing us that *Futuro 2006* was sponsored by the Illustrious Municipality of Cape Horn and Antarctica. The girls from this year's graduating class sold hot dogs and popcorn, and all of the town children who were not performing chased each other up and down the aisles and along the rows of chairs.

Most of the acts were about as good as you'd expect—six-year-olds miming and dancing to techno pop, a few brave adults mouthing lachrymose tango hits—but there were one or two surprisingly good sets that, night after night, the audience would call to be repeated. One favourite was a cute if cheesy song of childhood romance with a rosy-cheeked Grade 1 boy presenting a rose to his sweetheart of the same age as she sat at her school desk. Each night, about half of the hits of the previous night would be repeated, which meant that the show went on well past midnight. One night there was a pair of special guests who had come in "all the way from Ushuaia, Argentina!"—"Give them a big, big hand!" There were judges, *American Idol* style, but they were mercifully kind and brief in their comments, so that no one was left crying.

For other entertainment, the Dutch members of a well-meaning but underemployed NGO called ENVIU, whose mandate was to develop eco-tourism ("sustainable entrepreneurship") in Williams, ran occasional DVD movie nights at the school library. One night was *The Chronicles of Narnia*: with the beavers running around in a wintry landscape, it looked like Navarino. But the library was unheated and most of the village children understandably failed to see the attraction of freezing while watching a DVD they could just as well see at home. The local telephone call centre, which doubled as a DVD store, in fact had an amazingly good—if esoteric—range of DVDs. We watched *Finding Neverland* on our laptop in *Bosun Bird*'s cabin, the German (subtitled in English) *Der Untergang* (*Downfall*) with Bruno Ganz as Hitler and, to inspire just before we set off into the lonely and unknown world of the channels, Tom Wolfe's *The Right Stuff*.

The library became a haven for us. There was a small selection of English paperbacks left by passing yachts, but my Spanish is good and I spent hours browsing the surprisingly well-stocked shelves for works by Chilean writers. I got to know the librarian, a small bespectacled man known as El Profesor. At first the Professor struck me as fussy, following me around everywhere, but I soon realized what I should have known from the start: there weren't too many avid readers in Williams, and he was starved for conversation and company. He found for me obscure works on the history of the area, pointed out a couple of regional novelists who can scarcely be known beyond Patagonia, and steered me toward the difficult but rewarding José Donoso, away from overrated Isabel Allende.

"Frivolous," he would sniff. "Even a little trashy. All that magic realism. García Márquez got away with it, but he was Gabo; she can't...They like her abroad partly because they think she's Salvador Allende's daughter, it gives her some kind of aura, but she's nothing of the kind, just a distant relative; and more and more right-wing with every book..."

⁓ Our engine woes and many phone conversations with automotive and other workshops took me up for a few days to Punta Arenas.

223

The flight is one of the most spectacular in the world. From Williams's tiny strip, which is squeezed onto a rare patch of flat land parallel to the Beagle Channel, you first fly due west, straight up the channel that recedes ahead to a completely flat horizon. To the left are the jagged Dientes del Navarino and the myriad channels that wind through the islands all the way to Cape Horn, to the right the more solid but less threatening hills of Tierra del Fuego. Shortly after you have passed Ushuaia to starboard, the plane heads north, inland, and snow-capped mountains close in on both sides. Away to port now is the shining Monte Darwin, the highest in Tierra del Fuego, but the peaks to the right, as the little plane labours to gain altitude, seem hardly any lower. Then you slip down to Admiralty Arm, the land begins suddenly to flatten out, and you're approaching the Strait of Magellan. If you take the flight when the cloud is down, it can be terrifying. Then the only glimpses of land are sudden patches of vertical black rock seemingly only a few metres from the wingtips, and landing at Williams the thick tires of the Otter send up a spray of fine snow. The pilot flies with an old topographical map on his lap, usually half-obscured by his salami sandwiches.

Punta Arenas, which you reach after an hour, is laid out in a typically geometric Spanish pattern on flat and windblown moorland where the strait runs north–south: the "harbour," which you can see from the air, is just a long jetty that sticks out at right angles into the strait. There is protection only from westerly winds; when the wind comes from any other direction, the navy forecasters advise all vessels to cast off and seek refuge elsewhere.

Years before Jenny and I had stayed at the Residencial Ritz, down near the harbour. It was a cold, 1920s-era building at the confusing corner of Pedro Montt and Jorge Montt streets, with small rooms with worn lino floors, thin flowered curtains, and a pile of three or four heavy blankets on the bed that kept you warm but oppressed. Chatwin stayed here while researching *In Patagonia*. He recalls

meeting a madman over breakfast. When I asked about this, the
hotel manager said, "Yes, yes, I remember him. *Un tipo muy serio*—a
very serious guy."

He had shown me Chatwin's name in the registration book;
someone had added, in different handwriting, the term "writer"
where they asked you for your profession.

I didn't stay this time: the Ritz had had a new paint job, its
falling-down sign had been straightened, and it was definitely
at the expensive end of the spectrum (along with the Savoy, just
around the corner). Instead I chose a friendlier-looking, white-
clapboard place called the Residencial Fitz Roy; it was still cold and
I had to leave my bedroom door wide open in the hope that some
warmth would percolate through from the small wood stove on the
upstairs landing.

Up on Calle España, near one of my favourite oil-seal dealers,
was the strange, red-roofed, granite house—with a turreted
tower—that had once been home to Charles Milward, British
consul and the inspiration for Chatwin. It was almost obscured by
a high, well-kept box hedge, but by peering in over the green steel
gate I could make out a "For Sale" sign in a ground-floor window.
The gate was locked and there wasn't anyone around. Just across
the road was the brightly painted Jako Night Club, with a life-sized
poster of a naked woman looking sultry.

There were other relics of the days of British influence. The
British School, also white clapboard, trimmed with blue, was
thriving. I'd briefly known its headmaster, John Harrison, when he
was in charge of games at St. George's in the late seventies. I gave
him a call one night, and he remembered me without the slightest
hesitation; we arranged that he would come by next evening to the
Fitz Roy, but he never showed up or called again. Perhaps it was
just as well, I thought later: by now I had decided that it had been a
mistake to look up Mike at St. George's.

The British Club now housed the upstairs offices of a bank, but it had an ornate plaster exterior painted in brilliant white. Chatwin recounts that pinned to a green baize board in its doorway there used to be the visiting card of Admiral Cradock, which he left here en route to his death at the Battle of Coronel in 1914.

Over long breakfasts in the better-heated kitchen of the Fitz Roy, Misael the proprietor joined me in conversation with the other guests, most of whom were long-term residents. The country's public school students were on strike, demanding free school bus passes, school meals, and other benefits: it was the first major political crisis of Michelle Bachelet's presidency. Most of the guests were outraged by it all, thundering that today's kids didn't know how good they had it. But a young graduate student called Fernando disagreed.

"If you're interested," he said to me one day as I got up to leave, "there's something I'd like to show you."

He led me on a brisk walk, a few blocks, to a dilapidated, pale-blue, two-storey building, with no glass in the windows, where you could make out that street-level graffiti had been overpainted red. We stood on the opposite side of the road. Down one side of the nailed-up doorway was the word "*Memoria*" in large white letters.

"It's called the Casa de la Risa," he said. "The House of Laughter."

"The House of Laughter? But why?"

"In the years of Pinochet, they rounded up dozens of union leaders and students, anyone with long hair, anyone 'leftist.' This is where they brought them. It was a torture house. Most were never seen again. The political ones were taken over there..."—he gestured— "to Dawson Island. It was a kind of gulag, a prison camp. One of the prisoners was Bachelet's father, a dissident air force officer, in fact he died there..."

My friend didn't say much more, nor did he explain why he had brought me here. I think that he just wanted me to understand,

The Casa de la Risa, Punta Arenas, Chile.

to forgive those rowdy young students of today and perhaps even support them: they were exercising freedoms others had died for, and quite recently. I remembered Padre Armando, who had also pointed out Dawson Island; the Casa de la Risa must have been in full swing in those days.

Another day, Misael took me for a drive in his red jeep, southward along the strait. We passed the skeleton of an old, steel-hulled windjammer, the *Lord Lonsdale*, its bowsprit almost overhanging the road and covered with scratched graffiti. We stopped at two more mournful historical sites: the site of Port Famine (Puerto Hambre), where Spain's first attempt at colonizing this region ended in disaster with the death of nearly all the colonists. Nearby is Fuerte Bulnes, where a young new government in Santiago set up, in 1843, the first official but short-lived Chilean presence on the strait: a military log fort. Also close by is a bizarre monument that informs you that you are now at the geographical centre of Chile. Only when you contemplate the map do you understand that they mean you to take Chilean Antarctica (which nominally reaches all the way to the Pole) into account.

The strait that day was calm but grey, the clouds uniform and low: I watched a lonely Chilean gunboat steaming past, with Dawson Island as its backdrop, the splash of white and red on its stern the only colour in the landscape.

Our destination was the wide shallow bay just past Fuerte Bulnes. On our British Admiralty maritime chart ("From a survey by Capt. R.C. Mayne, R.N., C.B; HMS *Nassau* 1868") it was called Puerto Hambre, but that's actually the little bay to the north: this bay is really San Juan de la Posesión. About halfway along the western shore on the chart is the small inscription: "Tombs."

The *Beagle* wintered over here more than once. Darwin records in June 1834: "We anchored in the fine bay...It was now the beginning of winter, and I never saw a more cheerless prospect; the dusky woods, piebald with snow, could be only seen indistinctly, through a drizzling hazy atmosphere..."

He may have been feeling the weight of history. For not only had those hundreds of early colonists perished here, but more recently, Stokes, first captain of the *Beagle*, had blown his brains out. Exactly what had gone through Pringle Stokes's tortured mind in the weeks preceding August 2, 1828, is a mystery, for in those days communication between a captain and his subordinates—however small the crew and however great the common hardship—was not encouraged. He used a small pistol but it misfired; the bullet lodged in his head. He survived for days until gangrene set in and he died raving. The *Beagle*'s log for August 12 is laconic: "Light breezes and cloudy. Departed this life Pringle Stokes Esq., Commander."

His monument is the most conspicuous of the "Tombs": a three-metre-high white cross of rotting cement with the following inscription in bas-relief:

> In memory of Commander Pringle Stokes R.N; HMS *Beagle*; Who died from the effects of the anxieties and hardships incurred while surveying the western shores of Tierra del Fuego.

I was told that until recently all Royal Navy ships passing through the strait made it a custom to pause at the cemetery, tidy it up, and repaint the graves. But it had been many years since the cross had received a coat of paint, and of the dozen or so other crosses lying broken in the wet undergrowth, I could make out only one more inscription: HMS *Satellite*, 1883; someone had left a plastic red rose on it.

⌁ Choosing a date to leave Puerto Williams was as agonizing as usual. The common wisdom was that there were more calms in winter, and even some favourable easterlies and southeasterlies as depressions passed north of Tierra del Fuego. But the storms, when they hit, were worse and the days were a lot shorter. Nighttime navigation in these waters, especially without radar, was far too dangerous to contemplate, and we did not want to find ourselves meandering around at sea at dusk with no safe anchorage within reach. Graham and Avril on *Dreamaway* swore that every year there was a window of good weather around the equinox—September 21. Although we couldn't find anything in the Pilot Charts to back up this theory, aiming to reach the Strait of Magellan around that date seemed like as good a plan as any.

With Mauricio's active help and La Yésica's reluctant co-operation, we made bulk purchases of food from the navy supermarket and arranged a special shipment of cases of tins from Punta Arenas to come by the weekly ferry. The other main purchase was diesel:

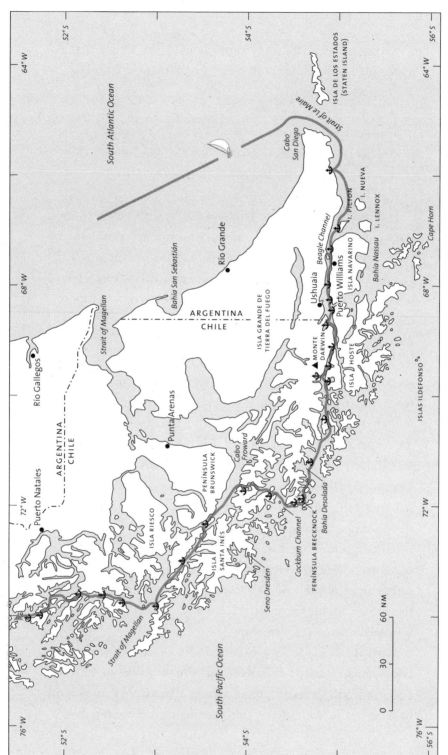

Tierra del Fuego and adjacent waters.

some boats, faced either with calms or adverse winds, had motored the entire 1,200 miles to Puerto Montt. We had every intention of sailing as much as possible, but in various nooks of the boat we stowed twenty-litre plastic jerry jugs that took our capacity from our normal 150 litres to four hundred. That should give us a range under power of somewhere between four hundred and six hundred miles, depending on the sea conditions.

Dawn on August 20. A silent and still wintry morning. It took us nearly two hours of untying and retying thick iced lines before we could extricate ourselves from the spider web that almost imprisoned us, and pull *Bosun Bird* around to the more exposed side of the *Micalvi*. With everything set, I turned the ignition switch.

There wasn't even a click. This was frustrating. We'd spent most of the past five months working toward this moment. We traced the problem to a faulty battery switch and, with the day half-gone, resigned ourselves to staying another night.

August 21 was similarly gloomy and overcast. But for a few moments, while the rising sun itself was still invisible behind the mountains of Tierra del Fuego to the northeast of us, its rays broke almost horizontally through the clouds and struck the Dientes. Everything was a brilliant red, fading then to pink—and then the sun was gone again, for the whole day.

The waterfront at Williams is protected by a sandspit that reaches out halfway into the Beagle Channel from the Navarino shore then curves away to the east, like a giant hook; it's called Banco Herradura (Horseshoe Bank). The outer part is underwater; at mid- or high tide it has a couple of metres over it, so we saved ourselves a mile by cutting the corner, heading northwest then west, in mid-channel.

The forecast was for northwesterly twenty knots, which could be uncomfortable, but we knew that often if the wind was only 5 or 10 degrees more northerly than westerly, then the channel would be mostly calm, with williwaws pouring down the occasional valley on the north shore. So it turned out to be. With the main and genoa hoisted, we were able to ghost along under sail all morning, learning to pay special attention when we reached one of those valley mouths and a blast of wind would hit us from the starboard. After months nestled up to the *Micalvi*, both of us were happy to be on the move again. A school of twenty or so fur seals gamboled around us for an hour, and a Chilean gunboat, the *Piloto Sibbald*, passed us from astern. He was punctiliously following the international border, which runs mid-channel, and he courteously called us on the VHF to enquire in excellent English as to our identity, course, and intended destination.

At 13:00, with nearly fifteen miles behind us and the wind starting to pick up, we nosed our way over to shore and into a well-protected bay called Caleta Mejillones (Mussel Bay). Although the anchorage was sheltered, if there was one thing every sailor who had navigated these waters had drummed into us, it was: "Always assume a gale will come up, and never try to guess what direction it will come from."

We followed a procedure that would gradually become routine but which, that first afternoon, took us nearly two hours before we were happy with things.

First, with the anchorage still a mile off, Jenny unlashed the Avon dinghy from where we kept it, half-inflated on the foredeck. She turned it the right way up and I passed her the foot-pump to finish inflating it. With a breeze now blowing, it took control to keep the dinghy from rearing up or even blowing away. She manoeuvred it over the port side rail and into the water, taking care to ensure the painter was already tied on.

By now we were a lot closer. Through the binoculars, I selected a tight corner of the bay that would give us good, all-round protection, but especially from westerly winds.

"Looks good to me, too," Jenny confirmed. "The trees are growing vertically, so the winds can't be too bad here."

With one eye on our Seafarer depth sounder, inside the cabin, and at dead-slow speed I made a couple of tight circles in the cove then, with the bows pointing out of the bay and the stern into the prevailing wind, gave Jenny the order.

"Ready?"

"Ready."

"OK, let her go. Depth six metres."

The chain rattled out, and Jenny snubbed it and gave me a thumbs-up. Gradually, I eased *Bosun Bird* into reverse. This is always a delicate moment, because the stern has a tendency to walk to one side when going backward. You need to be watching in all directions while carefully observing the surface of the water to see if you are pulling the anchor back or it is holding on the bottom. Meanwhile Jenny had her hand on the chain.

"Give her full throttle!" she called. "OK, she's holding..."

I eased the throttle back to hold us only in light reverse. Jenny came back to the cockpit, climbed quickly down into the dinghy, and I passed her the two wooden oars. Next, I handed her a nylon laundry bag containing one hundred metres of loosely stacked, ten-millimetre-diameter line, with one end tied to the interior of the bag, the free end clearly poking out from the neck; she stowed it in the bows of the dinghy. I picked up a second bag of line, fed Jenny the free end, which she tied around her waist, and kept the bag in *Bosun Bird*'s cockpit. As she hurriedly cast off, I gave her directions.

"Over there, try that small tree by the waterline...and for the port line take a look at that peculiar-shaped rock."

After a quick row with rope streaming out behind her, Jenny secured the first line then waited to see how the boat sat as I took up the slack. Taking her time now, she got back into the dinghy, checked out the rock on *Bosun Bird*'s other quarter, extricated the first bag of line, secured one end to the rock, and rowed the free end back. We now had the anchor chain down and two lines attaching

Stern-tied, off the Beagle Channel.

us to shore, both from the stern. But to be sure, and at our leisure, we added two more, from the bows.

All of this sounds straightforward, if tedious. But much can go wrong, especially if there is a hard wind blowing and the boat refuses to stay where you are trying to hold it. Lines get tangled or are found to be too short. Communication from boat to shore becomes difficult over the noise of the wind. Rowing the rubber dinghy to windward while trailing a line can become impossible. Sometimes there's nowhere obvious to land. Often there are no good trees or shrubs.

A further complication is that, especially in the Beagle, a fishing boat may turn up just before dark and after you are installed. This can be comforting: you know that if the fishing boats are using the place it must be OK. But fishermen have their own routines,

their own permanent lines attached to shore, and a good amount
of discussion and gesticulation is usually needed before everyone
is snug for the night. It's an unspoken rule that, as working boats,
they have priority over tourists like us.

Today there were still two hours left of daylight, so we went for
a walk on the shoreline. A kilometre to the west, on sloping ground
close to the water, was an old Yahgan cemetery; there were a
hundred or so small wooden crosses in rows and a few name boards
from the 1930s. At the end of the nineteenth century the Chilean
government had set aside land around here for the last Yahgans and
successfully persuaded them all to settle; when Puerto Williams
was established in the 1950s, they were moved on again. Ursula
Calderón, the sister of Cristina, is buried here. With the settlement
long gone and the afternoon closing in, it is a lonely place.

At night we'd already lost Jemmy Button FM. However, I found
on the AM dial a class in motor mechanics from Puerto Madryn,
far to the north in Argentine Patagonia, as well as Golden Oldies
from Calafate, also in Argentina, and a country and Western show
in English from Port Stanley. It blew hard and, in addition to my
regular 01:00 watch, I had to get up to replace some anti-chafe
padding on one of the stern lines that was moving under strain.

In the morning we carefully extricated the laptop from its
heavily padded and waterproofed locker, hooked up our new
Iridium satellite phone, and made a thirty-second call that gave us
in graphic form the weather forecast for the next three days: "what
the gribs say" would now become a regular topic of discussion
every morning on the Patagonian Net. Today they were indicating
ten to fifteen knots from the west, while Magallanes Radio (the
navy) was calling for eighteen knots falling to eight: as calm a day
as you get around here. Nick and Jan on *Yawarra* spoke to us from
Puerto Montt, where they'd arrived a week earlier, having opted for
a mid-winter ascent through the channels. There was no one else
on the net, except for the ever-cheerful Wolfgang.

Out in the channel and sailing close-hauled, we were soon off the red and white Les Eclaireurs light, marking the route into Ushuaia, the buildings of which we could now see at the foot of the spectacular jagged Monte Olivia. But we stayed left, passing a group of low tussocky islands named Despard, Bertha, Lucas, and Willie: the names of children of Thomas Bridges, who had many *Swallows and Amazons*-like adventures sailing their father's sloop in these waters. Turning hard left around Bartlett Point, we were soon in the calmer waters of Puerto Navarino. The depth sounder was not working that day, so it was with extra caution that we edged in backward, in our newly learned fashion, to a nook on the western shore of Isla Martínez. The head of the little bay was crossed by a heavy polypropylene line, a sign that fishing boats might be in later, so we tied off to that line, too, for good measure. We'd only done eleven miles but we knew from the tales of woe of many friends that every little bit counted and that later we'd be happy with days of only four or five miles.

We bushwhacked across Martínez to look into Puerto Navarino proper. It was blowing hard by now, thirty-five knots, and we had to lean forward to make any progress once we came out onto the open land on the west side of the island. Watery black clouds scudded past, the sea itself looked black, and there would be sudden twirls of white water and mist where a williwaw landed then seemed to fly off again like a miniature tornado. Occasionally a narrow sunbeam would break through: it was grandiose but threatening. A pair of Black Oystercatchers a few metres apart peep-peeped to each other as they explored the beach. Out in the bay I thought I saw the fin of a killer whale, but it could just have been a rock with the rising sea breaking on it.

When we got back, shivering, the *Ana Belén II*, a large blue and red wooden fishing boat, had tied up to the line close behind us. Their crew was all from Chiloé, whence almost all of Chile's fishermen hail.

"We've been out a month now from Punta Arenas," the skipper called out when we shouted our greetings. "Won't be heading back until Christmas. And you?"

"Bound for Chiloé...for Christmas."

"Ah, the Land of Men."

A mothership brought them new supplies every so often and took away their live *centollas* for canning at Puerto Williams. Out of the season they dived, using old-fashioned dry suits and great bronze helmets, for *erizos*, smallish, brown, spiny urchins whose flesh is eaten cold with lemon juice.

In what would soon become another habit, over a cup of tea, we had a close look at the charts and our reference books to map out our route and fallback anchorages for the next day. We'd already gone through all of our several hundred paper charts, measuring and marking up the obvious route north, and dividing it up, for the sake of manageability, into twelve sections of seventy to 130 miles. This was as much to check we actually had full chart coverage as anything. To accompany the charts we had our trusty blue Admiralty Pilot (now mildewed), but most helpful, as we had anticipated when browsing it on winter nights in Cape Town, was the Ardrizzis' encyclopaedic *Patagonia and Tierra Del Fuego Nautical Guide*—whenever in doubt we would find ourselves asking "what do the Italians say?" This volume we had by now annotated profusely with notes and comments from friends. Thus Caleta Víctor Jara, opposite Caleta Martínez, was marked in pencil: "Horrible; *Yawarra*."

In a glassy-still calm next morning, and with the sun reflecting brightly off the white mountains all around, we edged our way, under power, through a very narrow channel between Isla Martínez and the main island of Navarino—perhaps five metres wide—then past the alcamar. We had a chat on the radio with the young marine who remembered us from when we had come this way with our backpacks. Then in a perfect northerly breeze of five to ten knots, we floated gently across the mouth of the Murray Narrows, with every stitch of available sail up. Wulaia was away to our left, but we knew the channel was prohibited to us. All too soon, the wind switched to westerly, so we made it another short day, tucking into Caleta Eugenio, at the foot of high mountains on the northeastern tip of Hoste Island. Again there were fishermen's lines encumbering the bay, so we secured ourselves partly with our lines, partly with theirs. The log shows that we spent the rest of the day engaged in those typical minor boat jobs that you need to keep on top of: oiling a stiff sheet winch, cleaning the connections on the depth sounder. In the evening, as we'd half-expected, two fishing boats came in: the *Leonardo* and the *Enrique I*, both again from Punta Arenas, but with crew from Chiloé (in this case the old fishing port of Achao).

The Chilotes (chill-OTT-ays) are famous not just as fishermen, but as emigrants. For hundreds of years their island was the poorest part of Chile, yet it generated large families for whom potato farming and the local fisheries could not produce enough work. So throughout Chilean and Argentine Patagonia, there are Chilotes. Typically, they are short, dark, uncomplaining men who take on the hardest work. They are legendary for their stoicism, and if some find them a little slow-witted, others just say this is part of their mystical nature, for Chiloé is also the last stronghold in southern South America of witches. We never met a Chilote who was not honest, welcoming, evidently hardworking, and both curious and well-informed about the world.

Next day, a Thursday, the log reads:

It started blowing hard at about 04:30 and continued all day: 20 to 25 knots from the SW, often with sleet and snow, whitecaps visible in the Beagle Channel; it was not a day for moving on and the fishing boats didn't stir either.

We read, checked our charts, and in the evening cranked up our small heater: it blasts out warm air, which promptly rises and leaves you sweating, but with cold feet. And it's not safe to leave it on after you've gone to bed. Next day the forecast was worse—wind west to northwest twenty to thirty knots, gusting thirty-five to forty-five. In a lull we put out an extra line to shore and burned some of our paper rubbish on the beach.

On Saturday morning things were quieter, but it took nearly an hour to disengage ourselves. We motored out, but by 10:00 we were battling into a twenty-knot westerly, with a growing chop. We now had what would become a typical discussion.

"Shouldn't we think about going back?" Jenny would hazard.

"Not yet. We're still making headway."

"But it's going to get worse."

"Maybe, but getting back into that last anchorage in these conditions won't be easy anyway. We need to check off at least a couple of miles. Let's put a reef in."

We put the engine off and began tacking, reducing sail further every ten or twenty minutes as the wind ratcheted up a few notches. But still we found ourselves over-canvassed several times, with cold water streaming along the leeward deck and slopping back into the cockpit every time we lurched. A combination of the boat speed and the extreme angle of heel sent water shooting up the sink drain on the port side, making the sink overflow and cold seawater slop into the food lockers behind it. Jenny dealt with it stoically, but every time she passed up to me a bowl of mopped-up water to throw overboard I could hear the implicit "told you so."

The channel here is only a mile wide, and if we weren't snappy when going about at the end of each ten-minute board, half of the advantage won since the last tack was lost. By noon it was blowing a full gale, the black-blue waters ahead covered with foaming crests, my nose and exposed cheekbones numb with the cold. Holding the chart down with equally numbed fingers, I traced our planned route to a tiny nook on the south shore: Puerto Borracho, or Drunken Harbour. We had a reprise of our earlier conversation.

"We're really not getting anywhere now, we have to head in," said Jenny.

"Well maybe, but Borracho looks awfully tight. It could be tricky getting in, with this wind, and there's probably a fishing boat in as well, by now."

I moved my finger on the chart. "Let's try this large bay to star-board, Yendegaia, it won't be as sheltered but it'll be a lot easier to manoeuvre into."

We peeled off to a wide, six-mile-long arm on our right, whose entrance was just west of a white stone marker on shore that indicated the Chile–Argentina border. In the Yahgan language, Yendegaia means "Deep Bay," but I think in this case they meant "deeply indented."

Once we turned to take the wind on the beam and eased the sails, our white-knuckle angle of heel eased and the boat acceler-ated. Soon the chop eased as well. We anchored in an indentation, in between a low, cormorant-covered islet and the shore. As Jenny felt the tension on the chain, eventually giving me the thumbs-up, I saw on the beach a single, shaggy-coated guanaco—the wild cousin of the llama—eyeing us, motionless.

We spent much of the rest of the day drying out the food lockers; seawater had worked its way even into our plastic porridge containers, converting everything into a sticky mess. Jenny spooned out the worst of the soggy lumps and spread them out in the frying pan, in the hope they would dry out with a low heat. As we were barely on our way, we couldn't afford to throw anything out, but the mess looked unappetizing in the extreme as steam rose gently from it.

Next morning it was still blowing hard, but the sun was shining brightly. The solar panels and the wind generator combined were giving us lots of power, so as well as listening in to the net and downloading our grib files on the satellite phone, we hooked up the laptop to the ssb radio and downloaded the Chilean navy's twice-daily surface analysis. The process is a laborious one, taking twenty minutes or more. You often end up with the top half of the continent in the lower half of the page, and vice-versa, which demands careful attention when you try to read the pressure contours. But the satisfaction is in seeing a visual explanation for the verbal forecast. In this instance, we could make out an intense, high-pressure area moving in at the approximate latitude of Chiloé (42 degrees north), with a 980-millibar low rolling through the Drake Passage to the south of us. The result was a bunching up of the contour lines over Tierra del Fuego, spelling a strong westerly flow.

The wind stayed at thirty knots all day, but with a bright sun. Although we had a high rock wall to the west of us, the flow of air over the high ground of Tierra del Fuego was taking every possible avenue to the sea, so that it was westerly in the Beagle Channel, northwesterly in Yendegaia Bay. We strained at our chain, and in the afternoon we let out another thirty metres of line to decrease the angle of our line relative to the bottom and thus increase our holding power.

In a lull I judged I would be able to row to shore and, paddling frantically, just made it. I found several large patches of flattened grass and briefly surprised our local guanaco; he stared at me for a few seconds, whinnied nervously, and sprang off into the woods. Heading back to the boat it wasn't necessary to row: I just had to position myself upwind and drift fast down onto *Bosun Bird.*

Next day the forecast was bad again, so we decided to seek better shelter at the very head of the bay, which is identified as Caleta Ferrari. We anchored off an old ruined pier with some small, low, and apparently abandoned buildings lining the beach.

The *Romanche* anchored here in 1883. Captain Martial reports that:

> Close to the anchorage was a small settlement made up of half a
> dozen huts and a few vegetable patches where turnips and pota-
> toes grow; the Indians came on board to exchange vegetables for
> biscuits and old clothes. These creatures seemed tame and
> inoffensive...

The settlement was at the time in contact with Thomas Bridges's
Anglican mission at Ushuaia, a few miles to the east, and later with
Harberton. There was also a track from the head of the bay, up
along the side of a glacier, over a pass, and down the other side to
Admiralty Arm: a three- or four-day walk. Admiralty Arm gives
directly onto the Strait of Magellan, so this was the easiest route
across the big island of Tierra del Fuego.

We wandered around the settlement. It looked as though it was
periodically occupied. Doors were locked and the glass window
panes were intact. In the corner of one window was a red sticker
promoting Madrid's candidacy for the 2012 Olympic Games.
Behind the residential buildings were the ruins of a sawmill: it
looked to have blown down in a gale. A fat tabby cat, which Jenny
promptly christened Yendy, strolled out and rubbed against our
legs. In the meadow a pair of stallions grazed and neighed.

From behind the settlement a corduroy road—two-metre logs
laid crossways as paving—led northwest through meadows and
woodland. Handsome pairs of Kelp Geese browsed. On an old fence
post a rare Striated Caracara gazed at us fearlessly as we tiptoed
past him, and in the shallows at the head of the bay, where milky,
green, glacier outflow spread out into the deeper blue waters of the
bay itself, Steamer Ducks, oystercatchers, and gulls fussed around.
You could hear the wind rushing down the hidden glacier and onto
the surface of the sea.

By the time we were back at the settlement, a fishing boat had
come in, taking shelter from the gale; he was tied up to the rock

wall itself, next to what looked to be the ruins of a slaughterhouse. We weren't surprised, by now, to find that the friendly, two-person crew were both Chilotes.

It was another day before the wind went down. From the log for Wednesday, August 30:

> It snowed in the night and at dawn the boat was lightly coated. We were up at 06:00 to look at the gribs, which forecast 5 to 10 knots, so we decided to leave. It was glassy calm all the way back to Cape Hyades, but then we sailed into a two-hour squall of 20 to 30 knots...

By 10:00 it was calm again. At Isla del Diablo the Beagle Channel divides into two arms. Darwin's account could have been ours:

> ...we entered the northern one. The scenery here becomes grander than before. The lofty mountains on the north side compose the granitic axis, the backbone of the country, and boldly rise to a height of between three and four thousand feet, with one peak above six thousand feet. They are covered by a wide mantle of perpetual snow, and numerous cascades pour their waters, through the woods and into the narrow channel below. In many parts magnificent glaciers extend from the mountain side to the water's edge. It is scarcely possible to imagine anything more beautiful than the beryl-blue of these glaciers...

Chilote writer Francisco Coloane Cárdenas sets one of his short stories at this dramatic spot. The narrator, a passenger aboard the sailing cutter *Orion*, is a sheep-farm foreman on his way from Punta Arenas to Yendegaia to take up a new job. It is past midnight, the wind is blowing hard, and the captain has warned the helmsman to watch out for icebergs in the narrow channel:

A white mass drew nearer; it was in the shape of a pedestal for a statue and, on top of it...what a terrible sight! A corpse, a ghost, a living being, I can't tell you, but it was something unimaginable, with one arm raised and pointing into the distance that the night had swallowed. As it drew nearer, a human figure stood out clearly, standing up but buried up to its knees in the ice and dressed in rags that streamed in the wind. Its raised and stiff right arm seemed to say: "Get away from here!"

The ghostly figure on the iceberg, the narrator learns later, is the corpse of a young Yahgan hunter, lost a year earlier in a crevasse on the Italia Glacier.

We passed Isla del Diablo and radioed to the nearby, manned, Chilean light station that we'd be anchoring for the night at Caleta Olla, a well-protected bay on the north shore of the Beagle's northwestern arm, by the face of the Holanda Glacier.

"Okey *Bossun Beerd*...have a good voyage. We talk tomorrow," was the friendly reply.

The passage from Puerto Williams to Caleta Olla was the first and one of the shortest of what we'd mapped out as twelve legs of sailing on our way north. It had only been seventy-one miles, but we'd taken ten days. It wasn't hard to figure out that it could be four months before we were back in civilization. But we as we motored in, it was with a real sense of satisfaction. We looked forward to breaking out one of our carefully hoarded cardboard casks of Gato Negro red wine: we were on our way.

PUERTO WILLIAMS TO CALETA OLLA, BEAGLE CHANNEL: 71 N.M.; 10 DAYS.

~ *8*

In the Wake of the **Dresden**

CALETA OLLA LIES AT THE FOOT of the perpetually snow-capped
Monte Darwin (2488 metres). It was named by Fitzroy in February
1834, on the naturalist's birthday, but not climbed until 1962, by
Everest pioneer Eric Shipton; he describes the ascent in the evoc-
atively named but long-out-of-print *Tierra del Fuego: The Fatal
Lodestone.*

But most of the exploration of the area, after the *Beagle* that is,
was by Padre Alberto María de Agostini.

De Agostini (1883–1960) born in Pollone, Piedmont, was a Salesian
priest, posted from the age of twenty-seven to Punta Arenas as a

missionary. But by 1910 the Onas, Yahgans, and Alacalufs—the "benighted savages" whose souls the Salesians meant to save—were almost extinct, partly on account of the missionaries' misguided attempts to herd them into European-style settlements. With little else to do, de Agostini spent most of the rest of his life exploring the remotest corners of Patagonia, from hitherto unseen peaks in the Fitzroy and Paine massifs on the continent to the cloud-covered mountains of Tierra del Fuego. His best-known book is called *Ice Sphinxes*, but, like Shipton's, it has long been unobtainable. Fernando, the young man who had taken me to see the Casa de la Risa in Punta Arenas was editing de Agostini's letters, still buried in dusty archives in the huge and echoing Salesian monastery.

The priest used Caleta Olla, in 1914, as his base camp for the first attempt to climb a subsidiary of Monte Darwin, which he named Monte Italia. Like so many expeditions to this part of the world, the expedition had to be called off on account of incessant bad weather and poor visibility; the peak was eventually climbed by a German group in 1937. De Agostini returned in March 1956, at the age of seventy-three, and was this time successful.

A tall screen of pines growing on a sandy spur that juts at right angles into the Beagle's northwest arm gives unusually good shelter for boats, but behind the pines the high-sided channel runs straight as an artificial canal to the horizon. It was not difficult to imagine how hard the wind might blow down this gun barrel. We anchored in the usual fashion, stern to the sandy beach and lines to the pine trees, so close that even storm-force winds should blow safely above our masthead. At the south end of the beach, where it curled around to the east, two fishing boats were snugged up to the shore. A few minutes after we had settled in, a rowing skiff made its way over.

"*Hola Bossoon Beerd!! Centolla?*"

No payment was asked for or expected, but the young sailor looked more than happy with two packs of Derby cigarettes, and we had eight kilograms of crab, that in North America would fetch a couple of hundred dollars.

The cooking technique, we learned after some instruction, was to cram the legs into a pressure cooker, with maybe an inch of salt water, and steam them; the body had no meat to speak of and could be discarded. Once the legs had softened a little, you could slice them open with a sharp knife and scoop out the lobster-like meat. It was absolutely delicious, eaten cold with a little lemon, or hot in a stew or soup. The only snag was the hard work needed to extract the meat: the crab's spiky legs could leave your hands sore, even bleeding.

Next day it was gloomy and windy, and we thought it risky to row the mile or so that separated us from the terminal moraine of the Holanda Glacier (which de Agostini confusingly calls the Glaciar Francés): we might not be able to get back. So we cut through the pines behind the beach, tramped over a long expanse of peat bog, and then began to climb up to our right, in the hope of getting a good view over the channel. Soon we were in wet snow and whatever trail there might once have been disappeared; soft sleet began to fall and the grey waters of the channel became invisible. We turned back and, shivering, had a rapid wash where a stream came out onto the beach: it was so cold when you washed your hair that your head ached for a minute or two.

At dawn we got up to download the gribs. But it was snowing and miserable out, so we decided to wait for the navy weather forecast at 08:35. Westerly ten to twenty knots. Not bad. We walked through the forest to check what the open water looked like—a few whitecaps—and were off by 10:00.

All day the wind kept going up then down in what the Chilean forecasters call *chubascos*: short sharp squalls of thirty minutes or so, bringing snow, sleet, and rain and a rapid rise in the wind. We sailed patiently, first to one side of the channel, then the other, advancing two or three hundred metres with each tack. On the north shore, every mile or so a glacier tumbled to the water's edge: ghostly blue rivers of near-vertical ice creaking inexorably into the black water. First came Italia, then Francia, and finally Alemania. As a spectacle the Beagle surpassed all our hopes and expectations, but it is the loneliness, the sense of isolation, and the always nagging fear of bad weather to come, that I remember today.

One of the books we had on board was Maurice and Maralyn Bailey's *Second Chance*. Aboard *Auralyn II* they passed through these waters in 1975. The book is annoyingly sloppy in misidentifying many of the local features and misspelling others ("Hollandier" and "Hollandia," on the same page, for "Holanda"; "Pico Francis" for "Pico Francés"). But it was interesting and sobering to compare the book's grainy black-and-white photos of the glaciers in the Beagle with today's reality: several that then touched the water are now hanging glaciers; others are half their previous breadth.

But the main reason we liked the Baileys' book was that, unlike most of the "sailing" vessels that today transit these waters, they really tried to sail the whole way. By contrast, John Campbell's otherwise interesting-sounding *In Darwin's Wake* recounts an expedition on an eighty-three-foot yacht routinely capable of motoring one hundred miles a day, of powering directly into forty-knot winds, and of warming the crew's socks in the on-board tumble dryer. The Baileys' was incomparably the greater adventure.

With an hour or so to go before dark, we eased the sails on the starboard tack and coasted into the wide gap that had opened up in the steeply forested shores to our left: the four-mile-long and sock-shaped Bahía Romanche, so named by Martial on February 4, 1883. There were three possible anchorages, named Morning, Mediodía (noon), and Evening. We chose the first, partly because the Admiralty Pilot noted that the other two could freeze up in winter. The choice spot was between a vertical rock wall and a thundering waterfall just inside the entrance of the main bay; the

The Romanche Glacier, northwest arm of the Beagle Channel, Chile.

waterfall should keep the bay ice-free. This was a gloomy place, with nowhere to go ashore, and the steep sides meant williwaws could bounce around in here in heavy weather, but there were some old lines hanging down from the cliff, which was a sign that fishermen came here. Today's fourteen miles had taken us almost seven hours.

By now we had learned a new meteorological term from the navy forecast: *aguanieve*, literally water-snow. There was light *aguanieve* all night and for much of the next morning, which meant we hesitated to leave. But out in the channel the wind was only ten to fifteen knots, and mercifully there were no more of yesterday's *chubascos*. We beat our way over to the northern side of the channel and the Romanche Glacier.

It was probably here that Darwin and the little flotilla of whalers he had borrowed from the *Beagle* had a close call:

The boats being hauled on shore at our dinner hour, we were admiring from the distance of half a mile a perpendicular cliff of ice, and were wishing that some more fragments would fall. At last down came a mass with a roaring noise, and immediately we saw the smooth outline of a wave travelling towards us. The men ran down as quickly as they could to the boats; for the chance of their being dashed to pieces was evident...One of the seamen just caught hold of the bows as the curling breaker reached it; he was knocked over and over but not hurt; and the boats, though thrice lifted on high and let fall again, received no damage. This was most fortunate for us as we were a hundred miles from the ship...

Later in the morning, as we painstakingly zigzagged west, a fishing boat heading in the same direction overtook us. We waved at each other and followed the recommended VHF routine:

"*María Elena, María Elena*, this is yacht *Bosun Bird*..."

"*Bosun Bird, María Elena, Buenos días*..."

"*María Elena*, please report us to Alcamar Timbales. Port of registry, Victoria, Canada. Our intention is to anchor tonight in Seno Pía..."

"Okey *Bosun Bird*, tonight in Seno Pía. *Buen Viaje. María Elena fuera.*"

⌒ In theory we were supposed to report in by radio every day, but we were nearly always out of VHF range of the very few manned navy outposts. The alternative was to use our much longer-range SSB radio, but the problem was that once the navy knew you had such a piece of equipment, you could not elude the reporting requirement. They'd then raise the alarm if you missed a call. We didn't have enough faith in the reliability of our set to tie ourselves to this, and anyway, on a shorthanded sailing boat there were many occasions when you simply couldn't leave your post to wait for half an hour to answer a roll call.

By mid-afternoon we'd passed Caleta Voilier on our left and were opposite another gap in the mountain walls, to our right. The entrance to Seno Pía, a long fjord with three arms, was over a spit that only went below the surface for a short stretch. This was actually the lip of a now-receded glacier's terminal moraine, and the pass through it was maintained by the steady outflow of meltwater from the smaller glaciers still feeding into the fjord. We knew the only passable spot could shift from month to month, so we throttled the engine down to dead slow and, with the depth sounder showing only two metres (we draw 1.5 metres), we edged our way carefully in.

Our hope was to moor in a cove that all our friends had described as a "must visit": Caleta Beaulieu, in an arm to the east. But the main fjord was dotted with brash ice, and by looking through the binoculars I could see a line of solid white across the entrance to Beaulieu. Beyond, three separate glaciers cascaded down from cloud-covered plateaux, squeezed in by sheer, ice-scraped walls, and met the still black water. I never ceased to wonder at the colour of the glaciers, white but with a shifting and elusive shade of blue somewhere deep inside. As was usually the case when we nearing an anchorage, Jenny was too busy for sightseeing: she was unlashing then inflating the dinghy, flaking out the chain noisily. Later on she was perplexed at the pictures I'd taken with one hand, while holding the tiller with the other. "Where on earth was that?" she'd say.

With some Commerson's dolphins swishing through the mushy ice beside us, we turned sharp left, passed carefully through a five-metre-wide gap between a rock and the shore and moored in the wooded, lake-like Caleta del Sur. As usual we tied up with the stern to the west, which is where the wind normally blew from, but the topography was so complex here and the wind patterns so disturbed by the proximity of large expanses of ice that it blew easterly all night, making our halyards clank against the mast. I lay awake worrying that we might be driven back onto the beach.

Next morning the dolphins saw us out, but we were confused for several minutes by what sounded like the anguished wailing of a human on shore.

"Sounds like mountain goats," Jenny said.

"Well if they are, it's the first time they've ever been seen in these parts: congratulations."

Eventually, through the binoculars, we made out a dozen or so light-brown rocks that seemed occasionally to move: randy fur seals calling out to each other. Out in the main fjord there was a lot more ice than the previous evening, although I couldn't be sure if it was the glaciers calving or just the tide carrying out to the main channel that wall of ice we'd seen last night. Jenny stood in the bows as we motored at a dead-slow speed, pointing to where I should steer and prodding the occasional, sharp-looking bergy bit away with a boat hook. Going this slowly, the ice couldn't damage our fibreglass hull, but an awkwardly shaped piece could strike the propeller, which would be disastrous.

Today's was a short sail: southwest across the channel and into yet another fjord: Bahía Tres Brazos (Three Arms Bay). The Yahgans knew it as Takenawaia, and the *Romanche* found a few abandoned huts here. As we reached in, the wind and *aguanieve* started to pick up, but it was on the beam now and we were able to sail all the way to the cove we had identified as most suitable, Caleta Julia, on the west shore.

A narrow winding entrance, too tight for turning, again led to a small lake, but annoyingly there was in the very centre of the pond a plastic bottle evidently moored to the bottom. We never trust anyone else's mooring, but we didn't want to get tangled up in it either. It was more than an hour before we had a line from the bows to one shore and from the stern to the opposite side, with the plastic bottle floating free a metre or two to one side. Unusually, it took several attempts before the anchor held. The first two or three times Jenny retrieved it, she found that a great ball of kelp had

Caleta Julia.

formed around it and she had to hack the seaweed free with the boat hook. For the rest of the afternoon, the wind barrelled down the mountainside in great roars, laying us over first one side then the other.

Next afternoon we went for a long tramp in the hills. From three hundred metres up on the hillside we could see all the way to the end of Tres Brazos, five miles to the south, while on the north shore of the Beagle yet another glacier—Ventisquero España—thrust forward from the mist into the sea. We were standing overlooking a large, frozen, freshwater lake, almost surrounded by walls of sheer and shiny black granite, when I heard a gentle whooshing or whirring noise. I glanced up. There it was. Great black wings spread wide and motionless, its furry white collar unmistakable: an Andean Condor.

TUESDAY, SEPTEMBER 5. Up at 06:20; the gribs looked good. It was clear and cold, with thin ice on the surface of the caleta; it quivered and crackled as we hauled the lines in. We motored out to the west entrance point of Tres Brazos and hoisted the sails...

Gradually the northwest arm of the Beagle began to widen. To port, past the bulk of Isla Thomson and Isla Darwin, we could see right out to an unencumbered blue horizon: the open Pacific. This approach to the Fuegian channels is marked on the chart as Bahía Cook, and just down there were Seno Christmas and the Islas Christmas.

Captain Cook's second, and possibly his greatest, voyage had consisted in part of a circumnavigation of the Antarctic continent (although he never saw it). On November 10, 1774, the *Resolution* had sailed eastward from Queen Charlotte Sound, New Zealand. After a fast passage she sighted Cape Deseado, and from there she coasted down the wind-beaten southwestern shores of Tierra del Fuego, anchoring on December 20 in this island-studded expanse · of water that Cook called Christmas Sound.

The naturalist George Forster later wrote, "Barren as these rocks appeared, yet almost every plant which we gathered on them was new to us..."

But Swedish zoologist Anders Sparrman, in *With Captain Cook in HMS* Resolution, probably told the truth: "It was certainly true that, with goose-hunting on Christmas Eve and the dinner on Christmas Day, we did not much advance the cause of botany...it was not in the power of the botanists to choose the place for the digression..."

The *Resolution* left the sound on December 28. As they sailed for the Horn and back into the Atlantic, Cook's attention was caught by what he described as "a wild-looking rock" to port on what is now called Waterman Island. He named it after the massive cathedral of his distant native county: York Minster. Fifty-five years later, with Cook's log on board, Fitzroy noted in his own: "His sketch of the sound, and description of York Minster, are very good and quite enough to guide a ship to the anchoring place."

Jemmy Button's young friend was picked up by the *Beagle* near here and accordingly named after the rock. Today's Admiralty Pilot describes its historical provenance and then adds prosaically, "It is reported to be prominent on radar."

I found myself thinking how strange it was to be in a place with so much history—the Yahgans, Cook, the *Beagle*, the *Romanche*— and yet there was almost no sign humans had ever passed this way: just an occasional mound on a beach, a weather-beaten navigational marker, and (with fifty or sixty miles between them) those lonely alcamares. It was only as you looked at the chart that the story of these waters came alive, with every reef and island telling, in their name, a different episode.

With a rare fair wind and on sparkling seas we ran past Chair Island, named on account of its distinctive shape by Fitzroy and Darwin in 1833. Our Royal Cruising Club's guide book had unilaterally and whimsically christened a cove at its eastern end Caleta Cushion, but in an uncharacteristic and—to me—unfortunate example of pomposity, our Italian friends suggested English names were not suitable in this day and age; they urged cruisers to discard that name and call it Alakush (the Yahgan word for Steamer Duck).

We were able, reluctantly, to swallow this suggestion but would later have difficulty accepting other inventions: Caleta Desaparecidos (for the dead and disappeared of the Pinochet regime), Seno Venas Abiertas ("Open Veins," after a grim novel by a modern Uruguayan writer), and Caleta Violeta Parra (after a left-wing folk singer). It is a sure thing that if an anchorage is any good then, however remote, the local fishermen will already have some informal name for it, and it won't be on these politically correct lines.

We wove our way through a maze of tiny islands appropriately called the Timbales (Kettledrums) and tried in vain to call up the alcamar of the same name to tell the officer we were passing; perhaps he was taking a siesta. With the pathway to the open Pacific behind us, we finally entered a new channel, narrower than the Beagle: the ten-mile-long Canal O'Brien. On the south side is the irregularly shaped Isla Londonderry, named—surprise, surprise—by Fitzroy, after his grandfather, the first Marquis of Londonderry. The longer you follow the track of the *Beagle*, the more you sense its captain casting around ever more desperately for new names.

We anchored facing northeast in a small indentation on the north shore that the Italians had named Caleta Huajra. At first I thought we were too far out from the head of the bay, but in the morning I was relieved because a large rock had appeared, with low tide, a few feet behind us. We burned some more rubbish on the beach and walked up the hill for a fine view over the calm black channel. To the west we could see that the vegetation became noticeably sparser: many of the islands we could see ahead of us were bare grey granite with only a tuft or two of spindly brown grass. We were now approaching the stretch of islands and coast-line that bore the full brunt of the great Southern Ocean storms. On weather maps you could sometimes see how the depressions seemed to compress right here before squeezing past Cape Horn and popping out into the Atlantic. It was calm today, but we were now approaching one of the windiest places on Earth.

Next morning, the sailor manning Alcamar Timbales was awake early; he bade us farewell and warned us that the next human presence would be Fairway lighthouse, nearly 150 miles to the northwest. In an almost flat calm we motored out of O'Brien into the wide and long Canal Ballenero, "Whaler Channel"—so named because it was here that the *Beagle* had that whaler stolen and the mad chase began that ended up with Jemmy, Fuegia, York Minster, and Boat Memory as kidnap victims.

This would be a bad place to be in a heavy northwester. There is a fetch of twenty miles, and at its far end the channel is open to the Pacific swells. So we hurried and guiltily recorded our longest day so far under power alone: nearly thirty miles. There was a high overcast, but to the north we had a rare view of the twin peaks of Mount Sarmiento, at 2300 metres the second-highest on the big island, after Darwin. Also visible from the Strait of Magellan and even Punta Arenas and first noted by the Spanish sailor and colonist Pedro Sarmiento de Gamboa in 1580, it was generously given this name on the voyage of the *Adventure* and the *Beagle* by the *Adventure*'s captain, Philip Parker King, in 1827. The mountain even caught the attention of Captain Nemo and his crew aboard Jules Verne's *Nautilus:*

> ...we sighted land to the west. It was Tierra del Fuego, which the first navigators named thus from seeing the quantity of smoke that rose from the natives' huts. The coast seemed low to me, but in the distance rose high mountains. I even thought I had a glimpse of Mount Sarmiento, that rises 2,070 yards above the level of the sea, with a very pointed summit, which, according as it is misty or clear, is a sign of fine or of wet weather.

A fishing boat, the *Aries III*, detoured to come and see us, and the captain came out from his cabin to wave and take a photograph. We anchored for the night off the southwest shore of Isla Burnt (which is next to Isla Smoke). The *Don Mario* came past and offered us some king crab; we were frankly getting a little tired of this delicacy by now, but it seemed rude to say no, so we cut, scraped, and boiled far into the night.

This is as far as Darwin and Fitzroy came in their whaleboats. Darwin didn't like the place at all: "...we sailed amongst many unknown desolate islands and the weather was wretchedly bad.

One night we slept on large round boulders, with putrefying seaweed between them; and when the tide rose, we had to get up and
move our blanket-bags...".

We were just glad to have the open stretch of Ballenero behind
us, and the second of our twelve legs safely checked off. We washed
the *centolla* down with a glass of our precious red wine, celebrating
not only another leg but exactly one year since our departure from
South Africa. We settled into our sleeping bags at the daringly late
hour of 20:00.

CALETA OLLA TO ISLA BURNT: 93 N.M.; 6 DAYS.

⌇ It was a windy night. The halyards clanked and we swayed from
side to side as gusts hit us from different directions; I wished we'd
taken *Don Mario*'s advice and anchored around the corner, but
Jenny snored all night, unworried.

The forecast was for light winds, and in the morning we sailed
west, with Bahía Desolada (or Desolate Bay, as named by Cook) on
our right, another snatch of the open Pacific to the left.

The Admiralty Pilot gloomily but accurately comments: "The
entire bay is a confused welter of rocks and islets over which the
sea breaks almost incessantly, presenting a sombre and melancholy
appearance. The area is little known."

We were glad there wasn't too much wind, and that we could
see our way. This would be no place to be in heavy weather. Soon
we were in a narrow winding passage marked with a brightly
painted red buoy that leaned over hard in the strong tidal current.
Its red was a startling splash of colour on a day when the sea was
black, the rock walls of the mountains slate grey, and the cloud and
mist, which hung maybe a hundred metres up their slopes, only
slightly lighter. We skirted around another buoy, marking a shoal
and, with the wind now having died, motored past Isla Basket
(Fuegia Basket's long-since uninhabited home) and, with the
drizzle turning into cold rain, into Canal Brecknock.

To starboard there opened a narrow, Y-shaped bay: we manoeuvred carefully into the westernmost arm, as the eastern looked to be encumbered by kelp. It was an ominous location, with wet grey walls of rock rising in a steep semicircle behind the bay and only one or two stunted shrubs on the shoreline. It took Jenny nearly two hours to find two of these that looked to be sufficiently strong to hold our stern lines, as I shouted what were intended to be helpful directions from *Bosun Bird*, but which she soon (wisely) started to ignore.

When we talk about sailing, one of the things our friends ask us is, "Don't you argue a lot, being cooped up in such a confined space?" Yes, of course we have our disagreements, but probably less than on land. We have an unspoken agreement, first, that in decisions to be made while underway, the default position should be the most conservative: if one of us even thinks it might be time to reef, then we do so. The problem is that it is not always obvious what the safest option is, as in the case of going on or turning back. The unspoken agreement then, undemocratic though it may sound, is that the captain's opinion prevails. On a small sailing boat in adverse and possibly dangerous conditions there isn't always time to thrash things through, and the most important thing is sometimes to make a decision, any decision.

During the later afternoon at Caleta Yahgan, rachas (williwaws) swept down the mountainside with ever greater frequency, shaking *Bosun Bird* and laying us over first one side, then the other, until our rails almost went under. We secured the rubber dinghy tightly to one side, but the wind kept flipping it violently and noisily up on deck. Then indeed we would have disagreements: whose turn was it to get up and put things right? Sometimes the gusts came down almost vertically and bounced upward. Our solar panel, suspended in the rigging over the cockpit, simply turned over in one shrieking moment.

We didn't sleep much that night. It would be quiet for half a minute, then within three seconds the wind would go up to thirty or forty knots and just as quickly down again. The lines strained, our anchor chain growled on the bottom, but everything held. We were relieved to go in the morning. Later, Graham and Avril on *Dreamaway* said they'd had a terrible time here, too; they remembered Yahgan as "Racha City."

Whenever we had bad times like these, we consoled ourselves by telling each other, "Gerry wouldn't have even flinched..."

Gerry was Gerry Clark, New Zealand author and protagonist of *The Totorore Voyage*, accurately described on its cover as of "one of the most remarkable small boat adventures of all time." In his home-built, bilge-keel *Totorore* and starting in 1983 at the age of fifty-six, Gerry circumnavigated Antarctica over a period of several years. With the aim of logging bird life in the Southern Ocean, he ventured to the wildest imaginable corners of this, the wildest coast, and had one near-miss after another, terrifying his inexperienced and volunteer crew members in the process. He had one typical adventure right here, in midwinter:

The wind increased to thirty knots and the sea was rough with heavy obscuring showers of hail or rain, so progress was slow and wet...I was wondering at what unearthly hour we would reach Caleta Brecknock when there was a loud bang and the whole boat gave a jolt...Julia, down below, said: "I can smell something from the engine." The alternator was hanging loose; it had chewed up its own belt and some of the sound-proofing foam inside the case and was now bearing on the flywheel. In the dirty weather and pitch dark we had to find an anchorage quickly. An un-surveyed area of Península Brecknock looked quite promising but as we approached the gusts came out to meet us in a most daunting manner. I am always anxious when heading into tight corners which are not surveyed and this was no exception. As soon as the sounder showed

ten fathoms I yelled "let go!" just as another gust struck us. She paid
off so quickly that by the time the anchors were on the bottom we
were in 25 fathoms. Not very good at all but it was 23:30 and we
were whacked...

Gerry survived Patagonia, was dismasted in the South Atlantic,
rolled over three times in the Indian Ocean, but made it to Australia
using an orange plastic tarpaulin as a mainsail. We met him a few
years later when he gave a talk on Vancouver Island (and signed a
copy of his book for us), but soon after that he and his boat disappeared, never to be seen again, off the coast of New Zealand.

Canal Brecknock is really the open ocean, exposed to the Pacific
at its northwest and southeast ends, but shielded to the southwest by the high and wild Isla London. We were nervous here as we
motored under a heavy overcast, more afraid than we'd been since
we approached the Strait of Le Maire six months earlier. We had a
sense that the weather could change very rapidly and things could
easily get out of control. I found myself asking Jenny to check our
barograph every ten or fifteen minutes for a sudden rise or dip that
could spell a squall. After our night at Yahgan, where we'd taken a
heavy beating even though we were almost surrounded on all sides
by land and secured with three lines and the anchor, I was aware
that if we had a serious engine failure we would have difficulty in
sailing into anywhere protected enough to allow us to work on it.
And for the past several months, whenever we listened to the navy
forecasts at night, the weather at Brecknock seemed to be the worst
on the coast.

In the gloom, we turned right, into a narrow winding defile
then right again, into a cul-de-sac called Seno Ocasión: you
needed to keep your finger on the chart or risk losing your bearings. The smooth rock walls were now only fifty metres apart, but
then they opened up into a perfectly circular, steep-sided cirque:
Caleta Brecknock. It was like a set from *Lord of the Rings*: silent,

Caleta Brecknock.

threatening, overpowering. The water was black, everything
else grey.

The pool was deep, but by edging within a few metres of the wall
on the left-hand side you could find water shallow enough to anchor
in. On a low point off to our right as we faced outward Jenny found
a bonsai-like bush only thirty centimetres high to which we attached
our starboard bow line. We didn't dare test it lest we uproot the
bush. To port it was nearly one hundred metres to a slightly larger
shrub, but astern there were two good trees, and we were able to
pull ourselves back until it felt like we could step ashore.

Brecknock had let us past, but now we'd pay a price. For nine
days it blew a gale. In the only lulls it snowed so thickly that you
couldn't see past the bows.

I read *Crime and Punishment*, followed by *The Brothers Karamazov*, both of which had swelled to twice their already substantial size on account of the all-pervasive damp on board and which were diffi-cult to hold. We played up to three games of Scrabble a day and listened a lot to the radio; the log records that one day, with the word "cremated," I scored eighty-six points on my second turn at Scrabble, causing Jenny to quit in despair. Occasionally, through some freak condition, we were able to pick up BBC Radio Five on the AM band, as well as (more reliably) the Falkland Island Broadcasting Service, which is known without any apparent sense of irony as FIBS.

Tuning in to Wolfgang on the Patagonian Net in the morn-ings, we learned that there was finally another sailboat at sea and heading our way: Klaus and Maria on *Ludus Amoris*, whom we'd met briefly alongside the *Micalvi* months earlier. But as we sat and endured the gales, they were getting the same winds a few hours later in the Beagle Channel and were making slow progress.

The forecast we recorded for Wednesday, September 13, on Magallanes Radio from Punta Arenas was a typical one:

Canal Brecknock: sustained winds 40 to 50 knots, gusts 50 to 70, offshore seas to 14 metres.

One night the lighthouse report from the Evangelistas, at the west entrance to the Strait of Magellan, was a laconic one hundred knots, seas *montañosas*. From our tiny nook we could look out to furious, whitecap-covered waters just metres ahead, and I am not ashamed to say that I was again afraid. But although we reeled from side to side in gusts and in the wildest weather a swell worked its way in, we were never in breaking waves.

In the lulls we put out heavier lines, cleared snow off the decks and the solar panels, bailed water from the dinghy, and went for the occasional walk up the steep gully behind us and onto a rocky, lake-strewn plateau. But it never cleared for more than an hour, and twice we found ourselves carefully retracing our footsteps in the snow, in whiteout conditions. In spite of the enforced inactivity, it was a stressful time. There were times when we wondered if this could last for weeks; we felt lonelier here, and more isolated—on the very tip of Tierra del Fuego—than we ever had on an ocean crossing.

On Sunday, September 17, the wind finally eased. In the morning there were four centimetres of snow on deck and it was coming down thickly, but the water was black and still, the silence absolute. We laboriously unhooked our six lines to shore, upped the anchor and motored carefully out into Seno Ocasión, feeling our way in the falling snow with the shoreline only fleetingly visible. The next step was a delicate one, known to the fishing boats as the Paso Brecknock: leaving a maze of tight channels, we would make a long and lazy turn to starboard into the much wider and more exposed east–west-running Canal Cockburn. Here, for the first time since we had left Puerto Williams, we would turn east. If there was bad weather it would probably come from seaward, behind us, but it would bring heavy seas with it.

We felt our way out to the sinister-looking Roca Rompiente, an isolated black rock that invariably breaks in the heavy low swell entering Cockburn. Today the swells seemed sluggish and low, but they were deceptive and were sending spray ten metres into the air on the seaward side of the rock. Mid-morning the snow stopped and the sun came out: what a spectacular sight with the mountains all around white to the very level of the water and, as the blue sky spread, the water turning from a deep black to blue! Soon we were able to sail, with a sharp breeze pushing us from astern.

This area was poorly charted, and we extricated a set of detailed instructions from a boat that had preceded us by a year or two here. From rock to rock we navigated past one bay (which bore the pencil annotation "avoid at all costs—lethal" in our Italian guide) to a long narrow inlet known to cruisers as Caleta Cluedo. I could only presume that the name of the cove (which is also that of an old-fashioned English board game that I recalled playing at Christmas as a nine-year-old) came from some poor yacht having been marooned for days here. Its crew must have spent their time figuring out if the murderer was in fact Colonel Mustard in the library with the candlestick.

We were now back on Joshua Slocum's track. He'd not taken the *Spray* through the Beagle Channel at all, preferring the wider and shorter route to the Pacific: the Strait of Magellan. After many adventures he had battled his way through Magellan, out of the western entrance, only to be driven southeast by a tremendous gale. At one moment he thought he would be forced all the way around Cape Horn and then have to enter the strait all over again from the eastern side, but in a lull he thought he saw a way back into the archipelago:

> Night closed in before the sloop reached the land, leaving her feeling the way in pitchy darkness. I saw breakers ahead before long. At this I wore ship and stood offshore, but was immediately startled by the tremendous roaring of breakers again ahead and on the lee bow. In this way, among dangers, I spent the rest of the night. Hail and sleet in the fierce squalls cut my flesh till the blood trickled over my face. It was not the time to complain of a broken skin. What could I do but fill away among the breakers and find a channel between them...this was the greatest sea adventure of my life. God knows how my vessel escaped.

Slocum had entered Cockburn Channel through the myriad rocks and small islands, including the well-named Furies that encumber its seaward entrance, a location known on some charts as the Milky Way. Darwin sixty years earlier wrote in his journal: "Any landsman seeing the Milky Way would have nightmares for a week." Slocum, who had read this, commented, "He might have added 'or seaman' as well."

Through the night at Cluedo it continued to blow, sometimes with snow-squalls, but, encouragingly for our future progress, the wind direction was now easterly. We had a leisurely morning, clearing snow off the decks, because just ahead of us now was the narrowest passage on our route, the zigzagging Canal Acwalisnan. We would need to time our passage carefully so that a flood tide would carry us in, we would transit at high water, and an ebb tide would then carry us out of the northern end. With an error of only ten or fifteen minutes we could find ourselves battling currents of eight knots.

Acwalisnan would take us from the archipelago of Fuegian Islands and into the western portion of the Strait of Magellan. The more usual route, used by larger ships (and Slocum on the *Spray* after his adventure in the Milky Way), was called Canal Magdalena; this was wide and clear, but it would mean a lot of backtracking, and it emerged on the Atlantic side of Cape Froward, the southern-most tip of the continent. A third route called Canal Bárbara was the most direct of the possible options, but it had several tight tidal passages and was inadequately surveyed; the Chilean navy had formally forbidden yachts to use it.

It is a comment on how remote these waters are that Acwalisnan only began appearing on charts in the 1920s. The young Lucas Bridges recounts in *Uttermost Part of the Earth* how he was shown it by a Yahgan friend, Acualisnan, whom he had employed as a pilot on a voyage from Punta Arenas to Ushuaia.

For an hour or more we jilled around in the open water at the southern entrance of the passage, with Mount Sarmiento's snow-covered and encouragingly clear twin peaks jutting into the sky to the east of us. A blue fishing boat, the *Emisor*, chugged out of the pass and reported to us by radio that it was "*calma*." But I knew he could do ten knots under power, and we proceeded only with

great caution. We hit the narrows at 12:30, thirteen minutes ahead
of schedule. Here and there was a roiling effect on the otherwise smooth surface of the water, and we could see from an area
of eddies to starboard where a particularly dangerous underwater rock must be located. I remembered similar sets of rapids
between the mainland of British Columbia and Vancouver Island,
last cruised twenty-five years earlier. But we made our way through
without incident and, with light winds and a short distance to run,
tacked our way northward up Acwalisnan and into its northern
mouth, Seno Pedro. At the far end of Pedro was a chain of high
mountains that we knew must be the continent, the first time we
had seen it since leaving Puerto Deseado. We anchored as darkness set in at the head of a long bay called Caleta Murray, just before
Pedro debouches into the Strait of Magellan.

ISLA BURNT TO CALETA MURRAY (STRAIT OF MAGELLAN):
89 N.M.; 11 DAYS.

⁓ The problem with the Strait of Magellan is that west of Cape
Froward it points northwest and in a straight line, with steep
mountains on either side. This is precisely the direction from which
the prevailing winds blow, and the channel accelerates them,
frequently to gale force. The seas do not reach dangerous heights,
but their short period and steepness, in these conditions, can make
forward progress for a small sailing vessel almost impossible. What
we needed was to have a low-pressure area pass north of us, over
mainland Patagonia, creating a sequence of winds from northeast through east to southeast. But this only happened two or three
times a season, and some years not at all. Sir Francis Drake still held
the record for a westward passage of the strait under sail, but it was
not an encouraging one: eighteen days from end to end.

Almost unbelievably, it looked as though precisely the right
conditions might now be in place, although we worried that we
might already have lost a precious day of easterlies. The days were

Cape Froward, Strait of Magellan.

getting perceptibly longer now, and we were up at 05:45 to make
the most of things.

The first hour was a battle: fifteen to twenty knots of cold wind
from the north, apparently blowing straight into Seno Pedro. But as
we eased out into the famous strait the angle improved, and soon
we were racing along under full genoa, the rail under, the GPS occasionally hitting seven knots. Not bad considering our hull speed
(theoretical maximum) was only five. Far astern now, under a grey
sky, a massive granite cliff rose almost vertically out of the strait,
capped with snow: it must be Cape Froward. Not the Horn, not
Good Hope, but still one of the greatest and most challenging capes
in the world for a small sailing boat to round.

Later, I would remember the sight of Froward gradually receding
under the sharply defined horizon as one of the high points of my life.

The Admiralty Pilot warns: "At Cabo Froward exceptionally heavy squalls are experienced. The weather frequently changes to heavy rain or snow, and the shores are often obscured..."

But, with the predicted light snow falling in Froward Reach, we peeled off the miles. An eastbound freighter passed us, bound for Buenos Aires; we asked him to report us to Magallanes Radio in Punta Arenas. To starboard now was Fortescue Bay, with a protected inner anchorage called Caleta Gallant. This was a historic location: Thomas Cavendish named Gallant after one of his three ships as he battled his way to the northwest during what was to become the third circumnavigation of the world, in 1587. John Narborough named the outer bay Fortescue in 1670, in honour of one of his guests; then came Bougainville in *La Boudeuse* (1766), the *Beagle*, the *Adventure*, the *Spray*, Tilman's *Mischief*. Slocum, fearing an attack by the fearsome Indian known as Black Pedro, here sprinkled carpet tacks on his deck as a deterrent to boarders.

But the wind was fair: there was no question of stopping now. Soon we were in English Reach, with—up ahead—the large Isla Carlos III almost blocking the strait. Jenny had spent part of the morning down below, carefully tracking our course and, as she eyed the GPS, fretting that we were going too fast and that perhaps we should reduce sail. But in the mid-afternoon the wind began to fade and we slowed. The sky was overcast, steep mountains on either side simply disappearing into the cloud cover; their lower slopes were sparsely covered with stunted pines, still laden with the heavy snow that had fallen over the past week. As so often, everything was black, white, or grey, except for one brief moment when the red-painted *Alamo,* from Valparaíso, passed us eastbound.

With a good day's run of thirty-nine miles behind us, we pulled into a bay at the northeastern extremity of Isla Carlos III and anchored—swinging free for a change—at its head. I went for a row, but, except for a short stretch of pebbly beach, the shores were too steep for landing. All along the tide-line grew great clumps of fat and succulent looking mussels. Cavendish had named the adjoining Mussel Bay on this account. But the navy had warned us that virtually all the waters between here and Puerto Montt were infested by Red Tide and that eating any bivalve could be fatal.

That night we half-expected to hear the plaintive cry of "*Yammerschooner*" ("Give me!") that had plagued every navigator up to the time of Slocum, but it was nearly a hundred years now since the Yahgan and Alacalufs had plied these waters in their canoes. Fairway lighthouse was still eighty miles to the northwest.

⟿ The southern shore of the Strait of Magellan is here formed by Isla Santa Inés. Cutting deeply into its seaward shore, but with its exact limits tantalizingly marked only by dotted lines, is Seno Dresden.

September 28, 1914. The First World War is barely a month old. The British West Indies Squadron, made up of the cruisers *Good Hope*, *Glasgow*, and *Monmouth*, arrives off Punta Arenas. They ask British Consul Charles Milward and other members of the British colony if any Germans have passed this way. The answer is affirmative: the *Scharnhorst*, *Gneisenau*, *Nurnberg*, *Leipzig*, and *Dresden* are all thought to be in Chilean Pacific waters. The *Dresden* in fact has several times been seen at Bahía Orange, the *Romanche*'s old haunt. Admiral Christopher Cradock sets off, up the Strait of Magellan in hot pursuit, and out into the Pacific. He catches up with the German fleet off Coronel on November 1. But he makes a crass tactical error. He allows his ships to be silhouetted by the sunset, with the German fleet inshore. The British squadron is almost annihilated. It is the first British naval defeat in over a hundred years. On November 2, records the Punta Arenas port captain's log, the *Glasgow* limps back via Punta Arenas to lick its wounds at Port Stanley.

Once the news reaches London, Admiral Sir Frederick Doveton Sturdee hastily assembles a new fleet and orders them to rendezvous at the Falklands. They surprise the Germans. Only the light cruiser *Dresden*, commanded by Captain Fritz Ludecke, and an auxiliary, the *Seydlitz*, survive the ensuing battle; 2,000 German sailors are lost. In making off, the German cruiser almost bursts her boilers by running at twenty-seven knots.

The hunt is now on for the *Dresden*. On December 12, Consul Milward reports to London that she has briefly called into Punta Arenas again; the *Bristol* and *Glasgow* arrive in pursuit on December 14, leaving the *Inflexible* stationed off the southeastern tip of Tierra del Fuego. More British ships soon follow. For the next ten days the British steam frantically up and down the western Strait of Magellan. But the *Dresden* is hiding off the main shipping route, at remote Bahía Hewett near the seaward entrance to Canal Cockburn, along with a small German civilian freighter, the *Amasis*. On December 20 Ludecke dispatches the *Amasis* to Punta Arenas in search of coal, but she is immediately impounded by the Chilean port authorities.

Meanwhile, Albert Pagels, a German resident in Punta Arenas, has not been idle. Keeping clear of Milward, he mobilizes the entire German community, and, aboard his own cutter, he finds the *Dresden*, unloads tons of fresh supplies, and discusses with her captain the possibility of bringing further coal to her.

Then on December 24 a converted German passenger ship, the *Sierra Córdoba*, carrying 12,500 tons of coal, enters Magellan from the Atlantic. The *Carnarvon* and crew are suspicious and board her near Cape Froward; they let her go, knowing they cannot seize or sink her in Chilean waters; but they sense the *Dresden* must be near.

The German ship, warned by Pagels that the British may be closing in and that Hewett is too exposed, moves out to Christmas Bay, in the northeastern corner of Bahía Stokes and near the south end of Canal Bárbara. For the next five weeks a cat and mouse game goes on. The Chilean authorities become nervous and suspicious about Pagels. Under pressure from the Milward and the British, they deny him permission to leave harbour. He circumvents this by sometimes using the *Explorador*, which is owned by the Austro-Hungarian consul, who has diplomatic immunity.

The *Glasgow*, the *Bristol*, and now the *Carnarvon* are perplexed, all too aware that the *Sierra Córdoba* and her German-Chilean captain Henry Rothemburg have not yet moved on into the Pacific and are simply lingering. All of Punta Arenas is agog. Where is the *Dresden*?

On January 18 Pagels finds the *Sierra Córdoba* and clandestinely brings Rothemburg and his ship to Christmas Bay, where the next day she moors by the *Dresden* and starts unloading coal. A French fishing boat reports to Milward in Punta Arenas that he believes he has seen the German warship. But on the British ships, when they pull their charts out, they find no bay at the longitude and latitude indicated by the French skipper. The sighting is discounted.

On February 2 Pagels evades his watchers and comes out again on a tug, the *Kosmos*. With crew from the *Dresden* he scouts the neighbouring waters and, on February 4, they lead the German cruiser around to a then-uncharted, east–west-running fjord on the south coast of Santa Inés Island, off Canal Wakefield (it is now called Seno Dresden). Pagels returns to Punta Arenas and at Ludecke's behest sends a coded telegram to Germany: the cruiser will sail shortly, he says, and will wait for a German collier at 37 degrees south, 80 degrees west. In the late afternoon of February 14, the *Dresden* and the *Sierra Córdoba* set sail together and make for the open sea.

The British have lost her. After many rumoured but never confirmed sightings in the channels around Chiloé and at Quintupeu fjord, the *Dresden* is next heard of definitively when she sinks the *Conway Castle* off Valparaíso in late February.

Rothemburg later becomes a captain in the Chilean merchant marine and dies in Punta Arenas in 1931. Pagels, a national hero, is awarded the Iron Cross; he names his daughter Dresden and dies in 1966; his son, Gerardo, still lives in Punta Arenas and is a good friend of El Profesor, the Puerto Williams town librarian. Seno Dresden and Christmas Bay remain uncharted to this day. They were only recorded by aerial photography in the 1960s. Our German chart, Number 745, shows the approach to the bay as Dresden Hort (Dresden Refuge) and labels a point on its ill-defined western shore as Pagels Huk.

⚓ Next morning, Wednesday, September 20, we had another appointment with slack water, this time at Cabo Crosstides, where the tides from the Pacific and Atlantic meet. We didn't like hanging around but the forecast still held out hope of two more days of easterly winds. *Ludus Amoris* was fast catching us up and were already at Caleta Murray.

Jenny hoisted the anchor and we slipped out into Crooked Reach on the last of the contrary tide. Beneath the small unmanned light that marks the cape, making the most of the turbulent waters, a dozen or so orcas were milling around. They were big, and one or two of them had collapsed dorsal fins. They didn't seem interested in us; we recalled years ago sailing with the orcas in Sansum Narrows, our home waters inside Vancouver Island; that's where Jenny says she'd like her ashes spread one day.

Our course was northwest, the wind light northeast, so we made steady progress for most of the day. Up ahead on the starboard side, a ridge that came down to the sea had a distinctive dip in it, and we quickly identified it as the headland that must mark Caleta Notch, reputedly one of the safest refuges in the strait. We were tempted— the front cover of the RCC guide bore a spectacular photograph of it—but the wind was still favourable and we had another three hours or so of light. It would be foolish not to press on while the going was good.

In the early evening we were off another inlet to starboard: Caleta Playa Parda (Dark Beach), so named in the sixteenth century by Sarmiento. The entrance was a narrow one, opening up into a wide pool surrounded by steep mountains that were now turning deep orange and red as the setting sun briefly broke through. Those steep walls were ominous: as we had learned, around here they might spell flat water but they were no protection from strong winds.

Sure enough, it was another of those nights. Out in the strait it was probably blowing twenty or thirty knots, but in here we would have a minute or two of calm, then a fifteen-second gust of forty or fifty knots that would send us careering around on our single anchor line. There seemed to be no prevailing direction, which made us worry that our anchor would never set. Nowhere on the shoreline was there a nook where we could have backed in, and there were no trees to tie to, nor even bushes; we'd just have to endure being blown around in circles all night. Making things worse was the fact that there was no moon, it was heavily overcast, and it sleeted most of the night. Whenever we went out in the cockpit with a flashlight to see how far off the shore was, we could see nothing.

Next day, grudgingly, I had to admit that the Admiralty Pilot had warned: "squalls possible." But the unpredictability of the effects of the prevailing winds on a given location anywhere in these waters was highlighted by what Tilman, who anchored *Mischief* here in December 1954, had to say: "Save for the roar of the falls the place was profoundly still. Overhead and outside in the reach a gale raged. Curtains of rain swept ceaselessly across the cirque but not a ripple disturbed the steel grey water of the anchorage."

Next morning, after such a rambunctious night, it was surprisingly calm out in the strait, but there was a leftover chop that indicated it had been blowing a lot harder not very long ago. As we got underway we spoke by VHF radio with *Ludus Amoris*. The Germanic-sounding Klaus was cheerful.

"Ja, vee haf done sixty miles yesterday and haf reached Notch. Today I think we overtake you."

Gradually the wind picked up. Soon it was twenty-five, gusting to thirty knots, but mercifully from the right direction. Looking at the chart and over our starboard quarter, I wondered if the wind was being accelerated by cold air rushing down from the ice fields. By now, with some assistance from a favourable current, we were doing nearly eight knots over the bottom; the seas were building behind us and steering was starting to become difficult. But I was sure the effect was a local one, and we pressed on past several good anchorages to port.

One, a mile-long inlet known as Puerto Angosto, had been favoured both by Sarmiento (in 1550) and Slocum. The *Spray*'s captain found the bay, which he describes as "a dreary enough place," surprisingly busy. Chilean and Argentine gunboats called in; the captain of the Argentine *Azopardo* criticized him for not having shot Black Pedro when he had the chance. There was also a Swedish professor camped at the head of the bay, "with three well-armed Argentines along to fight savages." It took seven attempts before the *Spray* was eventually able to clear Angosto and make for the open Pacific, on April 13, 1896.

We had now passed from Long Reach and into Sea Reach, the westernmost portion of the strait, named, like the other reaches, by Sir John Narborough in 1670. Magellan was starting to widen out a little. Next, short of the open Pacific, we would hang a hard right into Canal Smyth and begin our long sail due north through the Patagonian channels, which are considered to be geograph-ically distinct from the Fuegian channels. There were very few good anchorages on the starboard (northern) side of the strait, so the priority today was to get as far as we could along the southern shore and spend the night in one of the more approachable coves. This would leave us well-positioned to cross to Smyth with virtu-ally any of the most common wind directions (northeasters being rare and weak). The "step" across the strait and into Smyth is

Bosun Bird *in the Strait of Magellan.*

known to Chilean sailors as the Paso Tamar, and, like Brecknock, the location has a bad reputation.

Ludus Amoris, five metres longer than *Bosun Bird* and consequently much faster, now caught us up. We photographed each other against a dramatic backdrop of snow-capped mountains and agreed to meet up later that evening at Caleta Uriarte. As we'd guessed it would, the wind faded and the sun came out: nearly twenty miles ahead on the port side we could see Cabo Pilar, which marks the western entrance to Magellan.

Just over the horizon, or perhaps obscured by the headlands we could see to the north, must be the fabled Evangelistas, site of the loneliest and most weather-wracked lighthouse in the world. With my finger, I found on the chart the nearby bay called Cuarenta Días, named because a lighthouse tender had once waited forty days there before the wind and seas abated sufficiently for it to reach the light. Like Slocum we now "felt the throb of the great ocean that lay before..."

Navigating into Uriarte meant dodging a number of rocks that had been inconveniently omitted by the cartographers, as well as making a sharp dogleg at the entrance of the cove. But by 15:00 we were securely tied up with two lines astern to shore, and *Ludus Amoris* only fifty metres away. We rowed over for an evening drink and spent an hour or two sharing stories. Except by radio, Klaus and Maria were the first people we had exchanged more than a few words with since leaving Puerto Williams almost six weeks earlier, and we all found ourselves strangely tongue-tied.

We hardly dared hope the wind would hold, but sure enough, next morning the gribs were showing a perfect east to southeast breeze of ten knots. With all our sails pulling, we set our course NNE, in pursuit of *Ludus Amoris* and almost directly across the strait. It was at first difficult to pick out the way ahead, but through the binoculars we were able to make out an islet with a clump of red and white buildings that we knew must be the lighthouse complex of Faro Fairway. There was a surreal moment when a submarine popped to the surface off our port beam and led the way into Canal Smyth.

The light keeper, who must have been a bit lonely, called us up. "*Bosun Bird, Bosun Bird*, Faro Fairway...please, I want you to visit me; you are most welcome."

He described a landing place on the north side of the tiny island, and the conditions were quite calm. But we knew we wouldn't be comfortable leaving *Bosun Bird* in such an exposed location for even a few minutes. We reluctantly declined the invitation and turned left into a wide complex of bays and inlets called Puerto Profundo.

There were dozens of possible mooring spots here, but the snuggest was at the end of a narrow winding inlet that cut deep into the headland protecting Profundo's southern entrance. It was like a river entrance: in one spot, to avoid a rock, you had almost to touch the rock wall on the port side. I was glad it was not blowing hard because here precision-steering was in order. The bay, which was not properly charted, had been explored by British sailors Ian and Maggie Staples on board their *Teokita*, and it was named accordingly.

We'd identified, before leaving Williams, three stretches that might be extra difficult: the short stretch from Caleta Brecknock, into Canal Cockburn was one of them; the long haul up Magellan was the next. We thought we'd been lucky with the weather but then recalled that *Dreamaway* had said there might be a good window at the equinox, which was...today.

CALETA MURRAY TO CALETA TEOKITA: 130 N.M.; 4 DAYS.

9

To the Gulf *of* Sorrows

FROM THE STRAIT OF MAGELLAN, a protected sailing route runs
north for 360 nautical miles, through the Patagonian channels,
before the next stretch of open water is met: the Golfo de Penas
(Gulf of Sorrows). Countless detours are possible, but of these only
the sixty-mile dogleg eastward to Puerto Natales is fully charted.
Many of the other channels are simply white on the chart, and
exploring these waters is known as "sailing on the white." The
Admiralty Pilot describes the passage:

> The general features of the channels are high and abrupt shores
> with innumerable peaks and headlands, remarkably alike in

279

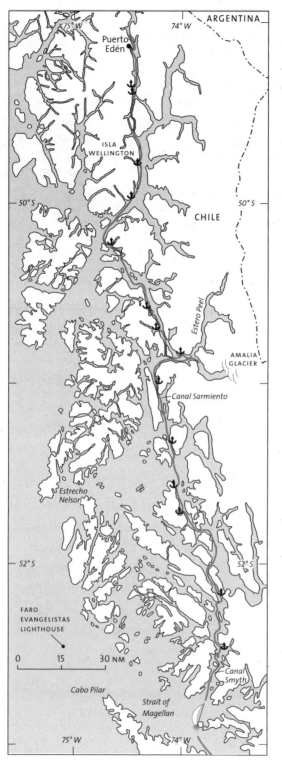

The Chilean channels:
Strait of Magellan to
Puerto Edén.

The wreck of the Santa Leonora, *Canal Smyth.*

character, giving an appearance of gloomy grandeur rarely seen elsewhere. The shores are generally steep-to and the channels open and free...

The course is actually few degrees west of north. As the prevailing winds blow from northwest through west to southwest, you might expect, on average, to have the wind on the beam: ideal sailing. In reality, the very slight skewing of the channels westward and the funnelling effect of the mountains mean that the wind in the channels is nearly always from the north, tending to rise in the afternoons. We could expect to be either tacking or taking advantage of calms to motor, for the entire way.

The first day's sail had us beating slowly northward up Canal Smyth in contrary winds of ten to fifteen knots, then resorting to the motor to negotiate the lazy S of Paso Shoal. As we were emerging, among a group of low islets to starboard was a reminder to keep well to the charted route: on its side, stern in the air, bows underwater, lay the vast rusting hulk of a steamship, its bridge and funnels pocked with holes. This was the 18,000-tonne *Santa Leonora*, wrecked on her maiden voyage in 1964. The holes were made by passing Chilean gunboats using her for target practice.

By afternoon, sure enough, the wind was up to twenty-five knots. We pulled into a perfectly protected lake-like inlet, explored by another yacht a few years earlier and now informally bearing its name: Caleta Dardé. Its shores were low and the trees upright. These were signs that the bay should be williwaw-free and the winds reasonable, so for a change we swung free at anchor.

Next day Smyth continued to trend north and, with the wind unusually having gone back to easterly, we were able to sail much of the day. But twelve miles out we found ourselves over on the left-hand side of the channel and needing to steer northeast as the channel briefly curved right. In no time the wind was up to thirty knots. The current was adverse, as well. For two hours, with the cold spray and wind stinging our faces, we battled with the engine on and our sails heavily reefed to make only a mile or so's progress. We had another of those conversations that would begin with Jenny's tentative, "Don't you think we should consider going back?"

Just where it looked as if we would in fact have to retreat, by using the binoculars to scan the surface of the sea we realized that if we could only get past that low point in the hills—Carnatic Bay, named after an old P&O steamer—we would lose the wind. We paid off to the left, found a glassy lee behind a small high island, and by the time we emerged back into the main channel, found the wind had almost gone.

We were now almost at the top end of Canal Smyth; conveniently to starboard was a wide inlet with, at its end, an enclosed pool. From Bahía Mallett it is only a short walk over low land to Canal Unión, which leads deep into the Andean Cordillera and terminates in the evocatively named Last Hope Sound. For centuries this was a portage place for the Alacaluf people, who could here save themselves thirty miles of paddling on their way to or from the interior. Because of its relative accessibility to sailing ships, the bay was later a popular stopping place for sailing ships and steamers. This, we presumed, accounted for the unusual presence of two large, now-rusting buoys marking hazards in the entrance of the bay and a broken-down framework tower on its northern point.

In Mallett it took us some time to find a location free of kelp. This is a long straggling form of seaweed that can grow in strands of ten metres or more. It is also often a warning indicator of shallow water. Small-boat anchors have difficulty penetrating it, and, as you swing and move at anchor, it has the annoying habit of tangling your propeller and rudder. Once we were safely secured, we pumped up the dinghy and went for a walk over the isthmus.

From the high point of the neck we looked inland to the mist- and snow-shrouded mountains and the maze of side-channels leading inland. The Spanish explorer Pedro Sarmiento stood exactly here on New Year's Day of 1580. He decided it was an appropriate spot and date to assert Spain's claim over the territory: a Mass was said, a cross erected, and the bay on the inland side of the peninsula was named Bahía Oración (Prayer Bay).

He was looking for Francis Drake. He thought the Englishman might come back this way after having passed through Magellan on that record-setting run in 1578, and after a subsequent season or so sacking Spanish settlements in Chile and Peru, which had earned him a place forever in Spanish folklore (*El Draque* came to be the equivalent of the English "bogeyman"). As he contemplated Canal Unión, Sarmiento must have been despondent in the knowledge of how easy it would be for a sailing ship to hide in these waters and never be detected. And what he was not to know was that instead of returning home through Magellan, Drake had continued westward to England. In fact he was already in the East Indies. One of Drake's support ships, the *Elizabeth*, commanded by Captain Winter, had indeed come past here, but six months earlier.

Among the knee-high sage grass were rotting fenceposts and other melancholy signs that the isthmus had once been inhabited. But that had been over a hundred years ago. A German sea captain, Herman Eberhardt, farmsteaded here for a few years starting in 1893, but he soon moved on to the upper reaches of Last Hope Sound. There he established a sheep estancia that still exists today and found, in a large cave, the remains of a giant prehistoric sloth called a mylodon.

Out here in the channels, we were in one of those rare parts of the world where man once tried to establish a foothold, failed, and where there is no evident reason for him ever to return.

Next day there was forecast an unusual southwesterly and sunshine. So as to slip out of Canal Smyth, which here trends northwest (to become Estrecho Nelson and enter the Pacific), we followed a set of doglegs also named by Fitzroy, in commemoration of the battle of Trafalgar: Paso Victoria (after HMS *Victory*), Estrecho Collingwood then Paso Farquhar (another captain at Trafalgar). These took us into the south end of Canal Sarmiento.

Outside in the ocean the wind probably was favourable, but here it was gusty on the beam whenever we passed low land to port and calm as soon as the hillsides steepened. We were alternately racing along with the starboard rail under, or becalmed with the sails slatting. In the late afternoon, we passed on our right a tight but safe-looking anchorage named after our American friend from Puerto Williams, Charlie Porter, but with the wind still acceptable we pressed on and near dusk we turned into a wide bay to port with the intriguing name Abra Lecky's Retreat. We carefully negotiated— in neutral—a kelp barrier into a small nook and dropped the anchor as darkness fell, a satisfying thirty-eight miles on the day's log.

Squire T.S. Lecky was yet another British sea captain, from the generation after Fitzroy's. As commander of the *Penguin* he surveyed these waters in 1872 but became much more famous for his book *Lecky's Wrinkles in Practical Navigation* (1881). For decades this was a kind of sailors' bible, combining explanations of celestial navigation with such words to the wise as, "It is as easy to be deceived in purchasing a sextant as in buying a horse," and, "There is nothing so distressing as running ashore, unless there is also doubt as to which continent the shore belongs."

We were stormbound for two days. We took bracing walks up the hills for views of the whitecaps on steely Canal Sarmiento, spent two hours pulling off long strands of kelp from the propeller by using a boat hook, and were consoled to some extent when we learned that *Ludus Amoris,* now some way ahead of us, was also waiting out heavy weather. Behind, another boat, also German, had now set out from Puerto Williams: Tom and Tatiana on *Break Point*.

The third day was so bright and warm and the winds so light that we decided—perhaps foolishly—to meander along entirely under sail, even if it meant we would not get very far. It was a busy days for ships: a freighter heading north, the big red Navimag ferry that plies once every ten days between Puerto Natales and Puerto Montt (and vice-versa), and a Chilean navy survey ship.

"Good morning *Bosun Bird,*" began the navy radio operator in perfectly accented English. "How is Victoria, and do they still serve afternoon tea at the Empress?"

It was strange to be talking to so many people after a week or more of hearing and seeing nobody, but from reading Tilman's account of sailing up here in the early 1950s it was clear that there was a lot less shipping now than before. In those days, we supposed, almost all communication between central Chile and the far south must have been by sea, but commercial aviation had displaced much of that business.

After only eleven miles, we turned sharp left into a narrow inlet a mile or so long, named in the RCC guide as Caleta Moonlight Shadow, and anchored stern-to at its head. I mentally applauded the pioneering spirit of the crew of the yacht that first ventured here "into the white" but wondered whether it was appropriate to name natural features in this Latin American country in this fashion; no Spanish speaker would have the slightest idea how to read the word "Moonlight." But then I thought that if Fitzroy had no such qualms, then who were we to complain.

Three kilometres of boggy walking across heath at the head of the bay took us to a point where we could see out into the open Pacific and across the broad inlet—Estrecho Nelson—that here cuts into the Patagonian archipelago at right angles. It is considered to be a possible route in from the sea for big ships. But it looked studded with small, but jagged and menacing, rocks and islets; they stood out sharply against a sea made silver by the setting sun cutting through storm clouds. Looking inland, a hundred miles of the Andean Cordillera, white and jagged as far as the eye could see, stretched across the horizon. Several of the peaks looked faintly familiar. I realized we were looking at the much-photographed and -visited Torres del Paine, but from an angle few people are privileged to enjoy. It wasn't just the angle that was special: for perhaps three hundred days a year the summits of those mountains were invisible from anywhere.

Next day the wind was thirty knots from the north to northwest, and the following morning we knew we had been right to stay put when we ran into a heavy leftover swell and a contrary current kicked up by the wind that had been pushing into Nelson. It eased once we were into the lee of Isla Vancouver. Another island of that name was our home; as we coasted along the dark and empty shores of this Vancouver Island, where we guessed no one might have set foot in decades, we recalled the bustle of Victoria and the four-lane island highway to Duncan and Campbell River.

The Canadian connection continued with our next anchorage, Puerto Mayne, a well-protected inlet on the east side of the channel. Captain Richard Mayne sailed these waters on HMS

Puerto Mayne, Chile.

Nassau in 1869, but earlier in his career he'd served aboard the *Plumper*, surveying the Gulf Islands of British Columbia and had Mayne Island named after him. It forms one shore of Active Pass, the narrow tidal narrows through which ferries from Vancouver to Victoria transit, and had been where we had learned to sail. From both Maynes you can see a Vancouver Island.

It was a still, cold, and clear night, the water and the steep mountains black all around us. All you could hear was an occasional creak or light clink of a halyard as *Bosun Bird* slumbered, and onshore the call of some strange bird. We were again 150 miles from the nearest human being. I was a little frightened by the isolation. But it was exciting, as well, to be in such a beautiful and wild place, to know we had got here by ourselves and would have to get out of here by ourselves.

The appropriately named Puerto Bueno was another perfect beautiful anchorage—or was it just because the weather was favouring us for a few days that it seemed idyllic? We washed in warm sunshine on a grassy slope where a stream gushed into the bay and bushwhacked inland to a still, peaty-brown, freshwater lake. This was one more place where the unfortunate Sarmiento, with the *Nuestra Señora de la Esperanza*, the *San Francisco*, the *Santiago*, and the *Nuestra Señora de la Guía* waited in the hope of catching Drake. From inside the bay you cannot see the outer channel. Even if Drake had come this way, he probably would have had a good chance of sailing past undetected. We supposed that, like Puerto Mayne, this had once been a favourite spot for coasters to spend the night, but now—at most—there might be one sailboat a year calling in, and the Alacalufs were long gone.

In the evening I performed what had now become a ritual. I was more and more conscious of how dependent we were on the engine, not so much for sailing up the channels—we could always tack, however painfully slow it might be—but for getting in and out of tight anchorages. I would lift off the engine cover, check the tension of the V-belt, squirt a little WD-40 into the alternator and onto the main electrical connections, make sure the impeller shaft was not slipping, scrutinize the oil level, and scan the body of the engine for oil leaks. Only after bidding good night to the engine did I feel comfortable going to bed myself.

TEOKITA (PUERTO PROFUNDO) TO PUERTO BUENO: 128 N.M.; 8 DAYS.

⁓ Until now, if the forecast was bad or there were whitecaps in the channel, we stayed put. We chose only the safest anchorages, ones that had been surveyed, and always attached lines to shore if it was practically possible. And we'd decided against a detour to Puerto Natales because it added 120 miles to the itinerary and meant having to pass twice through a difficult set of tidal narrows. But having come this far and with such effort, we decided now to be a little more daring and venture into the largely unsurveyed waters to the east of the recognized channel.

Barely had we exited the mouth of Puerto Bueno and begun to turn into Estero Peel when it became evident why this was not the favoured route. The winds were light but there were what looked from a distance like breaking waves. From closer up we could see they were bergy bits, moving out on the tide from the great glaciers that feed into Peel from the continental ice cap. As if to welcome us into these newly cold waters, a little squad of penguins followed us. A large aggressive skua, apparently fascinated by the flapping of the bright, red-and-white flag on our stern, kept closing in on it, veering away, and coming back.

We were aiming to anchor for the night in a bay close to the foot of the Amalia Glacier. This was the point at which Bill Tilman on *Mischief* had intended, in 1956, to launch his attempt on the first-ever crossing of the Patagonian Ice Field. He describes the scene:

> ...as we opened up the southeast arm, the glacier came into sight, a huge sheet of ice nearly two miles broad, cleft in its middle by a bald rocky hill, with its upper reaches shrouded in mist. [We] were profoundly impressed by its size and the way it flowed out into the deep waters of the fjord, suggesting to an observer the idea of an inexhaustible, overflowing abundance, an unmistakable hint of the vastness of the snowfield from which it came.

Motoring at four knots, we slowed gradually to a knot as the scattered miniature icebergs became more and frequent, and we found ourselves making long detours, looking for open water. With one finger on Tilman's narrative and an eye on the chart we eased our way ever so slowly into Amalia, hoping that any moment the glacier would open up before us. Soon I was sure that we must be past where Tilman had first seen it. But all we could make out were the scraped-bare mountainsides that once held the moving field of ice, and ever more loose brash ahead. It was clear that the glacier had receded at least a mile since 1956, possibly more, and we would not be able to get close enough to see it. It was little consolation that Tilman hadn't been able to reach the ice face either: at least he'd seen it. Turning around, we steered briefly up the main, north-going arm of Estero Peel, at whose head is another glacier.

Here Tilman had more success. With Charles Marriott he landed, crossed the Andes to Argentina and was back in two weeks. But while he was away, fellow-crewman W.A. Procter (to whom Tilman rather coolly refers only by his surname and initials, throughout his account, for reasons that will be apparent) decided to take *Mischief* farther up-inlet. Procter ended up running aground on a reef and had to unload six tons of pig-iron ballast before *Mischief* would float off again, buffeted all the while by strong in- and out-going currents and large ice floes. In the process, a bracket supporting the propeller shaft was irretrievably damaged and the engine rendered unusable. *Mischief* now had to find her way out of the channels by a complicated route under sail alone, much of it undertaken at night and in unsurveyed waters, and she limped to Valparaíso for repairs. Tilman's account of the voyage is a highly amusing one, but he concludes drily: "I will not pretend that at all times throughout this 20,000 mile voyage we were a band of brothers..."

It is not difficult to guess that the atmosphere on board, as they exited Peel, must have been tense. The shoal now bears the official name Angostura Mischief.

We should have known that if Amalia was clogged with ice, the upper reaches of Peel would be impossible. Soon, through the binoculars, we could see a solid white wall barring our way, and this time it wasn't just brash ice rising a foot or so above the surface: these were really large chunks that looked to be at least two or three metres high. Reluctantly, we retreated once more and found secure anchorage in a lake-like haven reached through a gap in the cliffs. For the first time in months we were bothered by flies, a sign both of spring approaching and of our gradual progress to the north. We did some laundry and hung it in the rigging. It would be another ten days before it dried.

Next day it was a real battle, still in the white: head winds of twenty-five knots, and the channel so narrow that each tack lasted barely five minutes. One fumbled rounding at the end of a board and we risked either heading straight into the wall or falling back and wasting the little progress we'd made since the last tack. As ever, once the wind had been up for a couple of hours, the current—regardless of what those little arrows on the chart said it was supposed to do—turned to run against us, as well, so that we'd sometimes go thirty minutes without making any perceptible progress. After eight hours and only sixteen miles covered, we reached off to the left into an officially unnamed inlet that another intrepid predecessor had informally called after his boat, Estero Plainsong. Anchoring was unusually worrying. The most suitable nook had large, mussel-covered rocks only a couple of metres off our starboard side, and Jenny had great difficulty in finding solid trees on shore; most were wet and rotten, a comment on the huge rainfall that this region receives.

For days we'd been tracking an enormous depression heading our way and next morning the radio and grib forecasts were frightening. But all was calm at daybreak. Uncomfortable in Plainsong, which had us broadside on to the expected direction of strongest wind, we decided to see if we could make another short run north to better shelter. A handwritten note from a friend, including a GPS reading, led us across a wide but protected unsurveyed approach, to the foot of a distinctive cone-shaped peak and a tiny south-facing indentation: the aptly named Caleta Pico.

Trees seemed to grow out of the seawater itself: there wasn't even a centimetre of beach. We dropped the anchor in deeper water than we like and very gingerly edged backward until we were only one and a half boat lengths from the trees. We laid out two

Downloading the weather forecast.

lines astern, and one from each bow. Unable actually to step ashore, so dense was the vegetation, Jenny had to tie these on from the dinghy. Over the bows we had a great view: an enormous cascade poured down five hundred metres of grey granite mountain, its top lost in the now-gathering cloud.

It rained for five days. There was no discernible lull, even for a few minutes, so that each morning we had to climb into the dinghy and bail it. The cascade grew by the hour. Most of the time, the wind blew hard, too. Through the binoculars we could see through the swirling rain that the open channel, to the south of us, was covered in whitecaps. Although we were almost under the trees of the mountain behind us, a swell came in around the point and every few minutes some wayward gust would blast us as well. To be safe, we laid out a second anchor and doubled up on one of our four shore lines, which was tied to a frail-looking shrub.

In Weather Zone Eight, which we had left behind us at Estrecho Nelson, the navy was reporting that winds of one hundred knots (well above hurricane strength) were coming through; we hoped *Break Point* was secured as snugly as we were. The log records, a typically promiscuous reading list: a pretentious book in Portuguese by Paulo Coelho that we had picked up at a junk sale in Puerto Williams, Margaret Atwood's *Life Before Man*, *Misteriosa Buenos Aires* in Spanish, and more Dostoyevsky. We played more games of Scrabble, but I was now on such a winning streak that Jenny asked to be allowed to play with eight letters. Jenny caught up on doing our accounts: we hadn't spent a cent, now, for two months. Just by leaving saucepans and other receptacles out in the cockpit to collect rain, we were able to top up our freshwater tanks.

At last, on Tuesday, October 10, the weather broke. It took us an hour and a half to extricate ourselves from Pico. Keen for a change of scenery, we motored all day in light winds: out of the north end of Canal Pitt and into another white section on the chart. Somehow things didn't quite look so deep here—there were little islets everywhere—so, following more handwritten notes, we moved very cautiously until the GPS told us we were near another possible anchorage, on the mainland side, called Caleta Colibrí (Hummingbird Cove).

The back route we had taken was quite devoid of any sign that humans even existed, but now there was an indication that we were entering waters that at some time in the not-too-distant past had been more frequented. We rowed to a beach at one end of the bay on which there was a vast pile of empty mussel shells and two or three wooden poles, indicating there had once been a shelter of some sort here. It had been years since a prohibition on mussel-gathering had been placed on nearly all of these waters, on account of the risk of Red Tide. Either the debris dated from the seventies or illegal mussel-gathering was still going on.

A front came through at 05:00, which meant that, waiting for things to settle, we were off late. We used the time by dialing up on the Iridium satellite phone, at the request of *Ludus Amoris*, a grib forecast for their area; they were now way ahead of us. We sailed out in light mist. This quickly dissipated, and for an hour or so we had glorious sailing across a sparkling blue sea, white spray flying. But, although we were here very close to the open sea and heading inland again, the flooding (i.e., rising) tide appeared to be running against us. We soon slowed. Close to an opening from the sea you expect the flood to move inward, the ebb outward: it was yet another example of the peculiar effects of the channels' complicated topography on winds and currents.

Next stop was an artificial-looking cut into the western shore of the enormous and mysterious Isla Wellington: Estero Dock. Mysterious because Wellington's rugged interior, almost perpetually shrouded in rainclouds and only recently photographed from the air, is still unexplored.

The entrance to Dock was wide but almost entirely blocked by a line of rocks, perhaps the terminal moraine of some long-gone glacier. The Admiralty Pilot warned, in its all-too-familiar way, that this inlet "should not be entered without local knowledge," but our RCC guide had an accurate drawing of the entrance, indicating exactly how much clearance, to port, should be given to the highest rock in the chain. With Jenny posted on the bows and looking anxiously over the side, we made our way over the sill without touching. Next day, in the familiar pattern, it was whitecaps all day in the open channel. By now we were blasé about such delays and were anyway happy just to be north of 50 degrees south for the first time in months.

To pass the day, we spent time on the radio catching up: *Ludus Amoris* was now twenty miles short of the Golfo de Penas; Tom and Tatiana on *Break Point* were slowly gaining on us and were at Moonlight Shadow; and a third German boat of which we had not heard for nearly a year, *Atlantis*, was today leaving Mar del Plata bound for Tierra del Fuego. *Atlantis*'s Inge and Ernst spoke only German, although the rule of the Patagonian Net was that it was to be in English. This led to some unintentionally comical moments when Wolfgang, from the net's home base, would ask the statutory, "Are there any medical emergencies or persons who need to check in first?"

Inge would reply with five minutes of German, not understanding she was jumping the queue; if *Ludus Amoris* and *Break Point* decided to respond in their own language, as well, our eventual burst of nonchalant English would provoke embarrassed silences.

One day, with almost no one else on the net, we asked Tom about the origin of his boat's name. His account was confused. He said he had originally been inspired by *Point Break*, a 1990s surfer movie with Patrick Swayze and Keanu Reeves. But the movie can't have made that much impact for Tom to have got the words the wrong way round; he admitted that he'd later rationalized the name as deriving from a computer programming term, which seemed to fit his and Tatiana's idea of taking a few years off work. It was all a bit strange: I couldn't imagine being so casual about naming a boat, nor could I see using a foreign language for it.

Leaving Dock, we dodged more glacier ice floating and readied ourselves for one of the narrowest sections of the entire voyage, through Paso Piloto Pardo, named after the Chilean tugboat captain who rescued Ernest Shackleton's expedition from the Antarctic ice (the sawn-off bow of his tug, the *Yelcho*, is now Puerto Williams's only civic monument). We were able to sail almost all the way, accompanied by porpoises. There is no great amount of current, but the turns are sharp and the steep-sided granite mountains create a sense of claustrophobia. It was easy to see why the Pilot mandates a one-way scheme for large vessels and adds: "Navigation at night is prohibited, even with moonlight and good visibility."

After a quiet night anchored off more mussel middens, I was doubtful about leaving in the morning; we could see white water only fifty metres away in the channel. But we were now nearing civilization again. Jenny was anxious to spend money and, hopefully, even find a few vegetables in the tiny settlement of Puerto Edén, now only sixteen miles away. Unusually, she argued for going on rather than staying put.

It was one of our worst days. The chop was even heavier than it looked, the wind (of course) was from dead ahead at twenty knots, and we had an adverse current of two knots. For two and a half hours we averaged only half a knot over the bottom. But I was still reluctant to concede defeat. We pulled into shelter having managed a meagre two miles.

Jenny was chastened but not to be deterred: still anticipating our imminent return to the bright lights, she upped our daily cookie ration from two to three and permitted us an extra slice of bread at lunch. *Ludus Amoris*, we learned, had had a similarly disappointing day: we commiserated together.

Next day it was two months since we had left Puerto Williams. By late morning, motoring along, we could see a dozen or so brightly painted wooden buildings at sea level on an island or peninsula to our left. I asked Jenny to start pulling the anchor chain out of its bow locker. For a moment I recalled the misty wet morning we had arrived here on the rusty *Río Baker*, nearly thirty years earlier. It was a brighter day, but Puerto Edén scarcely looked any bigger at all.

PUERTO BUENO TO PUERTO EDÉN: 149 N.M.; 14 DAYS.

⌢ Puerto Edén is built on the shores of a south-facing horseshoe bay on Wellington Island; it has no roads, just a boardwalk running along the shoreline, in the manner of some of the remoter villages on the coast of British Columbia. The only communication with the outside world is the big red Navimag ferry.

The first settlement here was a seaplane base, servicing the run from Puerto Montt to Puerto Natales and Punta Arenas, built in the 1930s. In the late 1960s the last remaining Alacaluf were offered free housing by the Chilean government and encouraged to move here. A dozen or so linger on in a group of yellow clapboard houses along the eastern shore of the bay.

The population today is about 160 and slowly declining. Local shell fishermen are still allowed to harvest mussels in certain designated and tested locations, but they must have every shipment checked for Red Tide in Puerto Natales or Puerto Montt. Many have decided it is no longer worth it. In summer, the Navimag deposits a few dozen tourists for an hour or so, and a small cruise ship, the *Skorpios III*, brings passengers for a morning, once a fortnight. Most people who have a regular job work for the government. There is an unnecessarily large modern school, with twenty students, a *carabineros* (police) detachment, a small navy post across the bay, a post office, and a government shop. The landscape is too steep, rugged, and heavily wooded to allow for any farming. It is difficult to see how the place will survive for another thirty years.

It didn't take long to find our way around. The most important person to know was Don José, a plump and balding man who ran the government shop, and who for years had served with the navy here.

"Don't worry," he said when we asked him if we could buy some more diesel. "We don't have any now, it's true. But there'll be some on the next Navimag from Natales. You see, they don't carry loose drums on the run from Puerto Montt, in case they break loose in heavy weather in the Golfo de Penas. We always have to ship in from the south."

But four days later, when the ferry came in, there was no diesel. Someone remembered having seen a few drums on the quayside as they had pulled out from Natales, but that was it. José scratched his head when we went to see him again.

"Well, I have an idea" he finally said. "But you must promise not to tell anyone, or we'll all be in trouble. If you go over to CONAF, you can ask them to lend you a hundred litres. Tell them I'll replenish their supply when the next boat comes in."

CONAF was the national park office; it maintained its own launch. On the net, *Break Point* was peremptorily informing anyone who would listen that they expected to find five hundred litres on hand when they arrived here in a few days' time; we decided to keep quiet.

There was no restaurant, but Doña María Vera was known to cook occasionally for government employees on various short-term missions to Edén. The first time we went to her place we found the living-room floor covered with what at first glance looked to be an exceptionally deep-pile brown carpet. In fact it was edible kelp, laid out to dry. The cheerful motherly María Vera nonchalantly cleared a space for us to sit at the table and didn't seem to mind when we inadvertently trod on the seaweed. We left with her two months' of dirty laundry to wash and put in a large order for fresh bread. I said she should advertise her services more aggressively to the occasional passing yacht and, in return for a free lunch for both of us, we painted a sign for her to hang outside: "Meals–Fresh Bread–Laundry–Crafts." I suggested she needed a name for her establishment.

"Since we're in Eden, why don't you call it Adam and Eve's?" I said jocularly.

< (top) The waterfront, Puerto Edén, Chile. (bottom) Doña María Vera, Puerto Edén, Chile.

She either didn't get the joke or thought me sacrilegious.

"Who is Adam? And my name is María Vera, not Eva," she finally said. "Let's Just call it Edén. I like that."

Shopping was a very haphazard affair. Don José's shop was large but nearly empty, and it was a matter of walking from one house to another, following directions, to see who had what. We found a camp gay man (he was known in the village simply as "*el gay*") who would sell us eggs. And up at the Almacén Lolo there was a lady who had a dozen or so chickens at the very bottom of a large freezer chest. They were stuck together in rock-hard clumps and we had repeatedly to throw one such boulder onto the wooden floor so as to separate out the individual chickens. Lolo was also the home of a spoiled tabby cat called Jacinta.

"Yes," said Sra Lolo, picking the purring cat up and stroking her. "And you have a boyfriend, don't you? Very handsome he is. Jack's his name, and he's a captain, too..."

Captain Jack was a black and white mongrel from a yacht that had passed this way a couple of months previously; later we would get to know him all too well.

Up at the school library we were allowed free Internet use, and there was also a little English book-swap, just like at Puerto Williams. We were truly impressed at the lengths the Chilean government had gone to, not just to stock a decent library in such a remote place but also to orchestrate Internet access (and free!) for the local people; later we learned that this was typical, and part of an ambitious and enlightened countrywide program.

Desperate for reading matter we unloaded our moisture-swollen Dostoyevskys and took on an equivalent thickness of new paper-backs, without worrying too much about the quality. This time around we collected some Stephen King, a collection of black-humour feminist stories called *Tart Noir*, a copy of *King Rat* missing the cover and first chapter, and a heavy-looking *History of the British Isles*, adapted from an old TV series we had not seen.

We had two or three days of brilliant sunshine, and the yellow-painted fishermen's boats, beached in groups or puttering across the channel against a backdrop of steep and snow-capped mountains, made for a colourful spectacle. But I knew this wasn't typical weather. On Thursday, October 19, I noted in the log:

...a clear night but the forecast is for strong winds to come.

Next day we laid out our spare CQR anchor at a 30-degree angle to the main Bruce anchor and, as the wind built, we retreated on board. On the evening navy report, the Evangelistas light was experiencing fifty knots with gusts to seventy-five, while Cabo Raper, one hundred miles north of us, was reporting forty-two knots, this with the main depression still to arrive.

The wind screamed all night, the halyards clanked, and I did not sleep at all. We adjusted the GPS to sound an alarm should we start to drag anchor, but it was frightening as the boat heeled first one way then the other, swinging from left to right and back again, at a speed you could sense from below decks. There were only fifty metres of open water between us and the head of the bay, to windward, but spray was breaking over the bows. On the two or three occasions when I was able to claw my way forward and feel the nylon anchor line, it was taut as a steel rod. The electricity failed on shore, which removed our reference points and made it more difficult to see if we might be dragging or if the wind had shifted direction. It seemed to me that the wind held above fifty knots for maybe six or seven hours, with periods of sixty or seventy. Later we heard that the Navimag had sought shelter all night in Puerto Ríofrío, six miles south of Edén. Don José said he had looked out for us.

"I thought you were done for."

⮑ After a week we had exhausted all the shops and *Break Point* was getting perilously close, still asking insistently not just about the diesel (of which we knew there to be none), but also about the availability of fresh water. As we were in an area where it rains about four metres a year, we thought this unnecessary. It was time to be off again.

A few miles up ahead was another tortuous section: a zigzag through a chain of islands known as the Angostura Inglesa. Tidal currents here could reach eight knots so it was important to pass at the right time. We arrived early, spent a couple of hours waiting at anchor in a protected cove at the south entrance, and set off through at the time indicated by the tide tables. In the tightest section, on an island, is a white statue of the Virgin Mary that can easily be mistaken, at a distance, for a navigational beacon. As always in these circumstances I found I had little time to admire the scenery. Here it was a matter of checking every minute or so to compare what I was seeing with what my finger was tracing on the chart, all the while studying the shore to gauge whether we were in strong current.

We emerged into Canal Messier—two to three miles wide— which leads due north into the Golfo de Penas. The winds weren't bad, but by now it was late afternoon. We reached across the north wind to the east side of the channel and into a tight, heavily wooded bay called Caleta Sabauda. It was a change to move out, at least temporarily, from waters explored by Fitzroy and other British navigators. Many of the names hereabouts come from the round-the-world research voyage of the Italian corvette *Magenta*, from 1865 to 1868; Sabauda is the Latin name for the House of Savoy.

Far to the south, a depression of 938 millibars was careering its way toward the Drake Passage. I'd never heard of a low this powerful, and in fact our barometer didn't go nearly that far down. We recalled how one morning a boat reporting the pressure in Ushuaia had cheerfully said it was at "G," i.e., the "G" of the "Made in Germany" on his gauge; today it would have been at the "Y." Fortunately, the South Pacific High was relatively weak: otherwise

it was possible to envisage a difference of one hundred millibars, which would have meant gale- and storm-force winds over
an expanse of at least 1,500 miles of the Chilean coastline. But we
decided to stay put for a day anyway.

Break Point had reached Edén and was reporting next morning,
unsurprisingly, their consternation at finding that Don José had no
diesel; *Atlantis* was in Puerto Deseado; and Bob, a radio amateur
from Port Stanley, reported that a week earlier the wreckage of a
small fibreglass yacht had been found near Steeple Jason Island, off
West Falkland: Antoine's little *Moustique*.

In the afternoon we fought our way up through dense vegetation above our anchorage for a view over the now-rough Angostura
Inglesa and north up the channel. Warming up over tea after our
walk, we researched the next day's run. The Admiralty Pilot on
Canal Messier, which we now faced, was to the point as usual: "The
area is subject to almost continual rainfall, with overcast weather
and strong gales. Violent squalls descend from the mountains."

Our first day out from Sabauda the wind was north at fifteen
knots. We probably could have sailed but we sensed Messier was
not a forgiving place and decided it was best to resort to power if
it meant gaining a few extra miles. An hour or two out, we passed
a very rusty freighter proceeding south. Or was it? The longer I
looked, the more immobile and rusty the vessel seemed. It was
actually a wreck, and it wasn't going anywhere: the Greek freighter
Captain Leonidas, perched horizontally and (apart from the rust)
apparently in good working order atop a shoal. Now that we were
here, I recalled also having seen it from the *Río Baker* in 1979, except
its white paint job at that time was as good as new.

Anchored that night, we encountered the first yacht since *Ludus
Amoris* had overtaken us in the Strait of Magellan a month earlier:
Starfire, from Victoria. She was a beautiful, fifteen-metre, white-
painted wooden ketch of classical lines, with an overhanging
transom. Once we were over the initial surprise of encountering

another Canadian boat in such a remote location, we were barely fazed at all when, in chatting, we learned that Kaspar and Trish were the former owners of our favourite sail chandlery in Victoria, Sailtrend. They had in 1981 rigged *Tarka the Otter*. Trish treated us to a gourmet, three-course dinner, with pork chops and drinks served in real crystal from a glass cabinet. On the cabin walls were sepia photographs of *Starfire* in full flight, winning Swiftsure races in the 1950s. It was all very nice and historic, Trish agreed, but the lines and balance of the boat were so demanding that—even with her fifteen-metre length—it had been impossible to accommodate a double bed.

Gradually we worked our way north up Messier, spending two or three days rain- or wind-bound for every day underway. At Caleta Connor we passed the time by carving the name *Bosun Bird* and the date into a piece of scrap wood and nailing it to a tree that marked the passage of boats from as long ago as forty years: there was the intriguingly named *Nine of Cups* and over here was *Mahina Tiare*, skippered by an old mentor last encountered twenty years earlier. Another evening, we had the strangely satisfying experience of working our way into a narrow inlet that just does not appear on charts. We had more handwritten notes on the area, passed down to us by a French yacht called *Chaski*, so found ourselves referring to it as Caleta Chaski. As we manoeuvred in reverse to set our anchor, otters cavorted on some nearby rocks, pausing occasionally to look over at us.

Ten days out from Edén we had most of Messier behind us. We tied ourselves into the very tight Caleta Lamento del Indio, a recommendation of our ever-present Italian companions. I found the name rather strange—it means "Lament of the Indian"—until I read Mariolina and Giorgio's explanation. This is the title of a 1970s-era song by "...the Inti-Illimani...the most famous Chilean ethnic band, appreciated all over the world for its high-level discography and commitment."

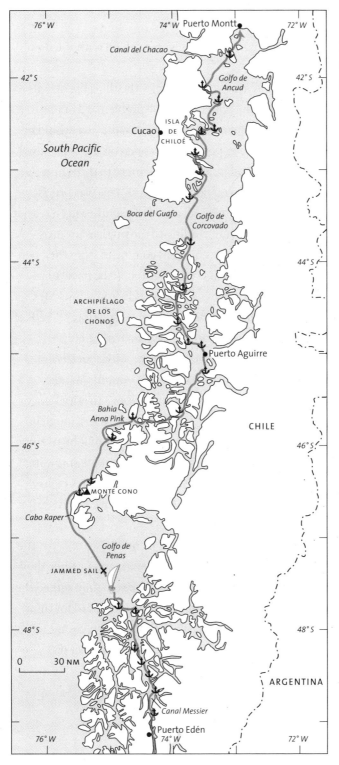

The Chilean channels: Puerto Edén to Puerto Montt.

We didn't think the name was likely to catch on with the dour local fishermen.

We were close now to the Golfo de Penas: the third big obstacle we'd identified on the long haul north. The problem wasn't just that here, for the first time since leaving the Atlantic, we would be exposing ourselves for a long period to the open ocean—the next refuge was about a hundred miles on—but, more to the point, the prevalent winds were between north and west. This was precisely the course we needed to lay to break out of the southeastern corner of the gulf, where we now were. Adding to the unpleasant prospect was the shallowness of the gulf. Seas coming in from the open ocean tended to pile up and reflect back, and could be particularly dangerous when they met a heavy outgoing tide from Canal Messier. As usual, it was no use turning to the Pilot for consolation: "Winds of great force, and very heavy seas, are experienced in the gulf."

We were up at 05:00 to scrutinize the gribs with special care. We needed, we estimated, thirty-six hours of westerly winds shifting to southwesterly, and preferably not above twenty knots. There was a brief window coming, but it didn't look as though it would last very long. We decided to make the most of it by heading west across the mouth of the channel to a very hopeful-sounding anchorage, Caleta Ideal. This would save us a dozen miles or so when we truly came to leave and would also improve the angle for leaving the gulf.

It was a bright sunny day, the winds light, and as we entered the broad tree-ringed bay, *Break Point* came up on the VHF radio. They were out in the main channel, about to overtake us. They agreed the window was short but they were prepared to motor hard for thirty hours or more, which we were not. We bade them bon voyage and took what we thought was a well-earned siesta in the cockpit.

PUERTO EDÉN TO CALETA IDEAL: 110 N.M.; 9 DAYS.

10

Wizards, Witches, and Ghost Ships

FOR THIRTEEN DAYS, we got up anxiously at sunrise every morning to download weather forecasts. The weather window did not come. The wind stayed in the north or northwest, or went calm.

One day a twenty-five-metre luxury yacht called *Leonore*, registered in Jersey, arrived from the north. The owner was an evidently successful investment banker but the paid crew, Kiwis Adrian and Jenny, were so desperate for some relief that they invited themselves over for dinner and brought with them two bottles of wine.

"The high life, mate? Not all it's cracked up to be. I gotta say, we'd rather be on a boat your size. You know what? We've got so many flippin' labour-saving devices, half of which aren't working at any given time, that we spend all day fixing them."

Adrian's Jenny chimed in, "And then there's the skipper. Likes his three-course dinner every evening, prime lamb or beef from the freezer, fine. But you know what? His wife's a vegetarian. That means two separate meals to be cooked every night, not counting ours..."

The captain and his wife indeed sounded peculiar. They separately called us up for long and rambling chats on the radio, ignored our invitation to come on over, and conspicuously failed to reciprocate. Jenny from *Leonore* told us that her boss spent half his time on the Satphone checking his share prices.

Gales came and went. It rained, hailed, and blew. One day Cabo Raper lighthouse, seventy miles north, was reporting fifty knots of sustained winds, but the next day was calm. On the news, we heard that an inter-island barge had capsized south of Chiloé and there were a dozen or more drowned.

We talked repeatedly with the navy personnel at Faro San Pedro, only a few miles away from us; they were friendly and several times called up Raper on our behalf to get the local weather conditions. Meanwhile, with Wolfgang away on holiday, Tom from *Break Point* mounted what Jenny unkindly called a putsch, commandeering the Patagonian Net and running it mostly in German; we were not amused.

When really bad weather threatened, we laid out an extra anchor. There really wasn't much else to do. Only at extreme low tide was there one small beach on one side of the bay, where we made a couple of runs ashore to load fresh water and burn rubbish. Otherwise there was nowhere to land. We played yet more Scrabble, read a lot, slept a lot.

⌇ The longer you dither, the more difficult it is to actually make a decision. But on the night of November 13 the navy was forecasting winds from the southwest to south at twenty-five to thirty knots, gusting forty to forty-five: a bit strong, but at last the wind was now forecast from the right direction. For once Jenny, who had lost a dozen Scrabble games in a row, was adamant, "Time to go."

Out in the mouth of Canal Messier next morning it was blowing westerly at twenty-five knots, with frequent squalls. Disappointed there was no south in the wind, we decided to duck into a small nook behind the San Pedro lighthouse to see how things developed.

As we worked our way in, through a minefield of barely visible rocks, a red inflatable zipped out to see us. I was distracted by having to steer but I understood from the crew's shouts that this was a diving expedition, looking for the wreck of Lord Anson's *Wager*, lost here in May 1741. It would have been nice to talk to them but the time wasn't quite right. They waved toward where they were camped, on the beach, but our chart showed perilously shallow water, and we carried on to the deeper water of Puerto Escondido.

A rapid front brought a hailstorm, but soon the sun was out again and the wind down. Cabo Raper was reporting only southwest at seventeen knots, and a ship out in the gulf confirmed it. Out we went again—only to run into yet another fierce squall that had us careering back across the mouth of Messier on our way to Lamento del Indio, last seen fourteen days earlier. Only by evening did things look to have settled once more. We came abeam the San Pedro light at nine o'clock and set a course into the gloom, to the northwest and the open sea.

The subsequent night was one of the worst I have ever spent at sea. We soon left the lee of the land and started reaching through an area of short steep swells that seemed to come from every direction. It was necessary to hand-steer but, with my eyes fixed on the wildly swinging, red-lit compass it wasn't long before I started to feel queasy. It had been many months since we had been in seas of this size. At about 23:00 the wind began to pick up to twenty-five knots. I called Jenny from below to help me put a third reef in the mainsail and steady us a little.

To reef you first have to head up a little into the wind so that the pressure is taken off the mainsail and it begins to luff (flap). You make sure the outer end of the boom is held up (with the topping lift), and you then release the mainsail halyard a short distance so that you can gather up canvas all along the foot of the sail. You secure the surplus to the boom and then tighten up on the halyard again. With the sail area thus reduced, the boat offers less resistance to the wind and you sail more steadily and more slowly.

Tonight, for the first time ever, as the main was coming down, its luff (leading edge) forming a series of loose Ss, one of those Ss was blown in front of one of the mast steps, about halfway up the mast. As a result, the sail could neither be pulled up nor let down and risked flogging itself to shreds.

I thought for a few moments, then halfheartedly asked Jenny, "Do you want to go up and free it?"

To which the answer was an unsurprising and emphatic, "You know I don't like heights."

Feeling more nauseated by the second, I passed the tiller to her, carefully climbed out of the cockpit onto the swaying side-decks—bereft of forward motion, *Bosun Bird* was rolling horribly—and, secured by a short tether to the wire jackstays that run along the deck just for this purpose, made my way forward to the mast. I uncleated the halyard of the stay-sail, which was not in use, secured it to my chest harness, and looked wearily up into the darkness, where the mast was whipping back and forth at random. At the signal Jenny tensioned the halyard and, running it around a winch, made ready to secure my climb.

I was used to going up the mast but had never done so out at sea, still less in twenty-five knots of wind, at night, and in cross-swells like these, which every few seconds were sending the tip of the mast weaving around in complicated patterns. After each long upward step—made more difficult by my cumbersome foul-weather gear—I had to hang on for twenty or thirty seconds, hugging the mast with both arms, while the motion settled a little. After ten minutes I reached the point where the sail was jammed. My arms were weak and I felt ready to vomit at any moment. I picked at the sail ineffectually with one hand, holding on with the other. Nothing. The white nylon was stretched too tautly to be just pried away. I realized there was no choice. I'd have to time it perfectly, let go of the mast and pull at the S with both hands and my body weight.

For a moment I thought it wasn't going to give. I leaned with all my weight and pulled so hard I thought the sail might rip. As it started to ease its way free I shouted to Jenny, "Hang on!" and gave a final desperate tug. I swung for a moment completely free. Jenny took most of the strain as I banged back into the mast and slid down it. I collapsed in an undignified retching heap.

The sail was free and the waves were washing over the side-decks so frequently and copiously that the mess was soon gone. I crawled to my bunk, placing a saucepan handily on the cabin sole, and spent the rest of the night trying to sleep and ward off further bouts of sickness while Jenny steered. The Gulf of Sorrows was living up to its name.

By dawn, when I emerged into the cockpit to spell Jenny off, we were close-hauled in light winds, with the steep wooded hills of the Tres Montes peninsula ahead. The forecast now was for a wind switch to the northwest, at up to twenty-five knots, which would make it very hard to get around the exposed Cabo Raper and into the first available secure anchorage. But if we gave up, reached away to the east, and made for one of the secure anchorages on the north shore of the gulf, it would be very difficult to get out in any kind of westerly wind at all. We had visions of another two weeks of playing Scrabble. So we persevered and were rewarded by the winds remaining light to moderate in the west.

Soon we were off the dramatic, rock-strewn headland that is Cabo Raper. I read that it owes its rather unlikely name (pronunci-

Cabo Raper.

ation "rap-AIR") to Captain F.V. Raper who had surveyed the River
Ganges in 1808 before venturing into Patagonian waters. A very
solid, heavily engineered lighthouse with its accompanying house-
like structure, white with a red roof, sits on a built-up ledge fifty
metres above sea level, just out of the reach of the heavy rollers
that surge in endlessly. The place is far too exposed to be served by
any boat, the cliffs too steep even for helicopters to approach, so
the British engineer who built the light in 1914, George Slight,
constructed a short railway to it from the head of a protected
inlet inside the gulf.

This is a place not only of notoriously rough weather but also
of great oceanic upwellings that bring shoals of fish and small
organisms to the surface; they attract whales, other large marine
creatures, and diverse bird life. For several hours we sailed
through swooping albatrosses, less beautiful and heavier Giant
Petrels, and delicate Cape Petrels: their geometrically patterned,

black-and-white wings earn them the Spanish name *dameros* (chessboards).

Now we were back in the wake of the *Beagle*. Unlike *Bosun Bird*, she didn't come up the channels, which were too narrow for a large ship to manoeuvre, but from the open ocean:

> DECEMBER 30, 1834: We anchored in a snug little cove at the foot of some high hills, near the northern extremity of Tres Montes. After breakfast the next morning the party ascended one of these mountains, which was 2400 feet high. The scenery was remarkable.

The cove in question is today called Caleta Suárez; at its entrance is the tall, cone-shaped pinnacle that Darwin climbed. In perfectly still conditions, we dropped anchor in the late evening to pass a well-deserved quiet night. The only disappointment was, in the fading light, seeing some plastic debris on shore: the first garbage of any sort that we had seen since leaving Puerto Williams ten weeks earlier. It was a sign that we were now entering more frequented regions.

The *Beagle*'s naturalist was restless here, evidently glad that the ship's long sojourn in the south was nearly over:

> JANUARY 1, 1835: The new year is ushered in with the ceremonies proper to it in these regions. She lays out no false hopes: a heavy north-western gale, with steady rain, bespeaks the rising year. Thank God, we are not destined here to see the end of it, but hope then to be in the Pacific Ocean, where a blue sky tells us there is a heaven...

Next day for us was a beautiful run north in the open ocean, with rugged cliffs and headlands to starboard, and glinting seas. Reaching along gently in these conditions we experienced a sense of freedom that we'd forgotten in the often claustrophobic channels, although an ironbound rocky shore like this to leeward at 47 degrees south was not a comfort. In the late afternoon, with fifteen miles on the log, we turned into a long and narrow fjord with a small lake at its end: Caleta Cliff. Later, a rusty fishing boat, the *Juan Antonio II*, joined us: the crew waved cheerily as they adjusted their lines and pulled themselves in close to the beach.

Next day, with a bad forecast, the *Juan Antonio*'s crew invited us to come over and raft up beside them. As we'd discovered farther south, it was always wise to take the fishermen's advice, so, in gathering rain, we manoeuvred our way gingerly in, put out every fender we had, and tied up snugly beside them.

Over the next few days, as flurries of white water whipped over the surface of our "lake," we realized we were in the only quiet patch of water. You might think that working fishermen would look down on rich foreigners who were here for fun, but the crew of the *Juan Antonio* were some of the friendliest and most open people we have met. All seven of them crammed into our tiny cabin, bringing as gifts not only two large gutted conger eels, but a box of herbal tea, some dried peas, and a bucket full of abalone. It's a cliché, but true all the same: the poorer people are, the more generous they often are, as well.

The *Juan Antonio* was based at Quellón, in southern Chiloé.

"We've been here for the best part of a month," the captain said. "But in twenty-three days we've had only five when it's been calm enough to fish."

They went after *bacalao*, which confused me as this word normally translates as "cod." Here it means Chilean sea bass (also known as Patagonian toothfish), a very large fish—two to three metres in length—whose exploitation is banned in many parts of the world, and which fetches high prices.

"But for the past two weeks a *cachalot*—a sperm whale—has been scaring them off; we've seen him, he's enormous...so we've been going after the conger instead."

The crew of the Juan Antonio II.

We asked about the economics of fishing this coast.

"Precarious, very precarious. Conger fetches—what?—1,000 pesos (2 USD) a kilo in Chiloé? Once we've deducted all our expenses—food, diesel, lines, nets—the *patrón* takes 50 per cent of earnings. The rest we split eight and a half ways. I'm the skipper, so I take two shares, the engineer one and a half, the other five one each."

One of the younger hands chimed in, without malice, "Sometimes, after three months at sea, there's not enough for the bus fare home."

But the *Juan Antonio*'s was a happy crew. As they brought us mug after mug of tea, and plates of freshly baked *sopaipilla* pastries, they joked about each other's cooking abilities (everyone took it in turns in the galley), and they argued intelligently but good-naturedly about politics. Like the rest of the country, they were divided down the middle over Pinochet and the years of dictatorship, but, "You have to say it: life for us is better than it was for our parents."

They'd all had at least a year or so of secondary education; they knew where Canada was. And although they were fishermen, they were passionate about the environment and fully aware of the dangers of over-exploiting the country's fragile fish stocks. They were genuinely surprised and concerned when we told them how rare the Patagonian toothfish was globally.

In the evenings we listened to Puerto Montt Radio, the naval station that now drowned out its sister to the south, Magallanes Radio. In the short time allotted prior to the weather forecast, fishing boats from all over the coast clamoured to check in, as they are required to do legally. It was farcical hearing boats shouting over one another to be heard, and there was even the odd foreign yacht pleading in brave but stilted Spanish. The *Juan Antonio*'s skipper shrugged. On any given evening, half of the boats at sea were left out, and so there didn't seem much point in getting aggravated about it; in any case, they said, they didn't want to have to depend on the navy.

Today as I turn to their carefully written names in our visitors' book, I feel proud and privileged that we met the crew of the *Juan Antonio*, and that they accepted us as friends in that remote bay on the edge of the Pacific.

CALETA IDEAL TO CALETA CLIFF: 117 N.M.; 2 DAYS.

~ Two more long days in the open ocean—thirty-seven miles, then thirty-five—took us first to an edgy lonely anchorage at the foot of towering granite peaks on the hauntingly named Skyring Peninsula, then into the much larger Bahía Anna Pink, which leads back into the next section of protected channels.

A pink is defined in my dictionary as "a sailing vessel with a narrow, overhanging transom"; the *Anna* was one of two such ships assigned to Admiral Anson's 1740–1744 circumnavigation of the globe as "victuallers." This was in most senses a disastrous expedition, with only five hundred men of the original fleet complement of 1,900 surviving, but there was some redemption in the capture of the annual Acapulco to Manila galleon, the *Nuestra Señora de Covadonga*. One and a half million pieces of eight were seized, and forty thousand ounces of silver.

Things had got off to a bad start when the five hundred soldiers Anson had decided he required had to be recruited from invalids at the Chelsea hospital: many had to be carried aboard on stretchers. As they headed south into the Atlantic the ships were struck by typhoid, then malaria and scurvy. French spies tipped off the Spaniards that the English were coming. In Le Maire and off Cape Horn, Anson ran into weather that was appalling even by that region's standards, provoking Captain (later Admiral) Saumarez to write gloomily in his log, "Really, life is not worth pursuing at the expense of such hardships."

The *Severn* and the *Pearl* were blown back into the Atlantic and straggled home via Brazil. The *Wager*, her captain drunk, was wrecked on the southern shores of the Golfo de Penas. There followed a *Lord of the Flies* saga with more drunkenness, mutinies, and at least one murder; a few of the *Wager*'s crew, including Foul Weather Jack, eventually made it to England via circuitous routes. The *Anna* lost contact with the main fleet in the same storm as the *Wager*, wandered haphazardly around, her rigging in tatters, and limped into the bay that now bears her name. After several months of refitting, she sailed again and rejoined Anson at the Juan Fernández Islands.

Most likely the *Anna* anchored, working into unknown waters under sail, in an easily entered southern indentation now named Puerto Refugio. We chose a more protected location in a steep-sided fjord of bare and streaked quartz to the north, with a soft sand beach at its head: Puerto Millabú.

This, a few months earlier, had been the site of a modern-day drama that echoed that of the *Anna*. We'd followed some of it by radio but only learned the full story weeks later. The French yacht *Jolie Brise*, manned by an elderly man and his younger wife, had been entering Millabú when a fire broke out in her galley—perhaps as a result of a leaking propane tank or hose, it was never quite clear. The fire burned through at least one hose carrying seawater and the boat started to flood. Her crew managed to run her into the shallows at the head of Millabú where she settled, stuck in the sand and her decks awash. They inflated their life raft, paddled it to shore, and spent the next two weeks living in it, on the beach, venturing out to the yacht periodically when the tide was low and the conditions calm, to rescue what they could.

Prior to the disaster, they had periodically been checking in with Wolfgang and the net. When there was a long interval with no radio contact and no sightings, the navy was alerted. An aerial search was mounted, the couple were rescued and taken to Chacabuco, a small town on the mainland. The boat was all they had. Eventually they were able to mount a salvage expedition, but by the time they got back to the *Jolie Brise* most items of any value had been stripped; the navy eventually floated the wreck for them, towed it to Chacabuco, and hauled it out.

Like most such steep-walled fjords, Millabú was gusty when it was blowing hard outside, as it did next day: the wind would rico-chet all the way down it, bouncing off the steep walls so that it would come at us first from one cliff, then the other. But there were lulls in the wind and the rain. We were able to fill up our water tanks from a stream on shore and took a walk on the sandy beach at the head of the tannin-stained shallows. Our friends on the *Juan Antonio* had told us there were secret fuel storage tanks hidden in the woods, for the use of the navy, but the undergrowth looked as dense as everywhere else and there were no paths, no sign that people went ashore here except very occasionally.

We sailed due east now to reinsert ourselves in the channels, choosing a little-used, narrow route appropriately named the Canal Abandonados. Puttering along under power one morning, feeling rather pleased with ourselves for having calculated the tidal currents so well that they lifted us to nearly eight knots of speed for a couple of hours, we heard the buzz of a distant aircraft.

Gradually it got louder and then we saw, up ahead and only a hundred metres above the water, a twin-engined Cessna apparently heading right for us. They made one pass, then turned around and swept back. I realized they might want to talk to us. Jenny went below, switched on the VHF and, sure enough, the plane came up on Channel 16. Over the next ten minutes, as they made two or three more passes, lower each time, we learned to our alarm that this was the navy, and that they were actually looking for us. We'd called Cabo Raper as we passed, ten days earlier, but hadn't found anyone to talk to since that point; we could have asked the *Juan Antonio* to check in for us, but then they'd have had to check in, too. The aircraft's crew seemed friendly enough but obviously found it difficult to understand how it was that we had covered such a small distance in such a long period: they kept asking if we were alright. Finally, with a polite *"Adiós,"* they flew off. We felt guilty for having put the navy to such inconvenience and expense, but then reflected that we hadn't done anything wrong; we'd just moved rather slowly.

The mountains around us were now less gloomy, the channels wider, and, as we headed into Canal Errazuriz, we started to feel we were on the homestretch. We turned briefly off the main channel to detour around a chain of low islands where yet another yacht of our acquaintance had met near-disaster earlier in the season: the Belgian *Olimir* (crewed by Olivier and Mireille, hence the name) had simply not seen a rock in their way, ripped half their keel off, and had to be rescued in a near-sinking state. Later, the navy fined them for using improper charts. It also transpired that poor

Mireille, on the helm at the time, was legally blind. The navy was even less amused.

At Caleta Rosita, it even started to feel warm. On a sunny beach in the bay a family was encamped, evidently for the season; their small, yellow-and-red fishing boat was tied up to a makeshift jetty, and they waved cheerfully at us as we anchored. Earlier in the day, we'd seen several of the sets of bright fluorescent buoys and floating walkways that indicate *salmoneras*, or fish farms. Not only were we moving into summer, we were getting close to civilization again. On Sunday, November 26, three and a half months out from Puerto Williams and a month from Puerto Edén, we came abeam only the second set of houses we had seen, Puerto Aguirre.

Aguirre, which is located on the southern tip of a small island, has a population of over a thousand, which makes it, when compared with Puerto Edén's diminishing 150 or so, a metropolis. The clapboard village straggles steeply down a hillside over-looking a little harbour with an L-shaped concrete wharf, where a landing-craft from the mainland calls in twice a week. Unlike at Edén, there's a road, too, along which three or four pickups ply. It leads to a smaller settlement called Caleta Andrade, where small, yellow-painted fishing boats are strewn on the dark sand beach. Traditionally, the people lived off harvesting then packing mussels, but the phenomenon of Red Tide has crippled that industry and most people were now involved, in one way or another, with the booming *salmonera* industry.

From here onward, we would encounter these complexes of semi-submerged cages anchored to the sea bottom, blocking many of the choicest anchorages. This was inconvenient for us, but we could hardly complain, given the evident importance of the industry to the local economy. By some accounts Chile had, over the past decade, cornered half the world market for farmed sea salmon, and Chiloé, where the industry is centred, was now seeing prosperity for the first time in its history.

Puerto Aguirre, Chile.

But salmon farming, which had been vigorously encouraged in the last years of President Pinochet in an attempt to reinvigorate the precarious economy of the far South, was controversial. We had a quiet beer at El Puerto—the only bar where it was more or less acceptable for women to be seen—with a garrulous and nearly unintelligible fish worker on his day off.

"These *salmoneras*, I shouldn't say it...but those greens, those ecologians, do you have them in Canada?...you know who I mean. Cunt—pardon my language— they're right! Yes sir, they're right. You see, these farms they contaminate so much, all that fish shit on the bottom—imagine it, sir—that every two years they have to move them. They ruin everything, then they move on. You wouldn't believe it..."

Later, a diver paid to maintain the nets and cages that protect the salmon from predators told us there were other problems, as well. Most of the farms were owned by large multinational outfits, unions were banned, wages were poor, and safety precautions were lax.

We were directed to the school, where (as we now expected) there were computer terminals open to the public for Internet use. As we chatted to the principal, he told us that at the island's other school—at Caleta Andrade—the Canadian Embassy in Santiago had just outfitted a small computer room. When we walked out there to see it, where we were proudly shown around, and we took pictures of the little centre, along with its posters made by the children, linking Canada and Chile on a coloured-in world map.

We were disappointed to find that no diesel fuel was available. As traditional fishing and mussel-gathering had almost disappeared, the only use people had for boats was for small runabouts to zip from one *salmonera* to another. These were powered by outboards, which took ordinary gasoline. But we stocked up with eight kilograms of specially baked, long-life bread, a frozen chicken, and fresh nectarines and cherries that had us drooling, so short of fresh fruit had we been for so long.

From Aguirre we crossed the five-mile-wide Canal Moraleda, which seemed exposed to us after so long in much narrower, higher-sided waterways. We entered a maze of channels to its west that would allow us to work our way farther up in more protected waters. As we did so, we glimpsed a white sail in the distance. Later we figured out it must be Peter, a German friend of Wolfgang's, on his way south.

It rained heavily at Caleta Canal, and we stayed a while, waving to the occasional fishing boat that came and went in the gloom. The log records that in our ever-lengthening series the captain beat the crew at Scrabble by a score of 307 to 305. It was now the end of November and we had come about 10 degrees north: it was a lot warmer, and we decided to take off the clear-plastic double-glazing that we'd installed eight months earlier to help keep the boat warm and minimize condensation.

On December 1, after an utterly still night, we rose to a spectacular dawn. On the net, Jenny today served as a relay between Wolfgang and Noel, an English net regular whom we'd first spoken with nearly a year earlier. After one season in the south, Noel and his *Sadko* had retreated north to spend the winter in Buenos Aires, but now he was heading down the Argentine coast once more, this time bound for Antarctica. *Sadko* was named after the Rimsky–Korsakov opera of the same name; Noel had been a British diplomat and had served in Russia. One of the problems of SSB and ham radio is that anyone else who tunes in can hear you. One day we heard Noel chatting with another old Canatabrigian somewhere in the Southern Ocean.

"I say, Charles. Remember Rutherford? Our old philosophy tutor at Caius? Bumped into someone who knew him, at the Club in London when I was back in UK a month or two back. Still going strong, would you believe it, must be ninety if he's a day..."

With summer here, one afternoon when we had stopped early, I persuaded Jenny to put her wet-suit on again and inspect *Bosun Bird*'s bottom, not just for growth but also to see if there was much corrosion on the two sacrificial zincs mounted on the exterior of the hull. These serve to neutralize natural corrosive electrolysis that exists between underwater metal fittings: the whole idea is that the zinc, being less "noble" (a real scientific term!) corrodes instead of the fittings. All was well. Afterward, we had a rare wash in the river at the head of the bay. Over the past few months, such affairs had been brief and far between; dousing yourself in glacier run-off in a cold winter wind was not an attractive prospect.

Next day, we took a narrow and only partially charted shortcut; it involved going over a sandbar supposedly covered by only two metres of water, but the route saved us nine miles. I was nervous when the depth sounder started indicating we were actually aground, but the bottom was soft sand and we kept moving. Soon we emerged into the wide mouth of Canal Moraleda. There is another small fishing port at its entrance, and it was tempting to stop in. But *Dreamaway* had told us that the current port captain— the senior navy official assigned to manage all comings and goings—had a habit of formally closing the harbour as soon as the wind rose above ten knots. Several yachts had passed long periods stuck at Melinka, not allowed to sail out even though the conditions were perfect for them. Instead, bucking a heavy chop raised by a spring tide running against the wind, we worked our way onward, turned to port, and ducked back into a narrow, well-protected inlet called Puerto Puquitín.

From the mouth of the inlet we could look north right across a wide-open stretch of water: the Boca del Guafo. Some twenty miles away, almost lost in the haze, was the southern tip of the great island of Chiloé, while to the left the Pacific opened up. Serving as a sentinel to vessels coming in from the ocean is the Isla Guafo light, in the middle of the Boca. We'd been hearing daily reports from it for weeks, on the radio.

After we'd anchored, we rowed ashore and walked along the beach to great granite shelves that slope gently into the ocean. It was quite calm this afternoon. But this is a deceptive stretch of water. Tidal currents rush in and out of the wide Boca del Guafo at rates of three to four knots, filling then emptying the enormous inland sea that separates Chiloé from the mainland. Ideally we thought we should try to leave Puquitín at the beginning of an incoming tide and put the bulk of the crossing behind us in the six hours available. Once the tide turned, the current would tend to wash us out to sea again. As always, we would need to be vigilant lest the wind turned against the tide: we recalled the disaster that had occurred here only a couple of weeks earlier, in which twelve people had lost their lives.

At the top of a lush grassy mound just where our stern lines ran
ashore was another reminder to be careful. Inside a white picket
fence were two slightly lopsided wooden crosses and a tiny chapel.
The graves were from a shipwreck in the Boca in the 1960s, one of
whose victims was a small child called Agustín Manado. The fishermen believe his spirit watches over them, and the chapel was
crammed with little statues, homemade crucifixes, and scraps of
paper imploring his help. One was from a fishing boat called the
Queen Elizabeth 2; there was a box of matches, a supply of candles,
and a visitors' book, in which we left a little message and found
one (in German) from *Break Point*.

CALETA CLIFF TO PUERTO PUQUITÍN: 229 N.M.; 15 DAYS.

≈ Crossing the Boca del Guafo, there was for once a disappointing
lack of wind. We kept putting the sails up whenever there was a
puff, taking them in when it went calm again. Consequently, we
went even slower than had we been either motoring or sailing and,
as we were approaching the big island, we started to feel the worst
of the outgoing tide running against us. Although I had the throttle
fully open, at times we were only making half a knot.

We anchored in a large bay on the southeastern corner of Chiloé,
where the *Beagle* spent several days in December 1835. Darwin
reports seeing, sitting on a rock on the shore, a fox said to be unique
to the region: *Canis fulvipes*. "He was so intently absorbed in watching
the work of the officers, that I was able, by quietly walking up behind,
to knock him on the head with my geological hammer. This fox...
less wise than the generality of his brethren, is now mounted in the
museum of the Zoological Society."

Later, Darwin and some of the crew tried to climb the ridge
overlooking the bay from the south, but they found the going so
hard, the vegetation so impenetrable, that they were for minutes at
a time ten or fifteen feet above the ground, "...so that the seamen as
a joke called out the soundings."

The ridge still looked to be inaccessible, but on the broad bay little boats came and went for most of the late afternoon. Puttering around in the rocky shallows was a pair of Kelp Geese—the male snowy white, the female dark brown with elegant flashes of white—with six tiny goslings in tow. A little way away, perched on top of a boulder, a carancho—a small local hawk—observed with interest. We wondered how many of the goslings would see the summer out.

Next morning we caught the flood tide going north and at times reached a heady seven knots. We passed alongside huge rafts of Sooty Shearwaters, thousands of them resting on the water over a square kilometre or more and much smaller schools of penguins, diving and surfacing in unison. Twenty-five miles on, with the landscape to port becoming ever more bucolic, with green fields reaching to the water's edge and shingle-clad farmhouses hugging the edges of the forest, we rode the last of the rising tide through a narrow estuary entrance and into the sheltered waters of Estero Huildad.

A family was encamped on the sandy beach of the spit. They made their living, although it cannot have been much of one, by bagging sand into old fertilizer and fish-feed bags, and stacking the bags in rows to be collected, later, by a launch. More runabouts came and went. Large fishing boats chugged past the entrance to the estuary. It was quite a different world from the severe uninhabited channels and islands that we'd known for the past three months. But next morning, on the net, there was a reminder of that harsher environment. Noel on *Sadko* and an American vessel called *Tamara* were gale-bound in our old anchorage at Spaniard Harbour, on the western tip of Tierra del Fuego.

PUERTO PUQUITÍN TO ESTERO HUILDAD: 58 N.M.; 2 DAYS.

◜ The island of Chiloé, which measures 250 kilometres by fifty kilometres, was isolated for the first two hundred years of the modern era from the mainstream of Spanish development in Chile,

yet when the Spaniards finally left South America this was the last
royalist holdout of all, succumbing only in 1826. In desperation,
the last governor offered the island to the British rather than turn it
over to the republicans.

The perennially bad weather, clinging fogs, and endless rain have
contributed to the aura of mystery that has shrouded the island for
so long. I wonder if the fact that this is a land where people have
always gone down to the sea—and died at sea—also has something to do with it. Chiloé has much in common with Ireland and
Newfoundland.

The most persistent myth tells of the *Caleuche*, a kind of *Flying
Dutchman*: a sailing vessel with fish-scales, only ever seen at night.
Ghostly music is heard, and the crew have their heads twisted to
one side, their right foot held back up against their spines. Then
there is the equally sinister Imbunche, who guards the cave of
Quicavi, the home of the island's wizards and witches. Raised by a
cat, he eats only dead bodies; he is mute and anyone who sees him
will die on the spot. The Caballo Marino (Horse of the Sea) is the
messenger of the wizards and witches: he gallops over the surface
of the sea, carrying a lantern fuelled by human blood, and can also
carry witches on his back. More benign are the dwarf-like Trauco,
who inhabits the forests of the interior, and the Camahuete, a kind
of small black unicorn, which can only be seen under the light of a
full moon and which can be captured only with a lasso of kelp.

These creatures all feature in the novels and short stories of
Francisco Coloane. The stories were familiar to him as a young boy
and widely believed; the last trial of a witch was held on Chiloé in
1879, and even today there are whispers that such people still exist.

Shortly after we had anchored in the beautiful wooded inlet
of Estero Pailad, just off a freshly painted, two-hundred-year-
old wooden church, with black-necked swans gliding smoothly
over the calm waters, an old fellow rowed out to greet us from his
rambling and dilapidated homestead on the opposite shore.

"Hola! Soy Héctor! Bienvenidos a mi estero!"

Héctor's craggy gnarled face, with leering fleshy lips, would be enough to give a small child nightmares. But he was friendly enough, lonely, and clearly dying to talk to someone, anyone. He showed us the old, broken-down water mill behind his farm, treated us to tea from cracked mugs in his dark, earthen-floored kitchen, and pressed on us some homemade gooseberry jam. Then he walked us up the dirt road to the nearest shop at Contuy, about three miles away. Héctor clearly had a bladder problem. Every twenty minutes or so, he would pause briefly, turn slightly to one side, and pee copiously into the ditch, all the while continuing to recount to us the details of some complicated dispute with his neighbours. He was very difficult to understand, but Jenny and I seemed to manage by intervening with appropriate "*Sí*"s and "*No*"s, whenever he turned to us interrogatively.

At the shop we shared a carton of wine with Héctor and a sheep-shearer, who had just dropped by and showed us his fine scissors. As we sat in velvet armchairs in the front room of the shop, which was actually just a private house with a spare room full of tins and dried goods, the conversation turned to the island's folklore. I asked Héctor with a smile if he had ever seen the *Caleuche*.

"No," he shrugged. "I never have. My father said he did once, but later people said it was the *Dresden*, that German warship..."

There was a long pause, and I thought Héctor was about to carry on and tell us that no one believed in these things any more.

"But I have seen two men fly," he finally said, very pensively, his lower lip hanging far down.

I looked over at the shopkeeper, but he wouldn't catch my eye. Neither would the sheep-shearer, contemplating his tooth-mug of wine. When we left, Héctor touchingly gave Jenny a single white rose, plucked from his garden. We carefully took down his address and later sent him some photographs of us all together.

Héctor and Jenny.

Our next stop was the small fishing port of Queilén. In 1835 Darwin recounts, this spot (which he spells "Caylen") advertised itself as "the end of Christendom." He found it a very poor place and tells the tale of a man who had walked for three and a half days to get here, just to sell "a small axe and a few fish." But we found ourselves in consumer heaven, marvelling at the selection of tins in the place's one small supermarket, and carrying home in triumph a few tired potatoes, carrots, and a single avocado. So excited was I that I took a picture of the shop, which bemused the man who was coming out at that very moment with his plastic bag full of shopping.

We worked our way slowly up the east coast of Chiloé, calling in at many more small islands and inlets. At the almost perfectly enclosed Estero Pindo was another of the old wooden churches that are so characteristic. They all date from the early eighteenth century, when the Jesuits held thrall, and most are built entirely of alerce wood, with pegs instead of nails. This one was painted a delicate shade of pink.

Under its spire, eight years after Darwin passed this way, the sixteen-metre schooner *Ancud* fitted out. Its captain was a Bristolian, John (or Juan) Williams, who had served for years in the Chilean navy as a mercenary but who had now been entrusted by Chilean President Bernardo O'Higgins (another mercenary) with the mission of claiming for Chile the Strait of Magellan. There were many tribulations on the journey south, but Williams and the *Ancud* were successful in entering the strait. In September 1843 her crew established a small wooden fort, to be called Fuerte Bulnes, overlooking the bay of San Juan de la Posesión, where Captain Pringle Stokes of the *Beagle* had shot himself that gloomy winter's day in 1828.

The location turned out to be a poor one, and only six years later the site was abandoned in favour of today's Punta Arenas. But by settling to the east of Cabo Froward (i.e., on the Atlantic side) Williams had set a critical geo-political precedent that, much to the frustration of Argentina, would later allow Chile to claim control of both shores of the Strait of Magellan, all the way between the two oceans. The pioneer's name lives on, of course, in Puerto Williams—although he almost certainly never went there.

In the shop at Pindo, we heard on the radio that Augusto Pinochet had died, and that there were disturbances on the streets of Santiago. The lady in the shop was unperturbed but said with studied nonchalance, as she packed our eggs, "There was order in Pinochet's time, you know."

She eyed me carefully, and I didn't know what to say.

A simple-minded young man in a checked shirt had attached himself to us now. Pinochet clearly meant nothing at all to him. We felt rather guilty as we loaded our bags into the dinghy and pushed off, leaving him standing forlornly on the beach.

At Mechuque, still farther north, most of the houses were *palafitos*: wooden and built on pilings over the water. Today they are regarded as quaint, but they have their origins in the grinding poverty of the nineteenth century when, by building out over the water, small householders were able to avoid paying rent or civic property taxes. In one old wooden house there functioned an informal museum, open by request. It was actually the repository of the junk of an old island family, arranged in no particular order, but the black-and-white pictures of 1930s Mechuque were evocative. They showed its little harbour crammed with the traditional Chiloé sailing boats: stubby, flat-bottomed, and black-painted wooden craft with a gaff rig. We remembered still seeing such craft being pulled up onto the beaches of the big island by oxen, in the late 1970s. But when we asked, it seemed that they were all now long gone.

The old man who dusted the place was the first aggressively anti-Pinochet person we found in Chile: he was grinning, almost cackling with laughter at the recent news.

"Por fin, el viejo Tata murió...!" he kept repeating, referring to the old general by his pejorative nickname (which normally means "daddy").

But he was angry, too: by dying, Pinochet was escaping the trial for corruption and massive human rights abuses that had at last been looking inevitable.

Our last anchorage on Chiloé was an inlet near the fishing village of Quemchi. This looked like a perfectly protected, fjord-like indentation on the chart, but we were disappointed to find it almost choked with *salmoneras* and mussel-farms (sets of ropes suspended in the water from chains of ugly white Styrofoam buoys). We spent a couple of hours weaving our way around them until we could find a nook that was both protected and gave us a little swinging

Fishing boats, Calbuco, Chile.

room. The bay is where the author Coloane was born, in 1910. His father, Juan, was captain of a small coaster called the *Victoria*, which used to help tow large sailing ships into Quemchi. Coloane records that in 1911, 278 such vessels docked at Quemchi. The first half of his novel *El Camino de la Ballena* (*The Way of the Whale*) is set here. It recounts the early years of a young orphan called Pedro Nauto, growing up among the mussel-divers and fishermen of Chiloé, before he sets sail aboard a whaler for Antarctica.

My Chilean visa was due to expire in a few days' time, and we made several visits into Quemchi to see if it would be feasible to catch a bus and ferry combination to Puerto Montt, from where I'd be able to take another bus over the border into Argentina, thus restarting the clock on the visa. But with a few days still to spare, on

December 18, the gale that had immobilized us for days blew itself out. With the odd squall still blowing in from the west, we set off on a northeasterly course. We moored for a night in the busy harbour of Calbuco but hardly slept: great, ocean-going fishing boats were coming and going all night with their floodlights on, engines thrumming, rocking us in their wake. It was a drizzly morning as we motored most of the last twenty miles to Puerto Montt.

Nick and Jan from *Yawarra* welcomed us at the marina dock with a bottle of champagne.

ESTERO HUILDAD TO PUERTO MONTT: 145 N.M.; 13 DAYS.

PUERTO WILLIAMS TO PUERTO MONTT: 1318 N.M.; 4 MONTHS.

$\sim$ *11*

Under the *Wide* and *Starry Sky*

WE HAD SEVENTEEN PEOPLE ON BOARD tiny *Bosun Bird* for
Christmas. Tom from *Break Point* studiously recorded the entire
event on video and posted it on his sponsored website. Every two
or three days new boats came and went, and there would be drinks
parties or potlucks most nights on one boat or another, or informal
gatherings in the Oxxean Marina's Internet café, with its incon-
gruous, overstuffed, blue couches.

Julian on *Harrier of Down*, the elderly Englishman whom we had
last met at Puerto Deseado, arrived by ferry from Puerto Edén, having
left the *Harrier* there, to seek spare parts. His sojourn in the South
had been a troubled one.

335

"One morning when I was climbing ashore from *Harrier* onto the wharf in Ushuaia," he recounted, "I grabbed onto a lamp post. It collapsed and knocked me out...A couple of days later I was run over in traffic."

Things hadn't stopped there. Julian's previous boat had no engine, and, until shown how by fellow yachties in Ushuaia, he had not learned how to change his engine oil or to change fuel filters. These basic skills he acquired only following his first attempted departure for the North, which had been aborted when his Yanmar failed on account of dirty fuel. All the way north he had experienced further mechanical difficulties. Julian was to be admired for his hardiness in undertaking such an enterprise at his relatively advanced age, and on such a small boat, but he did not always make himself popular with his constant need for assistance and advice. And it caught the attention of a number of us that while he was very happy to tell us all about Darwin and the book he was planning to write, he was not really following in the *Beagle*'s wake at all.

Alicia, a diminutive blonde American woman, was sailing with her Italian male friend who had an unusual line in introduction: "I am in exotic women's lingerie."

Alfredo—tall, suave, tanned, and with a roguish smile—was actually a former representative for the Senza underwear line. Aboard *On Verra*, the two of them had arrived amid drama from New Zealand. They were given incorrect advice by radio about the fast-running currents in the Canal del Chacao—the approach to Puerto Montt from the Pacific—and had a dangerously rough ride. Then their engine died on them completely: Tom and Tatiana generously towed them the last mile or so into the Oxxean Marina. Most of the next few months they spent in stressful and time-consuming negotiations by phone and Internet to purchase, import, install, and test an entirely new engine. Alfredo's Italian temperament and ability to get by in Spanish was helpful to them, but poor Alicia was sometimes reduced to tears by the agonizing process.

They had an interesting track record.

"Yes," Alicia would say blithely. "We lost our previous boat when we hit a rock off Brazil. In fact we swam away from the boat as it sank. Happily there was a diving platform on the rock, and even more happily my ex-husband then gave me his boat so we could keep sailing."

David on *Aqualung* was another quite senior British sailor, with a great deal of experience and—by his own frank admission— a lot more money than Julian. From David's casual references to his family castle in Scotland and his deceptively diffident, apologetic manner of speaking, we deduced he was from the minor British aristocracy, but he was not in the least soft; in fact he was currently nursing a recently dislocated shoulder, after having fallen off a bicycle when descending what is sometimes known as "the most dangerous road in the world," from La Paz to the lowlands of Bolivia. David's boat, which was mysteriously registered under a name other than that which appeared on its transom, had every possible modern convenience, including discreet, floor-level, red lighting below decks, but was so complicated that there was always something that needed fixing.

Edward's *Spirit of Rhema* was at the other extreme: a Herreshoff 26 that he had built himself in New Zealand, sailed single-handed and engine-less across the Pacific. It had no modern systems at all. The interior was bare fibreglass and wood, with no decoration, no electronics. Edward was an unduly modest, shy man whose sole source of income was a meagre, old-age pension but who had an impressive "can do" attitude, and for whom this voyage—which would culminate in England—was not just an adventure, but also the simplest and cheapest means of getting to Europe.

One morning as I was fingering his external lifelines, he commented very quietly, "What do you think? I should really have placed them a little closer together. A couple of thousand miles out from NZ, I fell through the gap and overboard. Somehow I held on with one hand; I can't remember how I managed to climb back on board..."

Edward was contemplating installing a small outboard to help him in tight corners on the way south through the channels.

Tied up next to us were Connie and Robert from Germany, on their white steel *Andiamo*. For the past year or so they had been ahead of us but had moved very slowly, even by our standards, and they had been delayed when in Puerto Edén Connie decided temporarily to move ashore, with an aggravated back condition. Robert had continued to Puerto Montt with, as crew, a local fisherman. We considered ourselves very cautious sailors, but Robert and Connie were even more so, to a point of almost chronic indecision at times.

Andiamo's crew included the lively, bouncy, and mischievous Captain Jack: a black and white mongrel cat who had adopted the vessel as his home in Puerto Williams and had not left it since, except for forays ashore to be with his girlfriend, Jacinta, whom we had met in Puerto Edén. Jack was always getting into trouble in the marina, nonchalantly padding across the cockpits of inveterate cat-haters like Graham and Avril on *Dreamaway*, wandering up to the bus stop, getting stuck up trees, pursued by stray dogs.

We spent a lot of time with our old friends Nick and Jan. Nick was a very practical kind of person, always cheerful and on hand with useful hints for our perennially difficult engine. He gave us hours of his time in Puerto Montt, climbing halfway up our mast to reinstall the corroding rivets that held our radar reflector and hanging over the side to help fix our wind vane. Jan was a nurse by profession, but also a semi-pro barber, who gave us both much-needed trims. We were able to repay them modestly by assisting

> *(top) Marina Oxxean, Puerto Montt, Chile. (bottom) Captain Jack.*

in various chores that required Spanish and in keeping an eye on Mischa and Tigs—their two cats—when they were away.

"The channels were hard," Nick admitted. "You know what? We've been out twenty years now, and we've done a lot of sailing. There's lots of places we still want to see, but we've decided we can't afford, at our age, to spend too much time waiting for wind any more. We've got a plan!"

"Oh yes?"

"Promise not to be shocked. When we get back to Oz, we're selling *Yawarra*. But we're gonna buy *Yawarra 2*; she's going to be an ocean-going power boat."

We were sad to see them leave. It's a cliché but such is the cruising life: departures and arrivals, meeting new people, saying goodbye to old friends.

The constant at Oxxean was Mani from Finland who has been sailing these waters for a decade as the skipper of *Biribi B*. He had become the cruisers' principal resource when it came to tracking down anything from high-grade Plexiglas to camshaft bearings in the industrial estates and was full of practical advice. He didn't own the boat though; once in a while the Finnish proprietor would fly in, and they'd go cruising for maybe two or three days. Mani was vastly experienced but frustrated to be in charge of someone else's boat and not his own. He was also touchingly out of synch with the modern world: we introduced him to the wonders of e-mail.

~ Located in a spectacularly beautiful, if rainy region, Puerto Montt is very much a working town, the end of the road for heavy traffic coming south, the beginning of several ferry routes, and the commercial centre for dozens of tiny fishing and logging communities. Like all ports, it has its rough edges.

If you walked into town from Chinquihue, where the marina was located, you went past strip joints like Pasiones and Lady Nigth (*sic*), and there was a good chance of running into a few drunks spending a month's fishing wages in a single night. In the port area and on soulless industrial estates behind town, you could also find most things you might need for refitting an ocean-going vessel: oil filters, V-belts, stainless steel, galvanizing paint, rocket flares. There were huge modern supermarkets and a multiplex cinema, and street stalls where you could buy punnets of fresh raspberries and every kind of shellfish imaginable, most with no equivalent English names.

Shortly after arriving, we joined Nick and Jan for a one-day outing to the roadhead at Petrohué, at the western end of Lago Todos los Santos: a bus journey of an hour or two. We'd come through here in the seventies, on our way to Argentina, but it had poured with rain and we had seen nothing at all except grey-green water and the lower slopes of forested mountains. Today the sky was a sharp blue, the near-perfect cone of Osorno Volcano dazzlingly white, and, at the head of the lake, we could see Tronador, site of one of our less successful climbing expeditions long ago.

This was a tourist route in those days, but it had been in the fifties, too, when Ernesto Guevara, his friend, Alberto Granado, and their inappropriately named motorbike, *La Poderosa* (The Mighty One), arrived here on their way into Chile and on to Peru. *Diarios de Motocicleta*, which recounts the journey, is—in the light of Guevara's later ascent to iconic status—touchingly innocent and ordinary in many places:

> The boat trip ended at Petrohué and we said goodbye to everyone, but first we had to pose for some Brazilian chicks who added us to their photo album of memories of southern Chile, and for a couple of naturalists from God knows where in Europe who very carefully took down our addresses so they could send us the snaps later. We met someone who wanted his truck taken to Osorno, which is

where we were going too, so he suggested I drive it...Just like in a cartoon, I set off in great starts behind Alberto, who was on the bike. Every bend was torture: brake, de-clutch, first, second, oh my God...

In the souvenir shops in Puerto Montt you can now find maps and guidebooks of "La Ruta del Che." I wondered if the Brazilian chicks (*negritas*) and the European naturalists had ever happened to leaf through their photo albums years later and realized whose picture they had taken that day in February 1952.

Later, we made another, longer trip—back to Chiloé, but this time to its west coast and the national park at Cucao. After taking a ferry across the narrows of Chacao, we had to change buses in Castro, the largest town on the island. Most of it is perched high on a hill overlooking a narrow inlet from the sea, with an enormous, twin-spired, wooden church serving as a focal point. Down at the waterfront a few fishing boats were tied up, and there was a lively market selling handicrafts and seafood. It was an unusually bright summer's day and the place had a bustle that Darwin found conspicuously absent when he was there.

> ...[this was] a most forlorn and deserted place. The usual quadrangular arrangement of Spanish towns could be traced but the streets and plaza were coated with fine green turf, on which sheep were browsing...No individual possessed either a watch or a clock; and an old man, who was supposed to have a good idea of time, was employed to strike the church bells by guess.

The road west, over the island, was narrow and rough with roadworks going on along several stretches, meaning we spent long periods waiting for vehicles to come past from the other direction. Until recently, it was necessary to take a boat across two successive lakes that almost bisect the island, which made reaching Cucao

On the beach near Cucao, Chiloé.

quite an adventure. It also meant that Cucao stayed remarkably isolated on what was already an isolated island.

The village was tiny: no more than half a dozen houses, with a long and low church that looked to have been converted from a cattle shed. We spent the night at the Hostal el Paraíso; although the surly landlady advertised a room as a double, in reality there were two single beds crammed into such a small space that you had to climb in over the foot of the bed. Next morning a thick fog was down and the place looked haunted. Shouldering our packs, we walked past the green bus that had brought us in the day before and observed that its left front tire was completely flat. It was a good job we were not planning to return just yet.

We spent the day walking northward up a huge, flat, sand beach, with rollers pounding in to the left. Every so often there were large stakes driven into the sand, with piles of nets nearby: when the tidal conditions are right, the Huilliche Indians fish the surf. Two hours out we saw coming toward us two men and a woman on horseback, driving four or five cows in front of them. I thought it made an evocative picture and, with the camera lens at maximum magnification, took a couple of shots. Fifteen minutes later the posse was approaching us, and the woman trotted up to me, stopping her horse only a metre or so in front. She raised a switch in one hand, in an unmistakably threatening gesture.

"*Dame dinero!* Money!"

I demurred and we walked on. Darwin, commenting on the "thirty or forty" Indian families that then inhabited the Cucao area, observed that they seemed only to survive on trade in seal oil and were "humble to a degree which it was quite painful to witness." Things had clearly changed.

We climbed up from the beach into dense dripping vegetation. Somewhere in the forest we took a wrong turn and we ended up high on a cleared hillside, looking down on the stretch of sandy beach where we were planning to spend the night. There was a small farm with an energetically barking dog, but no one in sight. We plunged down the hill, having to hack our way through bamboo thickets, and reached the beach in the late afternoon. Once there had been a *refugio* here, a simple, red-painted, wooden shack with a fireplace, for use by campers when the rain got heavy (as it often did). But it was in ruins, the roof and floor both rotten. We put up our tent instead.

As we sat later on the beach, watching the sun set, Senor José Pillampu of Cole Cole arrived. He wanted to charge us a fee for use of the refuge. When we pointed out that it was in a state of collapse and quite uninhabitable, he thought hard and long, then said, "Well yes. You are right."

He went away. But he was back half an hour later, this time to charge us 2 USD each for having crossed his land. Reluctantly we paid up, but our impression of the locals was by now not high.

Next day, leaving Jenny to guard the tent (Sr. Pillampu had seemed interested in what we had inside it), I followed the trail north for another two hours through dense Arrayán forest and bamboo clumps to a wide and deep river. There was another refuge, almost invisible from the path, so lush was the vegetation. With its grey shingle walls and roof it looked habitable, but this would be a lonely place.

It poured with rain all the way back to Cucao, and the breakers roared. I was reminded of the west coast of Vancouver Island. As Darwin rode on horseback along this beach, he also recorded: "...a terrible surf was breaking. I was assured that after a heavy gale, the roar can be heard at night even at Castro, a distance of no less than twenty-one miles across a hilly and wooded country."

Riding back in the bus to Puerto Montt, we could see on the eastern horizon the two great volcanoes of Osorno and Corcovado, their white cones pale and ethereal above the deep blue sea. In January 1835 the *Beagle*'s crew observed them both in spectacular eruption at night. Both have been dormant ever since, but the ever-inquisitive polymath Darwin observes in his journal that, as he later learned, both Aconcagua (800 kilometres north) and Coseguina (4300 kilometres north) erupted on the same night. Anticipating what is now commonplace tectonic theory, he wonders "if this shows some subterranean connection."

⮑ Our last trip on land was a double pilgrimage. First we wanted to meet face-to-face with the source of the disembodied voice that had for weeks on end, in the frozen South and in the wastes of the South Atlantic, been our tenuous, only link with the outside world: Wolfgang, controller of the Patagonian Cruisers' Net.

Wolfgang and Gabi had for years been cruisers themselves.

"Out of all the countries we went to," Wolfgang recalled, "we liked Chile the most. So we decided to stay; it was a bonus that we found some German speakers; that helped us settle in."

They'd bought an overgrown, bramble-infested piece of land with a sensational view over Lake Villarica and the volcano of the same name and, in a few years, had built a small farm and guesthouse. At night, through the panoramic windows of the guesthouse, you could see the mountain perfectly framed, its rim glowing red; in the daytime a few puffs of steam could be seen. Wolfgang and Gabi ran a few dozen sheep, a couple of goats, and also kept three llamas, which had just been sheared when we arrived and looked very skinny and unsure of themselves.

We listened in as Wolfgang made his morning calls, sitting at his kitchen counter. A regular these days was a young American woman called Donna, at this time just past Cape Horn and heading up the Atlantic bound for the east coast of the USA; her 8.5-metre boat was the aptly named *Inspired Insanity*. Her faint crackly voice from those rough waters sent a little shiver down our spines; soon we would be out there again. More prosaically, David on *Aqualung*, now sailing in the channels, was giving complicated instructions on how to transmit to the supplier of his satellite phone details of his credit card, so as to buy more airtime. David seemed to take for granted that Wolfgang would make all the necessary arrangements—which he did—but I wondered how many people really appreciated or understood the goodwill, effort, and time Wolfgang put into this service, with no tangible reward at all.

Still based at Wolfgang's we did some walking on the western slopes of Villarica: steep climbs through forests of monkey-puzzle trees to bare slopes of soft pumice, with snowfields intact on the southern slopes. Our longest walk brought us one day, puffing and panting, to a ridge with the view we'd been looking for. There, fifteen or twenty kilometres to the east and rising way above the

> *(top) Wolfgang, controller for the Patagonian Cruisers' Net. (bottom) Lanín Volcano, Argentina, twenty-nine years on.*

horizon, was Lanín Volcano. From this angle, its left—north-facing—slope was severe but steady all the way to the summit, the right-hand slope broken by a short and vertical-looking step just below the top.

Twenty-nine years earlier, laughably underequipped and with no map, we'd struggled to the foot of that step, only to have to turn back; when we walked out of the park days later we'd been stunned to find that Chile and Argentina were in a state of near-war. The following southern summer we'd gone up the straighter slope, the northern one. I remembered the morning we'd set off from the high-altitude *refugio*, with the sun just breaking the horizon over the Pacific, and had looked up to the summit, across shiny-hard fields of snow, pink in the early morning light.

For a few moments there were tears in my eyes. What for, I don't really know. Lost youth, I supposed, feeling maudlin.

⁓ Back at the marina, there were plans and decisions to be made. I'd been offered a final posting with the Canadian Foreign Service, in Islamabad, Pakistan, to start in the second half of 2007. For the past eighteen months we'd been in every sense removed from what was going on in Iraq and Afghanistan, where the sophisticated and powerful West seemed to be locked in an intractable struggle to the death with obscurantist Islamic forces. It seemed like a kind of Third World War was being waged. I wanted a taste of it before we sailed forever into the sunset. Jenny was ambivalent and would just as soon have spent the rest of her days on *Bosun Bird*, but—unlike Iraq and Afghanistan—a posting in Pakistan would at least allow her to accompany me, so she good-naturedly agreed that we could take a two-year break in the voyage.

Leaving the boat on land in Chile was possible in a prac-tical sense, but we would first have to import it formally, at great expense. After hours spent sitting at the marina's little Internet room, we decided to sail on into the southeastern Pacific and haul the boat out in French Polynesia. This way we'd make the fullest use of the six months remaining to us, and we'd be well positioned, after Pakistan, to sail in virtually any direction: down to New Zealand, up to Hawaii and British Columbia, or westward to Australia and New Guinea.

As always, careful perusal of the Pilot Charts was in order. It was important to leave when the South Pacific high-pressure area—which would give us favourable winds as we headed first north then west, following its northeastern quadrant—was still well in the South, before the onset of the southern autumn and winter drove it upward. But it was also important not to arrive in Polynesia too soon, for cyclones occurred as far east as the Gambier Islands up to and including April. The end of February or the beginning of March looked like the ideal time to head out through Chacao into the open ocean.

We gave away all the now-empty fuel jugs we'd carried on the way north though the channels. From here we expected to be sailing 99 per cent of the time. We checked every inch of stitching on the sails, had new lee cloths made, gave the engine another tune up, repainted our anchor chain with galvanizing paint, reattached the radar reflector that had come loose in those never-ending winds in the far South. And, of course, there were those ever-more frequent checks of forecasting sites on the net.

〜 On March 1, dead on time, the outlook was good. We bought as much fresh bread as we could carry, made a hurried visit to the port captain's to check out of Puerto Montt and, with all of our friends from the marina gathered on our wobbly pontoon, cast off at about 10:00. There were a few moments of panic. The throttle briefly stuck in reverse and we headed backward in a graceful circle toward the bank. I had to leave the helm for a few seconds, frantically pull off the engine cover, and reach in to the top of the gearbox to flick the control back to neutral. Jenny looked perplexed at my momentary disappearance, but no one on shore was tactless enough to laugh.

The day was drizzly, but we were able to sail most of the way through the maze of islands and channels that leads to the inshore entrance of the east–west Canal del Chacao. We anchored in the late afternoon behind a hook of land just short of the channel, with a few fishermen's houses on shore: Abtao.

I'm always nervous when going to sea after a long stretch attached to the shore, but the next twenty-mile stretch was of special concern. The current runs at up to nine knots between the continent and the big island, reversing with each tide. Although a westerly wind would not be unwelcome outside, we did not want to find ourselves being rushed along through Chacao at an accelerating pace with the wind in our face. The overall weather forecast was favourable and did not indicate anything too strong in the offing, but we would be going through at the time of month when the tides were only just past their strongest. Jenny was blithe about it all. I hardly slept at Abtao and was physically sick with worry in the night.

Next morning we motored out slowly, hoping to position ourselves at the entrance to the channel at exactly 13:56, the forecast time of high tide. For a while it was very slow going: we had two or three knots running against us. We crossed what the Admiralty Pilot informed us was a permanent line of turbulent white water, the Raya del Tique. Then, at about 14:00 and over the space of only five minutes, our speed increased from two knots to a hair-raising eleven. There was no perceptible slack water at all. It was best only to look at the surface of the water and not the banks either side, which were rushing past so quickly that it seemed we were running downhill. A couple of landing-craft style ferries were crossing the canal crab-like, moving sideways far faster than they were moving forward. Roca Remolinos—Whirlpool Rock—is in the middle of the channel at its narrowest part (one and a half miles wide) and it sped by. I was happy to see it receding astern, having feared its eddies could draw us in too close.

In only half an hour we were coming into the open ocean. *Yawarra* and *Break Point* had warned us that the worst could yet be to come: the point at which the outgoing tide meets the steep rollers coming in from the ocean. So we made a sharp turn right as soon as we could, through Paso Chocoi, which lies between the mainland and Isla Doña Sebastiana. Some careful judgement was needed to negotiate a shallow bank, but this way we were out of the main current far sooner than if we had continued due west. Soon we were back to our normal speed of about four knots.

On a brilliant afternoon, we set our course to the NNW and Robinson Crusoe Island, six hundred miles away.

The sun sank slowly, the wind picked up, South America faded into the night. Eyes fixed on the red-glowing compass, I tried not to think of the thousands of miles of open ocean that separated us from our next safe haven.

We'd lived our dream; for now that was enough.

Epilogue

AFTER LEAVING MAINLAND CHILE, *Bosun Bird* and her crew sailed
to Robinson Crusoe Island then made a long, 1,800-mile passage
across the Pacific to Easter Island. Here they anchored in the
shadow of the great carved heads for which the island is famous,
but were forced to return hastily to sea when enormous swells
began to roll in from some far-off storm in the Southern Ocean.
Past lonely Pitcairn, they then made for the Gambiers, the Australs,
and finally the island of Raiatea, west of Tahiti. *Bosun Bird* was
hauled out onto dry land, put to bed, and Nick took up a tumul-
tuous two-year posting at the Canadian High Commission in
Islamabad, Pakistan. These were years that saw the assassination of
Benazir Bhutto, the ousting of General Pervez Musharraf as president, and a wave of Taliban-inspired terror attacks that reached the
capital itself; it was the "real world" with a vengeance.

We re-launched in mid-2009 and hastened through the Cook
Islands, Tonga, and Fiji to spend the southern cyclone season in

New Zealand. After a partial refit, including the installation of a more up-to-date wind vane, we headed north again in May 2010, taking a beating in a fifty-knot storm en route, but then relaxing for four months in Vanuatu and another four in the Solomon Islands. By early 2011 we were cruising the unfrequented Federated States of Micronesia and starting to contemplate a return to cooler waters: Japan, Alaska, and British Columbia. All our travels are chronicled in our blog: www.bosunbird.com.

Meanwhile, most of our old friends from Patagonia have literally been scattered to the four winds. Tom and Vicky on *Sunstone* sailed east from Mar del Plata to South Africa and New Zealand—where we caught up with them in Auckland—but soon were off again, to Japan. Nick and Jan on *Yawarra* sailed home to Australia and exchanged their sailboat for a powerful motor cruiser, *Yawarra 2*, in which they are now cruising the Great Barrier Reef. Cor and Petra on *Simon de Danser*, after beating a strategic retreat from Puerto Deseado in 2006, have now returned to southern waters while Julian Mustoe, on tiny *Harrier of Down*, at least made it across the Pacific: we just missed him in Opua, New Zealand. Keith, our Puerto Williams neighbour on *Solquest*, is earning some money driving trucks in Australia; the intrepid Edward, on the twenty-six-foot *Spirit of Rhema*, whom we met in Puerto Montt as he was about to head south, reached Europe without incident, sailed the Scottish islands and is now preparing to sail home to New Zealand; he appears thoroughly to have mastered e-mail.

In Puerto Williams, Mauricio, la Yésica, and the irrepressible Beto are now among the village's longest-standing inhabitants; the pay must be good. Wolfgang, controller of the Patagonian Cruisers' Net, won an award from a well-known cruising association and recently sailed to Robinson Crusoe Island and the Galápagos aboard a friend's boat. Sadly, Captain Jack of *Andiamo* is no more: he fell overboard some distance short of Easter Island, and although Robert and Connie searched for him for hours, he could not be found.

Yves Robert, whose *Agur* was dismasted and rolled in the same storm that claimed the life of Antoine, returned to France and wrote a book about his experiences; he kindly lent me his log and allowed me to translate some excerpts into English for this narrative. Our warmest thanks are also due to Klaus and Maria Haeussler of *Ludus Amoris* for permission to use the photograph of *Bosun Bird* taken in the Strait of Magellan and featured on the cover and page 276. Klaus and Maria subsequently circumnavigated the Pacific via New Zealand, Micronesia, Japan, and Alaska. Their boat is berthed for the winter on Vancouver Island.

Select Bibliography

SAILING NARRATIVES

Bailey, Maurice and Maralyn. *Second Chance: Voyage to Patagonia*. New York: David McKay Co., 1977.

> The Baileys, who had become world-famous when they lost their first sailboat and survived for weeks adrift in a life raft, undertake a second voyage from England to Patagonia in 1975 aboard *Auralyn II*. The narrative is little more than the ship's log, interspersed with recollections of their earlier adventure reprised from an earlier book; the photographs are poor and the editing sloppy. But at the time this was a pioneering voyage and the Baileys, unlike many who later followed them, sailed almost all the way up the channels rather than resort to their engine.

Campbell, John. *In Darwin's Wake: Revisiting* Beagle's *South American Anchorages*. Dobbs Ferry, NY: Sheridan House, 1997.

Campbell and his professional crew take *Thalassa*, an eighty-three-foot luxury sailing yacht, around South America on behalf of an unidentified wealthy owner who periodically flies in to join the vessel. Some interesting historical narrative but, given the power and mod cons of *Thalassa*, this is hardly an adventure, and the owner's evident unwillingness to associate himself with the book leaves an odd taste.

Clark, Gerry. *The Totorore Voyage: An Antarctic Adventure.*
London: Ebury Press, 1988.

A modern classic. Unassuming New Zealander Gerry Clark undertakes a circumnavigation of Antarctica in his home-built *Totorore*, spending much of his time in the waters of Tierra del Fuego and the Chilean channels, with the aim of gathering new data on endangered seabirds. He and his motley succession of crew members have many hair-raising adventures, but the tale is modestly and engagingly told. Many superb colour photographs and line drawings.

Dumas, Vito. *Alone Through the Roaring Forties.* Columbus, OH:
McGraw-Hill Education, 2001.

An account of Dumas' epoch-making (but at the time unnoticed) solo voyage around the world in high southern latitudes in 1943. The book is self-promotional, but there was no doubting Dumas' courage and ability. Quotations in *Winter in Fireland* are my translations from the original Spanish edition, *Los Cuarenta Bramadores: La Vuelta Por la Ruta Imposible.* 1944. Buenos Aires: Ediciones Continente, 2002.

Robert, Yves. *De Tahiti à Bayonne par le Cap Horn.*
Paris: Éditions Atlantica, 2008.

French sailor Yves Robert, while sailing from Tahiti to France by way of the Patagonian channels on board *Agur*, became a close friend of Antoine Duguet, subsequently lost off the eastern entrance to the Strait of Magellan. Yves kindly supplied me with excerpts from his logbook, some of which I translated into English and which are included in this narrative. Yves has also published this full-length illustrated account of his entire voyage (in French).

Roth, Hal. *Two Against Cape Horn*. New York: Norton, 1978.

Roth and his wife Margaret sail their thirty-five-foot yacht *Whisper*
from California to the Chilean channels and, ultimately, around Cape
Horn. Superlative illustrations, but the narrative concentrates very
largely on one episode: Roth's near-loss of *Whisper* on a remote beach
north of Cape Horn.

Slocum, Joshua. *Sailing Alone Around the World*. New York: The Century
Company, 1900.

One of the great sailing adventures of all time and an entertaining
read. Slocum's wildest adventures aboard the *Spray* were in the Strait
of Magellan and adjacent waters, from his spreading of tacks on deck
to deter nocturnal boarders to his perilous negotiation of the rock-
strewn Milky Way by night.

Tilman, H.W. *Mischief in Patagonia*. Cambridge: Cambridge University
Press, 1957.

A highly amusing, understated account of one of this legendary
curmudgeon's early expeditions: under sail in his Bristol Channel
Pilot Cutter *Mischief* from England to the wall of the Amalia Glacier, in
Chilean Patagonia, and then on foot across the Patagonian Ice Field.

SAILING GUIDES

Ardrizzi, Giorgio and Rolfo, Mariolina. *Patagonia and Tierra del Fuego
Nautical Guide*, 2nd edition. Rome: Editrice Incontri Nautici, 2007.

Seven hundred pages, lavishly illustrated, with details and sketch
maps for over four hundred possible anchorages from Mar del Plata
(Argentina) to Valdivia (Chile); full GPS co-ordinates. The authoritative
guide to the area and a superlative example of its genre.

Mantellero, Alberto. *The First Yachtsman's Navigator Guide to the Chilean Patagonia / La Guía de Navegación del Yatista Para los Canales de Chile.*
A soft-cover bilingual (Spanish/English) guide by a former admiral in the Chilean navy. For many years it was the only such guide available, but it is now surpassed by the two other volumes described in this section. Self-published; a third edition was released in 2006.

O'Grady, Andrew. Original material by Ian and Maggie Staples and Tony and Coryn Gooch. *Chile: Arica Desert to Tierra del Fuego.* 2nd Edition. St. Ives: Royal Cruising Club Pilotage Foundation / Imray, Laurie, Norie & Wilson Ltd., 2004.
Large format, many sketch maps. The first professional cruising guide to the area.

CLIMBING/EXPLORATION

de Agostini, Padre Alberto María. *Esfinges de Hielo (Ice Sphinxes).*
Torino, Italy: ILTE, 1959.
Climbing and exploration from the Paine massif to Fitzroy and Tierra del Fuego in the first half of the twentieth century. A rare classic with many colour illustrations, not available in English.

Shipton, Eric. *Tierra del Fuego: The Fatal Lodestone.*
London: Charles Knight, 1973.
An account by a Himalayan veteran (a close friend of H.W. Tilman's) of climbing Mount Darwin and other peaks in appalling conditions; many of his routes have never been repeated.

HISTORICAL/LITERARY

Bridges, E. Lucas. *Uttermost Part of the Earth.*
London: Hodder & Stoughton, 1948.
A rich and moving account of the author's youth at Harberton, on the Argentine side of the Beagle Channel; of the history of his pioneering

family; and of the gradual disappearance of the Ona, Selknam, and Yahgan people. Many fine sepia photographs.

Chatwin, Bruce. *In Patagonia*. London: Penguin Classics, 2003.
One of the great modern classics of travel literature. Chatwin's relatively short book inspired a whole new style of travel writing but later attracted some controversy when some of the subjects of the book claimed he had been cavalier with the facts.

Coloane, Francisco. *El Camino de la Ballena (The Way of the Whale)*. Madrid: Ollero y Ramos Editores, 1998.
Chilean novelist Francisco Coloane is little-known outside his native country, and few of his novels and short stories have been translated into English. An exception is *Cape Horn and Other Stories From the End of the World* (Pittsburgh: Latin American Literary Review Press, 2003).

Cook, James R. *The Journals of Captain Cook*. London: Penguin Classics, 1999.
Cook spent about three weeks in and around Tierra del Fuego in December 1774, on his second voyage (aboard the *Resolution*). He describes the area around Adventure Cove, Christmas Sound, and Burnt Island in some detail.

Darwin, Charles. *The Voyage of the Beagle*. London: Penguin Classics, 1989.
A "must-read" for any traveller to the region. Although Darwin was in the end happy to leave the stormy waters of the South, it was the years aboard the *Beagle* in and around Tierra del Fuego that formed him as a scientist and observer, and his discussions with Captain Robert Fitzroy that planted in him the seeds of "awful doubt."

Giménez-Hutton, Adrián. *La Patagonia de Chatwin*. Buenos Aires: Editorial Sudamericana, 1998.
Argentine writer Giménez-Hutton sets out to retrace Chatwin's travels twenty-five years on; at best a partial de-bunking. Giménez-Hutton finds that while Chatwin changed many names and other minor

details, this was as often as not at the request of his subjects. Available only in Spanish.

Guevara, Ernesto "Che." *Diarios de Motocicleta: Notas de Viaje por América Latina.* Melbourne: Ocean Press, 2004.

Had Che not subsequently gone on to greater things, the *Diarios de Motocicleta*, which recount a motorcycle trip undertaken by Che and Alberto Granado, from Buenos Aires to Bariloche, into Chile and north to Peru, would surely never have seen the light of day. With hindsight, however, the short and mainly lightweight narrative is of some interest; it was recently made into a movie and is available in English as *The Motorcycle Diaries.*

Martial, Louis-Ferdinand. *Mission Scientifique du Cap Horn, 1882–1883.* Vol. 1: *Histoire du Voyage.* Paris: Gauthier-Villars, 1888.

A brief, readable account of the 1882–1883 voyage of the *Romanche* to Tierra del Fuego to observe the passage of Venus and make other scientific observations. Remarkable for its rare photographs of the last of the Yahgans. Also available in a recent Spanish translation (*Misión al Cabo de Hornos.* Ushuaia: Zagier & Urruty Publications, 2005), but not in English.

Nichols, Peter. *Evolution's Captain: The Dark Fate of the Man Who Sailed Charles Darwin Around the World.* New York: HarperCollins, 2003.

Notwithstanding the ponderous title, this relatively recent, balanced account of the life of Captain Robert Fitzroy (who deserves to be remembered as one of the founders of modern meteorology, as much as for his role as Darwin's foil on the *Beagle*) is a good read. Like Pringle Stokes, Fitzroy committed suicide.

Index

Page numbers in italics refer to photographs. Page numbers with an italicized m refer to maps. JC and NC are abbreviations for Nicholas and Jenny Coghlan.

25 de Mayo, 178

Aboriginal peoples, 42–43, 176–77, 246, 344. *See also* Alacaluf people; Yahgan people
Abra Lecky's Retreat, Chile, 284–85
abrolhos, 109–10
Active Pass, British Columbia, 287

Admiral Graf Spee, 127
Admiralty Arm, Chile, 242
Admiralty Pilot guides. See *British Admiralty Pilot* guides
aguanieve, 249, 252
Agulhas, Cape, 55–56
Agur, 189–92, 355, 358
Alacaluf people, 246, 270, 283, 288, 297
Alamo, 269
albatrosses, 46, 86, 124–25, 155, 171, 312
Alcamar Timbales, Chile, 250, 256
Allara, Jorge, 180
Allen Gardiner, 43, 175, 214
Allende, Isabel, 223
Allende, Salvador, 24, 223

Alone Through the Roaring Forties
(Dumas), 135, 358
Amalia Glacier, Chile, 67, 280*m*,
289–90
Amasis, 271
Ana Belén II, 236
Ancud, 330
Andean Condors, 253
Andiamo, 338, 354
Angostura Inglesa, Chile, 302–03
Angostura Mischief, Chile, 290
Angra das Voltas, Namibia, 89
Angra dos Reis, Brazil, xii*m*, 120
Anna, 316–18
Anson, George, 309, 316–17
Antarctica, 39–46
Aqualung, 337, 346
ARA *Bouchard*, 178–79
ARA *General Belgrano*, xii*m*, 178–
81, *180*
ARA *Piedrabuena*, 178–79
Ardrizzi, Giorgio, 67, 237, 304,
359
Argentina, xii*m*, 230*m*. *See also*
Beagle Channel; Falklands
War; Perón, Juan Domingo
and Evita
economy of, 18–19, 38–39, 139
governments, 17–24
human rights abuses, 19–21,
140
military, 18, 22, 25–26
nationalism, 21–23, 25–26
Patagonia as soul of, 26–27
train travel, 27–29, 136–37, 169

Aries III, 257
Ascension Island, United
Kingdom, xiii*m*, 98
Astarte, 189
Atao, 172
Atlantic Spray, 90
Atlantis, 295, 303
Auralyn, 67
Auralyn II, 127, 248, 357
autopilots, 85
Azopardo, 275

BA. *See* Buenos Aires, Argentina
Baba del Diablo (Devil's Dribble),
128
Bachelet, Michelle, 195, 226
Bachelor, 161
Bahía Aguirre, 40
Bahía Aguirre (Spaniard Harbour),
Argentina, 175–77, 326
Bahía Anna Pink, Chile, 305*m*, 316
Bahía Blanca, Argentina, xii*m*,
29, 41
Bahía Buen Suceso, 40–41, 44, 174
Bahía Buen Suceso, Argentina, 40
Bahía Cook, Chile, 254
Bahía Cuarenta Días, Chile, 276
Bahía Desolada, Chile, 230*m*, 258
Bahía Hewett, Chile, 271
Bahía Mallett, Chile, 282–83
Bahía Nassau, Chile, 205, 230*m*
Bahía Oración, Chile, 283
Bahía Orange, Chile, 205–06, 270
Bahía Romanche, Chile, 248

Bahía San Sebastian, Argentina, 230*m*

Bahía Santiago, Chile, 190

Bahía Stokes, Chile, 271

Bahía Tres Brazos, Chile, 252–54

Bahía Windhond, Chile, 196

Bailey, Maurice and Maralyn, 67, 127, 248, 357

Banco Herradura, Chile, 231

Banner Cove, Picton Island, Argentina, 176–77, 181

Bariloche, Argentina, 32–33

Bartlett Point, Chile, 236

Battle of the River Plate, 127

Battle of the River Plate, The (movie), 127

Bay of Curves, Namibia, 89

Bayly Island, Chile, 205

Beagle. See HMS *Beagle*

Beagle Channel, *201*, 230*m*, *234*. *See also* Puerto Williams, Chile; Ushuaia, Argentina

  Argentine/Chilean conflict, 23–26, 30, 181, 196

  Darwin on, 249–50

  features of, 243, 247–54, 253, 258

  glaciers, 247–51, *249*, 253

  names and history, 254–55

  weather generally, 247–48

beavers, 203

Belgrano. See ARA *General Belgrano*

Benguela current, 84

Berg River, South Africa, 81

Biggs, Ronald, 119–20

Biribi B, 340

Black Oystercatchers, 236

Black Pinnace, 160

Blue Nile Sailing Club, Khartoum, Sudan, 185–86

Boat Memory (child). *See* Yahgan people

Boca del Guafo, Chile, 305*m*, 324–25

Bonzo, Héctor Elías, 179–80

Booby Island, Brazil, 124

Borges, Jorge Luis, 5

Bosun Bird

  autopilot, 85

  communications, 64–65, 166, 235, 241, 250, 292

  dinghy, 232

  engine repairs, 71–72, 111, 129, 156–57, 173, 217–20

  exterior of, 47, 57, 70, 76, 83, 110, 148, 201, 234, 253, 262, 276, 287

  heating and insulation, 71, 187, 199, 239, 322–23

  history and design, 50–55

  interior of, 292

  maintenance routines, 117, 263, 288, 323, 349

  naming of, 56–57

  repair of bottom (fibreglass osmosis), 75–76, 76

  repair of deck, 69–71, 70

  repairs, 117, 123, 144–45, 156

  solar panels, 240–41, 259

  steering system, 84–85

wind generator, 240–41

wind vane, 87, 354

Bosun Bird, life on

daily routines, 82–84, 96, 263

decision-making process, 259

entertainment, 68–69, 223,
263, 293, 308–09, 322

flags, 91, 98, 116–17

food, 87, 229, 239–40, 247, 257,
296, 299–300, 322, 329

fuel, 229, 231, 297, 299, 302,
349

navigation, 65–68, 83–84, 121,
181, 237

radio at sea, 65, 107–08, 153–
55, 183, 235, 250, 263, 295

radio in port, 163, 165, 199,
221–22

reading, 68–69, 106, 129, 199,
223, 263, 293, 300

reference books, 67–68, 357–
62

reporting to shore, 250

security routines, 114–15, 118

water supply, 293, 302, 318

weather information, 64–65,
199–200

website about, 354

winter routines, 199–201

Bosun Bird, travel on
(chronological order)

overview, 58–61, 258

preparing for, 58, 74–77, 76

route, xii–xiii*m*, 60–61, 82,
230*m*, 280*m*, 305*m*

weather patterns, 58–64

with icebergs, 289–90, 295

with ships, boats and rigs, 85–
86, 96, 109, 121, 174, 234–35

Laaiplek, SA, to Lüderitz,
Namibia, xiii*m*, 81–88

Lüderitz to St. Helena, UK,
95–98, 99

St. Helena to Rio de Janeiro,
Brazil, 107–11, 110

Rio de Janeiro to Ilhabela,
120–23

Ilhabela to Mar del Plata,
Argentina, 123–29

Mar del Plata to Quequén,
145–47, 148

Quequén to Puerto Deseado,
153–60

Puerto Deseado to Bahía
Aguirre, 172–76, 230*m*

Bahía Aguirre to Puerto
Williams, 181–83, 230*m*

Puerto Williams to Caleta Olla,
230*m*, 231–44, 234

Caleta Olla to Isla Burnt, Chile,
248–58

Isla Burnt to Caleta Murray,
257–67

Caleta Murray to Caleta
Teokita, 267–78

Caleta Teokita to Puerto
Bueno, 279–88, 280*m*

Puerto Bueno to Puerto Edén,
280*m*, 288–96

Puerto Edén to Caleta Ideal,
280*m*, 301–06, 305*m*
Caleta Ideal to Caleta Cliff,
307–16
Caleta Cliff to Puerto Puquitín,
316–25
Puerto Puquitín to Estero
Huildad, 325–26
Estero Huildad to Puerto
Montt, 305*m*, 326–33
Puerto Montt, Chile, to French
Polynesia, 348–51
French Polynesia to British
Columbia, 353–54
bosun birds, 57, 95
Botafogo Bay, Rio de Janeiro,
Brazil, 115–16
Bouvetoya (Bouvet Island), 96
Brazil, xii*m*, 109, 114, 118–19. *See
also* Rio de Janeiro, Brazil
Break Point
in Beagle Channel, 285, 293,
295
in Chilean channels, 299, 301,
303, 306, 308, 325
in Puerto Montt, 335, 351
Brecknock Peninsula, Chile,
230*m*, 260–63, *262*, 276
Bridges, Clara Mary (Clarita),
44–45
Bridges, Lucas and Mary, 42–45,
175, 211, 214–15, 266, 360
Bridges, Thomas, 42–43, 236, 242
Bristol, 271–72
British Admiralty Pilot guides
on Beagle Channel, 258
on Brazilian oceanic islands,
109
on Chilean channels, 296, 303
on Strait of Magellan, 279–80,
294
overview of, 67–68
British/Argentine conflict,
Falklands. *See* Falklands
War
British/German conflict (WWI),
Strait of Magellan, 270–73
Brown Boobies, 124
Buen Suceso Bay, Argentina, 174
Buenos Aires, Argentina, xii*m*, 127,
136–42. *See also* St. George's
College, Buenos Aires
Byron, John, 161

Caballo Marino (mythical), 327
Cabo Blanco, Argentina, 157
Cabo Crosstides, Chile, 273
Cabo de Hornos, Chile, 161
Cabo Frio, Rio de Janeiro, Brazil,
110
Cabo Froward, Chile, 23–24,
230*m*, 266–69, *268*, 330
Cabo Pilar, Chile, 276, 280*m*
Cabo Raper, Chile, 305*m*, 308–09,
311–12, *312*, 319
Cabo San Diego, Argentina, 24,
230*m*
Calbuco, Chile, *332*, 333
Calderón, "Abuela" Cristina, 200,
204, 235

Caleta Andrade, Chile, 320, 322

Caleta Beaulieu, Chile, 251

Caleta Brecknock, Chile, 260–63, 262, 276, 278

Caleta Canal, Chile, 322

Caleta Cliff, Chile, 314

Caleta Cluedo, Chile, 265–66

Caleta Colibrí, Chile, 293

Caleta Connor, Chile, 304

Caleta Cushion, Chile, 255

Caleta Dardé, Chile, 282

Caleta del Sur, Chile, 251

Caleta Desaparecidos, Chile, 255

Caleta Eugenio, Chile, 238

Caleta Ferrari, Chile, 241–42

Caleta Gallant, Chile, 269

Caleta Huajra, Chile, 256

Caleta Ideal, Chile, 306

Caleta José, Chile, 204–05

Caleta Julia, Chile, 252–54, *253*

Caleta Lamento del Indio, Chile, 304, 309

Caleta Martínez, Chile, 237

Caleta Mejillones, Chile, 232

Caleta Moonlight Shadow, Chile, 285

Caleta Murray, Chile, 267, 273

Caleta Notch, Chile, 273

Caleta Olla, Chile, 244–48

Caleta Pico, Chile, 291–93

Caleta Playa Parda, Chile, 273–74

Caleta Rosita, Chile, 320

Caleta Sabauda, Chile, 302–03

Caleta Suárez, Chile, 313

Caleta Teokita, Chile, 277–78

Caleta Uriarte, Chile, 276–77

Caleta Víctor Jara, Chile, 237

Caleta Voilier, Chile, 251

Caleta Yahgan, Chile, 259–60

Caleuche, 327–28

Camahuete (mythical), 327

Campbell, John, 248, 357–58

Canal Abandonados, Chile, 319

Canal Acwalisnan, Chile, 266–67

Canal Ballenero, Chile, 256, 258

Canal Bárbara, Chile, 266, 271

Canal Brecknock, Chile, 258–61, 263, 276

Canal Cockburn, Chile, 264, 271, 278

Canal del Chacao, Chile, 305*m*, 336, 350

Canal Errazuriz, Chile, 319

Canal Magdalena, Chile, 266

Canal Messier, Chile, 302–04, 305*m*, 306, 309

Canal Moraleda, Chile, 322, 324

Canal O'Brien, Chile, 256

Canal Pitt, Chile, 293

Canal Sarmiento, Chile, 280*m*, 284–85

Canal Smyth, Chile, 275–76, 277, 280*m*, 281, 281–84

Canal Unión, Chile, 282–83

Cape Agulhas, 55–56

Cape Columbine, South Africa, 72

Cape Cross, Namibia, 89

Cape Desolation, Chile, 208

Cape Froward, Chile, 23–24, 230*m*, 266–69, *268*, 330

*Cape Horn and Other Stories
From the End of the World*
(Coloane), 361
Cape Horn islands, Chile, xii*m*, 24,
63, 161, 230*m*
Cape of Good Hope, South Africa,
xiii*m*, 55–56, 79, 89
Cape Petrels (bird), 86, 312–13
Cape Pillar, Chile, 208
Cape Point, South Africa, 79
Cape Town, South Africa, xiii*m*,
49–50, 65
Captain Leonidas, 303
Caretta, 123
Carnatic Bay, Chile, 282
Carnival Two, 174
Casa de la Risa, Punta Arenas,
Chile, 226–27, 227, 246
Castro, Chile, 342
Catch the Wind, 218–19
Cavendish, Thomas, 160, 269, 270
Cerro Catedral, Argentina, 33
Cerro Torre, Argentina, 34
Chair Island, Chile, 255
charts, 65–66, 83–84
Chaski, 304
Chatwin, Bruce, 45, 171, 224–26,
361. See also *In Patagonia*
(Chatwin)
Chichester, Francis, 33
Chile, xii*m*, 230*m*, 280*m*, 305*m*.
See also Pinochet, Augusto
air service, 223–24, 285, 297
Bachelet government, 195, 226

Beagle Channel conflict, 23–26,
30, 181, 196
British/German conflict
(WWI), Strait of Magellan,
270–73
churches, 330
fishing industry, 314–16, *315*,
320–22, 326, *332*
human rights abuses, 37, 226–
27, 227, 255, 331
mussel industry, 297, 320, 322,
331
salmon farming, 320–22, 331
Spanish colonies, 227–28
*Chile: Arica Desert to Tierra del
Fuego*, 360. See also Royal
Cruising Club's guide to
Chilean coast
Chilean channels, 37, 302, 305*m*,
312
Chiles, Webb, 99
Chiloé Island, Chile, 207, 236–38,
305*m*, 320, 324–33, 342–
45, *343*
Chilotes, 238, 243–44
China Moon, 148
Chinquihue, Chile, 340–41
Christmas Bay, Chile, 271, 273
chubascos, 247, 249
Chubut, Argentina, 169
Clark, Gerry, 67, 260–61, 358
climbing guides, 360
Cockburn Channel, Chile, 230*m*,
265–66

Coghlan, Jenny, *10, 150, 164, 292,*
    329. See also Coghlan,
    Nicholas and Jenny, travels
    of; St. George's College,
    Buenos Aires
    careers, 2, 17, 20, 48, 49–50
    in England, 1–6, 221
    in South Africa, 49–50
    interests, 2, 30, 34, 35
    wedding, 4–5, 113–14
Coghlan, Nicholas, *1, 8, 31, 70*
    as photographer, 35, 251
    at Oxford University, 2, 5–6
    at University of Nottingham,
      1–4
    childhood, 4, 17, 33–34
    wanderlust, 17, 33–34, 172
    wedding, 4–5, 113–14
Coghlan, Nicholas, careers. *See*
    also St. George's College,
    Buenos Aires
    in Pakistan, 348–49, 353
    in South Africa, 49–50, 56, 64,
      74, 81
    in Sudan, 49, 185–86
    with Canadian Foreign Service,
      48–49, 74, 81
Coghlan, Nicholas and Jenny,
    travels of. See also
    Bosun Bird, travel on
    (chronological order); *Tarka*
    the Otter
    Antarctica (1970s), 38–41,
      45–46

Argentina (1970s), 15–17, 32–
    38, 41–46
Lanín Volcano, Argentina
    (1970s), 27–32, *31*
Richards Bay to Cape Town
    (1987), 55–56
website on, 354
Cole, Alfred, 214–15
Cole Cole, Chile, 344–45
Cole Island, Chile, 215
Coleridge, Samuel Taylor, 160–61
Coles, Adlard, 68, 73, 74
Coloane, Francisco, 186–87, 243–
    44, 327, 332, 361
Columbine, Cape, South Africa, 72
Commerson's dolphins, 159, 251
CONAF (National Forest
    Corporation, Chile), 299
condors, 253
Cono, Mount, Chile, 305*m*
Conway Castle, 272
Cook, Capt. James, 254–55, 361
Cook, Frederick, 43–44
Cook Islands, 353
Corcovado Volcano, Chile, 345
Córdoba, Argentina, 15
cormorants, 81, 210, 240
Cradock, Christopher, 270
crawler vessels. *See* diamond
    dredgers, Namibia
Crooked Reach, Chile, 273
Cross, Cape, Namibia, 89
cruising guides and narratives,
    357–62
Cucao, Chile, 305*m*, 342–45, *343*

Curves, Bay of, Namibia, 89

da Silva, Luiz Inácio Lula, 118-19
Dark Beach, Chile, 273-74
Dársena Norte, Buenos Aires,
    Argentina, 40, 140
Darwin, Charles
    at Queilén, 329
    by Chiloé, 325
    in Beagle Channel, 243
    by Chilean channels, 313
    in Patagonia, 255
    in Puerto Deseado area, 161-62,
        170
    in Rio de Janeiro area, 115, 120
    on Beagle Channel, 249-50,
        257-58
    on Cockburn Channel, 265-66
    on Cucao area, 344-45
    on natural history, 115
    on St. Helena, 103-04
    on volcanoes, 345
    recreation of voyage of, 143
    The Voyage of the Beagle, 360-
        61
    Yahgan children and, 209-10,
        213-15
Darwin, Mount, Chile, 224, 230*m*,
    245, 246
Davis, John, 160
Dawson Island, Chile, 37, 226-28
Day, Marcos Oliva, 170
de Agostini, Alberto María, 245-
    47, 360
de Castro, Raimunda, 119-20

*De Tahiti à Bayonne par le Cap
    Horn* (Robert), 358
Deceit Island, Chile, 205
Desire, 160-61
Desire, Port. *See* Puerto Deseado,
    Argentina
Desolate Bay, Chile, 258
Desolation, Cape, Chile, 208
Despard, George, 214-15
Devil's Dribble (insects at sea), 128
Dexter, Dave, 93
diamond dredgers, Namibia, 86,
    90-91, 91
diamond mining, Namibia, 93-94
Diarios de motocicleta (Guevara),
    341-42, 362
Dias, Bartolomeu, 89-90, 94-95
Dias Point lighthouse, Namibia,
    88, 94-95
Dientes del Navarino, Chile, 192,
    224, 231
Dientes del Navarino café, Puerto
    Williams, Chile, 193-97
dolphins, 87, 125, 159, 251, 252
Don Mario, 257, 258
Don Segundo Sombra (Güiraldes),
    5, 163
Donoso, José, 223
Dozo, Lami, 141
Drake, Sir Francis, 160, 267, 283-
    84, 288
Drake Passage, 45, 62, 302
Dreamaway, 155, 229, 260, 278,
    324, 338
Dresden, 270-73, 328

Dresden Hort, Chile, 273

Drunken Harbour, Chile, 240

Duguet, Antoine, 142–43, 154–55, 165, 189–92, 303, 358

Dumas, Vito, 134–36, 358

Easter Island, 353

Eberh'ardt, Herman, 284

Eendracht, 161

Egger, Toni, 34

Egmont, Port, Argentina, 170

El Calafate, Argentina, 33

El Camino de la Ballena (Coloane), 332, 361

Elizabeth, 284

Emisor, 266

Enrique I, 238

Esfinges de Hielo (de Agostini), 360. See also de Agostini, Alberto María

Estancia Harberton, Argentina, 43–45, 44, 175, 242, 360

Estero Dock, Chile, 294–95

Estero Huildad, Chile, 326

Estero Pailad, Chile, 327–28, 329

Estero Peel, Chile, 289–90

Estero Pindo, Chile, 330

Estero Plainsong, Chile, 291

Estrecho Collingwood, Chile, 284

Estrecho Nelson, Chile, 280m, 284, 286, 293

Evangelistas, Chile, 276

Evita (Webber and Rice), 5

Evolution's Captain (Nichols), 362

Explorador, 272

exploration reference guides, 360

Falkland Island Broadcasting Service (FIBS), 263

Falkland Islands/Islas Malvinas, xii*m*, 22–23, 46, 58, 101, 160, 175

Falklands War, 22–23, 140–41, 178–81, *180*, 196

Famine, Port, Chile, 227–28

Faro Evangelistas lighthouse, Chile, 280*m*

Faro Fairway, Chile, 277

Faro San Pedro, Chile, 308–09

Feng Shui, 122

fibreglass osmosis, 75–76, *76*

Fiji, 353

Fireland. *See* Tierra del Fuego

First Aid Afloat, 68

First Yachtsman's Navigator Guide to the Chilean Patagonia, The (Mantellero), 360

Fitzroy, Mount, Argentina, 33–34

Fitzroy, Robert
in Tierra del Fuego area, 162, 176, 257, 284
life of, 207–10, 361, 362
naming of geographical features, 245, 286

football, 6–7, 196–97

Forster, George, 254

Fortescue Bay, Chile, 269

French Polynesia, 349

Froward, Cape, Chile, 23–24, 230*m*, 266–69, *268*, 330

Fuegia Basket (child). *See* Yahgan people

Fuerte Bulnes, Chile, 24, 228, 330

Furious Fifties weather patterns, 62–64, 173

Gable Island, Argentina, 45

Gannet, 131–33

Gardiner, Allen, 176–77, 181, 213–14

Gardiner Island, Chile, 181–82

gauchos, 163, 164

General Belgrano. See ARA *General Belgrano*

German/British conflict (WWI), Strait of Magellan, 270–73

Germany's claim to Namibia, 89

Giant Petrels, 312

Giménez-Hutton, Adrián, 171, 361

glaciers
  in Beagle Channel, 247–51, 249, 253
  in Chilean channels, 280m
  in Strait of Magellan, 289–90, 295

Global Positioning Systems (GPS), 65–66, 68, 84

Gneisenau, 270

Golfo de Ancud, Chile, 305m

Golfo de Corcovado, Chile, 305m

Golfo de Penas, Chile, 38, 39, 279, 297, 302, 305m, 306

Gondwana, 187, 199

Good Hope, Cape of, xiiim, 55–56, 79, 89

Goodall, Anne and Abby, 41–42, 44–45

Goodall, Tommy, 44, 44–45

Goree Roads, Chile, 210

Graf Spee, 127

Granado, Alberto, 341–42, 362

Great Train Robbery, 119–20

Grevy Island, Chile, 205

gribs, 65

Guanabara Bay, Brazil, 110, 116–17

guanacos, 15, 240, 241

Guevara, Ernesto "Che," 341–42, 362

Gulf of Sorrows, Chile, 38, 39, 279, 297, 302, 305m, 306

Gulf of St. George, Argentina, 156

Hansen, Al, 135

Happy Event Bay, Argentina, 174

Harberton Estancia, Argentina, 42–45, 44, 175, 242, 360

Harrier of Down, 143, 168, 335–36, 354

Harris, Robert, 51

Heavy Weather Sailing (Coles), 68, 73, 74

Hermite Island, Chile, 205

Herschel, 133

Herschel Island, Chile, 205

Heyerdahl, Thor, 97

Hiscock, Eric, 68

historical reference guides, 360–62

HMS *Achilles*, 127

HMS *Adelaide*, 207

HMS *Adventure*, 207, 257, 269
HMS *Ajax*, 127
HMS *Beagle*
  by Chilean channels, 313
  by Chiloé, 325
  crew and Yahgan people, 208–
    10, 254–55
  in Patagonia, 255–57
  in Puerto Deseado area, 161–62
  in Rio de Janeiro area, 115
  in Strait of Magellan, 228–29,
    269
  in Tierra del Fuego, 176–77
  name of, 207
  recreation of voyage of, 143
HMS *Carnarvon*, 271–72
HMS *Conqueror*, 179–80
HMS *Dolphin*, 161
HMS *Exeter*, 127
HMS *Glasgow*, 270–72
HMS *Good Hope*, 270
HMS *Hermes*, 178
HMS *Inflexible*, 271
HMS *Invincible*, 178
HMS *Melik*, 185–86
HMS *Monmouth*, 270
HMS *Nassau*, 228, 286–87
HMS *Penguin*, 284–85
HMS *Plumper*, 287
HMS *Resolution*, 254
HMS *Satellite*, 229
HMS *Swift*, wreck of, 169–70
HMS *Victory*, 187–88, 197–98
HMS *Wager*, 309, 317
Holanda Glacier, Chile, 247

Hoorn, 161
Horn, Cape, Chile, xii*m*, 24, 63,
  161, 230*m*
Horn Island, Chile, 205
Horse of the Sea (mythical), 327
Horseshoe Bank, Chile, 231
Hoste Island, Chile, 34, *201*, 202–
  03, 205, 230*m*, 238
Hudson, W.H., 15
Hummingbird Cove, Chile, 293

Ice Sphinxes (de Agostini), 246
Ilha de Saõ Sebastiaõ, Brazil,
  123–24
Ilha dos Alcatrazes, Brazil, 124
Ilha dos Porcos, Brazil, 123
Ilha Grande, Brazil, 120, 123
Ilha Laje, Rio de Janeiro, Brazil, 111
Ilha Rasa, Brazil, 110
Ilhabela, Brazil, xii*m*, 123
Imbunche (mythical), 327
immigration and customs
  in Argentina, 134
  in Brazil, 116–17, 124
  in Chile, 181–83
  in South Africa, 80–81
  in St. Helena, 101
In Darwin's Wake (Campbell), 248,
  357–58
In Patagonia (Chatwin), 6, 26, 31,
  171, 224–26, 361
Inspired Insanity, 346
International Meteorological
  Conference (1879), 205
Isla Basket, Chile, 258

Isla Burnt, Chile, 257–58

Isla Carlos III, Chile, 269–70

Isla Darwin, Chile, 254

Isla de Chiloé, Chile. *See* Chiloé Island, Chile

Isla de los Estados, Argentina, 173, 175, 230*m*

Isla del Diablo, Chile, 243, 244

Isla Doña Sebastiana, Chile, 351

Isla Grande de Tierra del Fuego. *See* Tierra del Fuego

Isla Guafo, Chile, 324

Isla Hoste, Chile. *See* Hoste Island, Chile

Isla Londonderry, Chile, 256

Isla Martínez, Chile, 236–37

Isla Navarino, Chile. *See* Navarino Island, Chile

Isla Nueva, Chile. *See* Nueva Island, Chile

Isla Picton, Chile. *See* Picton Island, Chile

Isla Riesco, Chile, 230*m*

Isla Santa Inés, Chile, 230*m*, 270

Isla Smoke, Chile, 257

Isla Thomson, Chile, 254

Isla Vancouver, Chile, 286

Isla Wellington, Chile, 280*m*, 294

Islamabad, Pakistan, 353

Islander, 154–55

Islas Christmas, Chile, 254

Islas Ildefonso, Chile, 230*m*

Islas Malvinas/Falkland Islands, xii*m*, 22–23, 46, 58, 101, 160, 175. *See also* Falklands War

Isle of Pigs, Brazil, 123

Italians' sailing guide. See *Patagonia and Tierra del Fuego Nautical Guide* (Ardrizzi and Rolfo)

Jackass Penguins, 155

Jamestown, St. Helena, 97–107, 99

Jemmy Button (child). *See* Yahgan people

Jemmy Button (radio), 221–22, 235

Jolie Brise, 318

Journals of Captain Cook, The (Cook), 361

Juan Antonio II, 314–16, 315, 318–19

Kaap Bol, 93

Kalahari Railway, 95

kelp, edible, 299

Kelp Geese, 242, 326

Keppel Island, Argentina, 43, 214

Khartoum, Sudan, 185–86

King, Philip Parker, 207, 257

Kolmannskoppe, Namibia, 93–95

Kon Tiki Expedition (Heyerdahl), 97

Kosmos, 272

La Boudeuse, 269

La Paloma, Brazil, 125

Lago Lácar, Argentina, 29

Lago Todos los Santos, Chile, 341

Lake Nahuel Huapí, Argentina, 33

Lament of the Indian, Chile, 304, 309

Land of Fire. *See* Tierra del Fuego

Lanín National Park, Argentina, 29–31

Lanín Volcano, Argentina, xii*m*, 28–32, *31*, 347, 348

Lapataia, Argentina, 35

Las Heras, Argentina, 169

Last Hope Sound, Chile, 283–84

Latorre, 186

Le Boulard, 198

Le Maire, Jacob, 161

Le Maire, Strait of, Argentina, 43, 173–74, 230*m*, 314

Lecky, T.S., 284–85

Lecky's Wrinkles in Practical Navigation (Lecky), 285

Lehg II, 134–35

Leicester Galleon, 160

Leipzig, 270

Lennox Island, Chile, 24

Leonardo, 238

Leonore, 307–08

Lindblad Explorer, 39

literary reference guides, 360–62

Loerisfontein, 81

London Island, Chile, 208

Long Reach, Chile, 275

Lord Lonsdale, 227

Los Cuarenta Bramadores (Dumas), 134–35, 358

Lowe, Sir Hudson, 104

Ludecke, Fritz, 271–72

Lüderitz, Alfred, 90

Lüderitz, Namibia, xiii*m*, 88–95, *91*

Ludus Amoris, 263, 273–74, 276–77, 285, 294–96, 303, 355

Lula da Silva, Luiz Inácio, 118–19

Macarena, 181–82

Maestri, Cesare, 34

Magallanes Radio, 199, 235, 263, 316

Magellan, Ferdinand, 160

Magellan, Strait of. *See* Strait of Magellan, Chile

Magenta, 302

Mahina Tiare, 304

Malulu, 93

Malvinas Day, Argentina, 23

Malvinas/Falkland Islands, xii*m*, 22–23, 46, 58, 101, 160, 175. *See also* Falklands War

Mantellero, Alberto, 360

Mar del Plata, Argentina, xii*m*, 129–36, 142–45, *144*

María Elena, 250

Marie Galante, 122

Márquez, Gabriel García, 223

Marriott, Charles, 290

Martial, Louis-Ferdinand, 205–06, 241–42, 248, 362

Martin Vaz Island, Brazil, xii*m*, 109

Mayne, R.C., 228, 286–87

Mayne Island, British Columbia, 287

Mechuque, Chile, 331

Menem, Carlos, 141

Micalvi, 186–87, 198–99, 222, 231

Milward, Charles, 225, 270–71

Mischief, 67, 127, 269, 274, 285, 289–90, 359

Mischief in Patagonia (Tilman), 67, 274, 289–90, 359

Mission Scientifique du Cap Horn (Martial), 362. *See also* Martial, Louis-Ferdinand

Mitre Peninsula, Argentina, 175

Mladineo, Luis, 211

Modesta Victoria, 33

Moitessier, Bernard, 63, 135

Monte Cono, Chile, 305*m*

Monte Darwin, Chile, 224, 230*m*, 245, 246

Montevideo, Uruguay, 127

Motorcycle Diaries, The (Guevara), 341–42, 362

Mount Fitzroy, Argentina, 33–34

Mount Sarmiento, Chile, 257, 266

Mount Scott King, 205

Mount Tronador, Chile, 33, 341

mountaineering scandals, 34

Moustique, 142–43, 154–55, 165, 189–92, 303

Murray Narrows, Chile, *201, 202,* 238

Mussel Bay, Chile, 232, 270

mussel gathering, 293–94

mussel industry, 297, 320, 322, 331

Nahuel Huapí, Lake, Argentina, 33

Namibia, xiii*m*, 82, 86–95, *91*

Nancy, 215

Napoleon Bonaparte, on St. Helena, 100, 103–05

Narborough, Sir John, 161, 269, 275

National Forest Corporation (Chile) (CONAF), 299

National Oceanic and Atmospheric Administration (NOAA), 65

Nautigal, 107

Nautilus (Verne's fictional submarine), 257

Navarino Island, Chile, 24, 181–83, *182,* 210–14, *211,* 230*m,* 237

navigation systems, 64–68, 84–85

Necochea, Argentina, 146

Neuquén, Argentina, 29

New Zealand, 354

Nichols, Peter, 362

Nine of Cups, 304

Nott, John, 179

Nuestra Señora de Covadonga, 317

Nuestra Señora de la Esperanza, 288

Nueva Island, Chile, 24, 230*m*

Nujoma, Sam, 92

Nurnberg, 270

O'Brien, Conor, 135

Ocean Queen, 177

O'Higgins, Bernardo, 330

Olimir, 319–20

On Verra, 336–37

Ona people, 246

orcas, 273

Orion, 243

ornithological expeditions, 67

Osorno Volcano, 341, 345

Ostoic, Antonio Vrsalovic, 211

Owen, Port, South Africa, 58, 74, 77, 79–81

oystercatchers, 242

Pagels, Albert, 271–73

Pagels Huk, Chile, 273

Paine National Park, Chile, 36

Pampas, 187–88

pamperos, 127–28

Paraty, Brazil, *121*, 122–23

Paso Brecknock, Chile, 264, 276

Paso Chocoi, Chile, 351

Paso Farquhar, Chile, 284

Paso Piloto Pardo, Chile, 295

Paso Shoal, Chile, 281–82

Paso Tamar, Chile, 276

Paso Victoria, Chile, 284

Patagonia, 26–27, 46

Patagonia and Tierra del Fuego Nautical Guide (Ardrizzi and Rolfo), 67, 237, 304, 359

La Patagonia de Chatwin (Giménez-Hutton), 171, 212, 361–62

Patagonian Channels, 275

Patagonian Cruiser's Net, 153–55, 171, 189, 235, 263, 295, 308, 318, 345–46, 347

Patagonian Ice Field, 289

Patagonian toothfish, 314, 316

Paternoster, South Africa, 72

Patience, 90

Pearl, 93, 317

Pelagic, 198

penguins, 95, 159, 160, 171, 289, 326

Península Brecknock, Chile, 230*m*, 260–63, *262*, 276

Península Brunswick, Chile, 230*m*

Península Skyring, Chile, 316

Península Valdés, Argentina, 41

Perón, Juan Domingo and Evita, 5, 13, 18, 141–42

Perón, Maria Estela Martinez de (Isabelita), 18–19

Petrohué, Chile, 341

Philips, Garland, 214–15

Picton Island, Chile, 24–25, 176–77, 181, 210, 230*m*

pigs, wild, 203

Pillar, Cape, Chile, 208

Pilot Charts, 64–65

Pilot guide books. *See British Admiralty Pilot* guides

Piloto Sibbald, 232

pink, definition of, 316–17

Pinochet, Augusto, 25, 36–37, 195, 226, 255, 316, 321, 331

Pipe Dream, 51–55, 57, *57*, 71, 75. See also *Bosun Bird*

Plate, River, Argentina, 126–27

Point, Cape, South Africa, 79

Polynesia, French, 349

Ponsonby Sound, Chile, 205–06

porpoises, 295

Port Desire. *See* Puerto Deseado, Argentina

Port Egmont, Argentina, 170

Port Famine, Chile, 227–28

Port Owen, South Africa, 58, 74, 77, 79–81

Port Stanley, Falkland Islands, 175, 183, 235

Portuguese explorers, 89–90

Prayer Bay, Chile, 283

Pringle Stokes, Robert, 207, 228–30

Procter, W.A., 290

Pronk, Tom, 93

Prosser, Natalie, 44–45

puerto as term for anchorage, 200

Puerto Aguirre, Chile, 305*m*, 320–22, *321*

Puerto Angosto, Chile, 275

Puerto Borracho, Chile, 240

Puerto Bueno, Chile, 288–89

Puerto Deseado, Argentina, xii*m*, 157, 160–71, *164*, 189–91

Puerto Edén, Chile, xii*m*, 38, 280*m*, 296–301, *298*, 305*m*, 320

Puerto Escondido, Chile, 309

Puerto Eugenia, Chile, 183

Puerto Hambre, Chile, 227–28

Puerto Inútil, Chile, 204

Puerto Isorna, Chile, 202

Puerto Madryn, Argentina, 41

Puerto Mayne, Chile, 286, *287*, 288

Puerto Millabú, Chile, 317–18

Puerto Montt, Chile, xii*m*, 37, 305*m*, 335–42, *339*, 349

Puerto Montt Radio, 316

Puerto Natales, Chile, 35, 230*m*, 279, 288, 297

Puerto Navarino, Chile, 200, 202, 236

Puerto Profundo, Chile, 277–78

Puerto Puquitín, Chile, 324–25

Puerto Refugio, Chile, 317

Puerto Ríofrío, Chile, 301

Puerto Williams, Chile, xii*m. See also* Beagle Channel
  air service, 223–24
  Beagle Channel conflict, 24–26, 196
  beavers, 203
  canning, 237
  civic monuments, 295
  engine repairs at, 217–20, 223
  entertainment, 222–23
  features of, *182*, *183*, 231
  hiking in area of, 200–07, *201*, 211–13
  immigration and customs, 181–83
  overview of, 192–93
  radio stations, 221–22
  residents, 187–88, 192–98, 217–21, *218*, *220*, 284
  restaurants and cafés, 193–98
  sailing club, 186–87, 198–99
  weather information, 199–200, *201*
  weather patterns, 229–30

Punta Arenas, Chile, xii*m*, 230*m*
  air service, 211, 218, 223–24, 297

Beagle Channel conflict, 24–26
British/German conflict
(WWI), 270–73
explorers and missionaries,
245–47, 330
features of, 35–37, 42, 224
human rights abuses, 226–27,
227
in fiction, 186–87
radio station, 199, 235, 263, 316

Queen Elizabeth 2, 325
Queilén, Chile, 329
Quellón, Chile, 314
Quemchi, Chile, 331–32
Quequén, Argentina, xii*m*, 145–51,
148, 150
Quilmes, Argentina, 7, 15, 23, 139

Radio Globo, 107
Raiatea Island, 353
Raper, F.V., 312
Raya del Tique, Chile, 350
RCC guide. *See* Royal Cruising
Club's guide to Chilean
coast
Red Tide, 204, 270, 294, 297, 320
Restless, 154, 177
Resurgam, 99
Richards Bay, South Africa, 52, 55,
57, 77
Rime of the Ancient Mariner
(Coleridge), 160–61
Río Baker, 37–39, *39*, 58, 296, 303

Rio de Janeiro, Brazil, xii*m*, *110*,
113–20
Río Gallegos, Argentina, 167–68,
230*m*
Río Grande, Argentina, 230*m*
Río Matanza, Chile, 214–15
River Plate, Argentina, 126–27
RMS *St. Helena*, 102
Roaring Forties weather patterns,
62–64, 135, 192
Robert, Yves, 358
Robinson Crusoe Island, 351, 353
Roca Beagle, Argentina, 159, 162
Roca Foca, Argentina, 158
Roca Remolinos, Chile, 350–51
Roca Rompiente, Chile, 264
Rolfo, Mariolina, 67, 237, 304, 359
Romanche, 205–06, 241–42, 252,
255, 270, 362
Romanche Glacier, 249, 249–50
Rose, Alec, 135
Roth, Hal, 359
Rothemburg, Henry, 272
Royal Cape Yacht Club, Cape
Town, South Africa, 58
Royal Cruising Club's guide to
Chilean coast, 67, 255, 273,
285, 294, 360
Ruta Tres, Argentina, 35

SA. *See* South Africa
Sadko, 323, 326
Sail Rocks, Argentina, 175

Sailing Alone Around the World
(Slocum), 67, 359. *See also*
Slocum, Joshua
sailing guides and narratives,
357–62
sailing navigation, 65–66, 83–84
sailing terms
drogue, 74
heave to, 73
lying ahull, 73
on the hard, 74
pitchpoling, 74
running downwind, 73–74
running under bare poles,
156–57
stern-tied position, 252–53,
259
Salas, Marcelo, 196–97
Saldanha, South Africa, 80
salmon farming, 320–22, 331
Samborrombón River, Argentina,
128
San Juan de la Posesión, Chile,
228, 330
San Martín de los Andes,
Argentina, 29
San Pedro lighthouse, Chile,
308–09
Santa Inés Island, Chile, 272
Santa Leonora, 281, 282
Santa Maria, 198
Saõ Sebastiaõ, Brazil, 123–24
Sarau, 131
Sarmiento, Canal, Chile, 280m,
284–85

Sarmiento, Mount, Chile, 257, 266
Sarmiento, Pedro, 257, 273, 275,
283, 288
Saumarez, James, 317
Scharnhorst, 270
Schouten, Willem, 161
Scott King, Mount, 205
sea bass, 314
Sea Reach, Chile, 275
seals, 87, 146, 232, 252
Second Chance (Bailey), 67, 248,
357
Seno Christmas, Chile, 254
Seno Dresden, Chile, 230m, 272,
273
Seno Ocasión, Chile, 261, 264
Seno Otway, Chile, 207
Seno Pedro, Chile, 267–68
Seno Pía, Chile, 251
Seno Skyring, Chile, 207
servo-pendulum vanes, 85
Severn, 317
Seychelles tortoises, 105
Seydlitz, 271
Shackleton, Ernest, 12, 295
Shearwater Bay, Namibia, 95
Shipton, Eric, 245, 360
Sierra Córdoba, 271–72
Sierra de la Ventana, Argentina,
15–16, 28
Silver Katonkel, 81
Simon de Danser, 143, 354
Sirio, 136
Skorpios III, 297
Skyring Peninsula, Chile, 316

Slipper Bay, South Africa, 72

Slocum, Joshua, 67, 105, 107, 117, 127, 135, 265–66, 269, 275, 277, 359

Smooth Island, Brazil, 110

Snipe Island, Chile, 181, 183

Solquest, 198, 218, 354

Sooty Shearwaters, 326

Sorrows, Gulf of, Chile. *See* Gulf of Sorrows, Chile

South Africa, xiii*m*. *See also* Port Owen, South Africa; St. Helena Bay, South Africa

NC as Consul General, 48–50, 56, 64, 74, 81

race relations, 80, 92

South America, xii*m*

South Atlantic weather, 59–60

Southern Ocean, 62

Spanglish, 8–9, 27

Spaniard Harbour (Bahía Aguirre), Argentina, 176–77, 326

Sparrman, Anders, 254

sperm whale, 314

Spirit of Rhema, 337–38, 354

Spray, 105, 107, 117, 127, 265, 269, 275, 359. *See also* Slocum, Joshua

Squeek, 51. See also *Tarka the Otter*

squid industry, 163, 173

St. George's College, Buenos Aires

JC at, 6–10, *10*, 17, 20, 48

NC at (1978–1981), 4, 6–16, *8*, 48, 127, 128

overview of, 6–11, 21–23, 47

return visit (2005), 138–40, 225

sports, 4, 10–13

staff, 6–9, 16, 21–23, 27–30, 32–33, 41, 138–39, 225

student life, 7–16, *8*, *10*, 21–22, 31, 41–42

St. Helena Bay, South Africa, 72, 77–78, 81

St. Helena Island, United Kingdom, xiii*m*, 97–107

Stanley, Falkland Islands, 175, 183, 235

Staples, Ian and Maggie, 360. *See also* Royal Cruising Club's guide to Chilean coast

Starfire, 303–04

Staten Island, Argentina, 173, 175, 230*m*

Steamer Ducks, 242

Stompneus Bay, South Africa, 72

Stormkop, 81

Strait of Le Maire, Argentina, 43, 173–74, 230*m*, 314

Strait of Magellan, Chile, xii*m*, 230*m*, 280*m*

conflict over, 23–24, 330

Drake in, 267

features of, 267–69, *268*, 275, *276*, 279–80

HMS *Beagle* in, 207

isolation of, 287

naming of geographical features, 286

Slocum in, 265–66

visit to (1979), 37

Straw, Jack, 6

Striated Caracara, 242

Sturdee, Frederick Doveton, 270–71

"Submerged Iceberg" (Coloane), 186–87

Sugar Loaf Point, St. Helena, 97

Sunstone, 130, 354

Sweepstakes, 161

Tamara, 326

Tarka the Otter
circumnavigation (1985–1989), 48, 55–56, 80–82, 87, 95, 98, 105–06, 108
history and design, 48, 50–52, 54, 71, 304

Teokita, 278

Terra Nova, 77

Terry, Belaúnde, 180

Thalassa, 357–58

Thatcher, Margaret, 180–81, 196

Three Arms Bay, Chile, 252–54

Tierra del Fuego, xii*m*, 230*m*. *See also* Beagle Channel; Puerto Williams, Chile; Ushuaia, Argentina; Yahgan people
anchorages, 173
beavers, 203
isolation of, 264
missionaries in, 42–44, 176–77, 210, 213–15, 242, 245–47
weather patterns, 63–64

Tierra del Fuego: The Fatal Lodestone (Shipton), 245, 360

Tilman, H.W. (Bill), 67, 127, 269, 274, 285, 289–90, 359

Timbales (Kettledrums), Chile, 255

Tonga, 353

Torres del Paine, Chile, 286

tortoises, Seychelles, 105

Totorore, 67, 260–61, 358

Totorore Voyage, The (Clark), 67, 260–61, 358

Trafalgar, Battle of, 284

Trans-Kalahari Railway, 95

Trauco (mythical), 327

Tres Montes, Chile, 311, 313

Trindade Island, Brazil, xii*m*, 109

Tristan da Cunha, United Kingdom, 96

Tromen Pass, Argentina, 31, *31*

Tronador, Mount, Chile, 33, 341

tropicbird, 57

Two Against Cape Horn (Roth), 359

Urca Bay, Brazil, 111

Ushuaia, Argentina, xii*m*, 230*m*
features of, 24–25, 34–35, 42, 44
missionaries, 215, 242
visit to (1979), 41–45

Uttermost Part of the Earth (Bridges), 42–45, 266, 360. *See also* Bridges, Lucas and Mary

Valdés Peninsula, Argentina, 41
Vancouver 27 (design), 51–53. See
    also *Bosun Bird*
Vega 27 (design), 51. See also *Tarka
    the Otter*
Ventisquero España Glacier, 253
Verne, Jules, 257
Vianini, Andrea, 165
Victoria, 332
Videla, Jorge Rafael, 6, 18, 22
Vito Dumas Yacht Club, Quequén,
    Argentina, 147–48, *148*
Voice of the Falklands (radio), 183
volcanoes, 345
Voyage of the Beagle, The (Darwin),
    360–61
Voyaging Under Sail (Hiscock), 68

Walvis Bay, Namibia, 89
Waratah, 55
Waterman Island, Chile, 254
Way of the Whale, The (Coloane),
    332, 361
weather maps, 59–60, 64–65
website, Coghlan's, 354
Wellington Island, Chile, 297. *See
    also* Puerto Edén, Chile
Whaler Channel, Chile, 256
whales, 87, 236, 314
Whirlpool Rock, Chile, 350–51
Whisper, 359
Wilde Mathilde, 153–55
Williams, John (Juan), 330
Wilson's Storm Petrel, 86
Wind Pilot, 84–85

Windhoek, Namibia, 92
wind-powered vanes, 84–85
With Captain Cook in HMS
    Resolution (Sparrman), 254
Wolfgang and Gabi, 153–55, 345–
    46, *347. See also* Patagonian
    Cruiser's Net
Wollaston Island, Chile, 205
World Cup, 5–6, 25–26, 196–97
World War I battle, hunt for
    Dresden, 270–73
Wulaia, Chile, 202–03, 210–15, *211*

Yacht Club Argentino, Mar del
    Plata, Argentina, 134
Yahgan people, *206*
    archaeological sites, 203–04
    as boat pilots, 266
    Beagle's crew and, 176–77,
        208–10, 213–15, 254–56
    Boat Memory (child), 209, 256
    cemetery, 235
    extinction of, 206–07, 246, 270
    Fuegia Basket (child), 209–10,
        213, 256, 258
    in fiction and reference works,
        243–44, 360–61, 362
    Jemmy Button (child), 176,
        209–10, 213–15, 255–56
    language, 43, 240, 252, 255
    last living Yahgan, 200, 204,
        235
    Martial's crew and (1882),
        205–07

missionaries and, 42–44, 176–77, 210, 213–15, 246

York Minster (child), 209–10, 213, 255–56

Yamaná (tugboat), 158, 166, 168, 170

Yamaná-English Dictionary, 43

Yawarra

  in Beagle Channel, 149

  in Gulf of St. George, Argentina, 156

  in Mar del Plata, Argentina, 125–26, 130

  in Puerto Montt, Chile, 235, 333, 338–41, 351, 354

in South Africa and Namibia, 56, 77, 93

Yawarra 2, 354

Yelcho, 295

Yellow-nosed Albatross, 124

Yendegaia Bay, Chile, 240–43

York Minster (child). *See* Yahgan people

York Minster (rocky headland), 254–55

Zanzibar, 143–44, 160, 167–68, 170, 191

Other Books in the Wayfarer Series

Prodigal Daughter
A Journey to Byzantium
MYRNA KOSTASH

352 pages | Map, bibliography, index

978-0-88864-534-0 | $34.95 (T) paper

Travel Memoir/Creative Nonfiction

Bosnia
In the Footsteps of Gavrilo Princip
TONY FABIJANČIĆ

264 pages | 45 B&W photographs,
    maps, index

978-0-88864-519-7 | $29.95 (T) paper

Travel Writing/Politics/World History

Under the Holy Lake
A Memoir of Eastern Bhutan
KEN HAIGH

296 pages | B&W photographs, map, notes,
    suggested reading list

978-0-88864-492-3 | $29.95 (T) paper

Adventure Travel/Literary Memoir